Praise for *DotCom Secrets*

"A simple process that any company can use to geometrically improve their traffic, conversion, and sales online."
— Tony Robbins

DOTCOM
SECRETS

ALSO BY
RUSSELL BRUNSON

Expert Secrets

Traffic Secrets

DOTCOM SECRETS

THE UNDERGROUND PLAYBOOK

FOR GROWING YOUR COMPANY ONLINE
WITH SALES FUNNELS

RUSSELL BRUNSON

BUSINESS

HAY HOUSE, INC.
Carlsbad, California • New York City
London • Sydney • New Delhi

Copyright © 2015, 2020 by Russell Brunson
Published in the United States by: Hay House, Inc.: www.hayhouse.com®
Published in Australia by: Hay House Australia Pty. Ltd.: www.hayhouse.com.au
Published in the United Kingdom by: Hay House UK, Ltd.: www.hayhouse.co.uk
Published in India by: Hay House Publishers India: www.hayhouse.co.in

Cover design: Jake Leslie and Rob Secades
Interior design: Julie Davison
Interior photos/illustrations: Arturo Alcazar and Vlad Babich
Cover photography: Brandan Fisher and Erin Blackwell

A previous editon of this book was published under the same title (ISBN: 978-1-63047-4775).

Library of Congress has cataloged the earlier edition as follows:

Names: Brunson, Russell, author.
Title: Dotcom secrets: the underground playbook for growing your company online with sales funnels / Russell Brunson.
Description: First edition. | Carlsbad, California: Hay House, Inc.,
    Identifiers: LCCN 2020005092 | ISBN 9781401960469 (hardback) | ISBN 9781401960605 (ebook) | ISBN 9781401960810 (Audiobook)
Subjects: LCSH: Internet marketing. | Customer relations. | Electronic commerce.
Classification: LCC HF5415.1265 .B777 2020 | DDC 658.8/72--dc23
LC record available at https://lccn.loc.gov/2020005092

Tradepaper ISBN: 978-1-4019-7059-8
E-book ISBN: 978-1-4019-6060-5
Audiobook ISBN: 978-1-4019-6081-0

13 12 11 10 9 8 7 6 5
1st Hay House edition, May 2020
2nd Hay House edition, August 2022

Printed in the United States of America

SUSTAINABLE
FORESTRY
INITIATIVE

Certified Chain of Custody
Promoting Sustainable Forestry
www.forests.org
SFI-01268
SFI label applies to the text stock

This product uses papers sourced from responsibly managed forests. For more information, see www.hayhouse.com.

*To my dad, who helped inspire me
to become an entrepreneur.
To my mom, who always knew my true worth.
And to my wife, Collette, for supporting
me through all my crazy ideas and running
our home in a way that has allowed
me to chase my dreams.*

CONTENTS

FOREWORD

WHAT THE 'ONLINE MARKETING WIZARD FRATERNITY' DOESN'T WANT YOU TO KNOW . . . (AND: IS THIS BOOK A 'FRAUD'?)

Yes, there IS an 'online marketing wizard fraternity.' Many of them hang out together, scheme together, and work together. And yes, there ARE a few things they'd rather you *didn't* think about while they perform their wizardly shows. This book is the first of its kind to actually reveal what is really happening behind the scenes in their fast-growing companies.

Don't misunderstand: Few of these wizards are actually *evil*. Most bring valid 'magic tricks' to the show. Many do guide businesspeople to treasure. But often there is a discernible pattern behind everything they say, teach, promise, and promote: a deliberately engineered and exacerbated lack of solid ground. This book doesn't just focus on magic tricks, but the core strategies you must have in place to scale a company with online media.

It is in the wizards' best interest for you to believe everything in the online media, marketing, and business world is shiny and new, constantly changing, and untethered from the old rules, principles, facts, and math of successful advertising and marketing.

This book by Russell Brunson is different. While teaching you about the "shiny" secrets of the internet, he shows you how to build these tactics and strategies into your business on solid ground—tactics and strategies founded in true direct response marketing. It is **your responsibility** to resist the seduction of short-lived, bright and shiny lures, popularity and peer pressure, and the siren songs of superficially knowledgeable promoters of 'new' tactics with no knowledge of its original direct response genealogy. **You** must exercise discernment.

I'm *for* challenging norms and breaking rules. But I also like solid ground, not ever-shifting sand. I like being confident and in control of things—particularly my money and the making of it—not in constant high-anxiety and at the mercy of wizards.

I taught myself direct marketing as a *science*. I'm a reliability guy. I'm far more interested in a car that starts and runs well and predictably every time you turn the key than one that looks sexy and is popular with some 'in' crowd but might stall at 80 mph or not start at all. I like evergreen, not frequently obsolete. In my roles as a strategic consultant and a direct response copywriter, I am all about creating advertising, marketing, and sales *assets* of lasting value for my clients—not moneymaking devices written in disappearing ink.

That's why I agreed to write the foreword for *this* online marketing wizard's book. I admire the truth Russell has put between these pages. Unlike many of these whiz kids, Russell Brunson is grounded in direct marketing *disciplines*.

Discipline is good. General Norm Schwarzkopf (of Operation Desert Storm fame) once said:

"Shined shoes save lives."[1]

Norm went on to explain that in the heat of battle, the fog of war, under pressure, *the undisciplined die.* So it is in business. I sit now, as infrequently as possible, in meetings with young online marketing people demonstrably devoid of any disciplined thinking. They are full of opinion and youthful hubris but very short on facts. I would not want to share a foxhole with them or depend on them. I would risk it with Russell.

This book offers solid ground in the very ethereal world of online marketing and commerce. It properly treats internet media *as media*—not as a business. It utilizes the science of split-testing. It builds on long-proven marketing funnel and sales architecture. It takes a very disciplined approach.

It is, in one way only, a *fraudulent* book. The title is deceptive. It really is not about "DotCom Secrets" nor is it a playbook for "growing your company *online*." It is that, but such a narrowed and limiting characterization is deceptive.

In truth, this is a *solid* book about *reliable* marketing 'secrets' that can be applied to 'DotCom' business activities—and that are 'secrets' to many who've come of age only paying attention to what they see occurring online. In truth, this is a *proven* playbook for growing your company with effective lead generation and sales/conversion methods, which can be used online and offline.

'Solid' and 'reliable' and 'proven' aren't the sexiest positioning terms, so Russell can be forgiven for holding them back, waiting to carefully reveal them inside the book. 'Growing Your Company ONLINE' sounds cooler and less work than 'Growing Your Company,' so he can also be forgiven for playing to people's fascination of the moment. He is a wizard, and as such must be permitted some legerdemain. But let's you and I be very clear about reality. Let me serve a useful purpose for you here.

My advice: Don't settle for or be distracted by mere tricks. Be a responsible *adult*. Invest your time 'n treasure in information, skills, and properties that can yield harvest after harvest after harvest—not fleeting fads or not sexy ideas that age very poorly. And don't fall for the idea that any new media gets to defy gravity and live untethered to reality, math, or history.

Don't go into this book in lust for a new, cool, quick, easy "fix" or nifty "toy" or clever gimmick that might make you money today but require you to find another and another and another at a frantic pace.

Go into this book in search of deep understanding and profound clarity about the structure and science of effective marketing to be applied in the online media universe.

—Dan S. Kennedy

Dan S. Kennedy is a trusted strategic advisor to hundreds of seven-figure-income professionals, direct-marketing pros, and CEOs. He is also the author of over 20 books, including *No B.S. Ruthless Management of People and Profits* (2nd Edition). For more information about Dan, visit NoBSBooks.com and GKIC.com.

PREFACE

WHAT THIS BOOK IS ABOUT
(AND WHAT IT'S NOT ABOUT)

Hey, my name is Russell Brunson.

Before we get started, I want to introduce myself and let you know what this book is about (and more importantly, what it's not about).

This book is NOT about getting more traffic to your website—yet the "DotCom Secrets" I'm going to share with you will help you to get exponentially MORE traffic than ever before.

This book is NOT about increasing your conversions—yet these DotCom Secrets will increase your conversions MORE than any headline tweak or split test you could ever hope to make.

If you are currently struggling with getting traffic to your website, or converting that traffic when it shows up, you may think you've got a traffic or conversion problem. In my experience, after working with thousands of businesses, I've found that's rarely the case. Low traffic and weak conversion numbers are just symptoms of a much greater problem, a problem that's a little harder to see (that's the bad news), but a lot easier to fix (that's the good news).

Recently, I had a chance to fly to San Diego to work with Drew Canole from FitLife.tv. He had built a following of 1.2 million followers on Facebook, but because of some changes at Facebook, his traffic had dropped by 90 percent. He was now spending $116 to sell a $97 product. He was no longer profitable.

Drew's team called me because they wanted help with two things: traffic and conversions.

I smiled because that's why most people call me. They usually assume that I'm going to help them tweak a headline or change their ad targeting and solve their problems. But I knew that, like most companies I work with, FitLife.tv's problem wasn't a traffic or conversion problem.

It rarely is.

More often than not, it's a FUNNEL problem.

After listening to Drew and his team share with me all their numbers, their pains and frustrations, and their ups and downs, I sat back in my chair and told them they were in luck.

"You don't have a traffic or conversion problem," I said.

"What are you talking about? Our traffic is down ninety percent, and we can't break even converting our customers!" Drew said.

"The problem is you can't spend enough to acquire a customer, and the way to fix that problem is to fix your sales funnel," I replied calmly.

One of my mentors, Dan Kennedy, says, *"Ultimately, the business that can spend the most to acquire a customer wins."*[2]

The reason Drew's business wasn't making money was because he wasn't able to spend enough to acquire a customer. If we fix his sales funnel so that instead of making $97 for every $116 he spends, he can start making two to three times as much money for each sale—then the whole game changes. Suddenly, he can afford to buy more traffic from more places, he can outbid his competitors, and he can spend two to three times more than he is now, all while becoming exponentially more profitable.

So what changes did we make to Drew's business? How did we take a sales funnel that was losing money and transform it into a tool that allowed FitLife.tv to spend MORE money than its competitors while gaining more traffic, more customers, and more sales?

THAT is what this book is about.

This book will take you on a journey similar to the one I took Drew and his team on. It will help you understand how to structure your company's products and services in a way that will allow you to make two to three times as much money from the same traffic that you're getting now. When you follow the steps, you'll open the floodgates, allowing you to spend a lot more money to get a lot more new customers. This book will also show you how to communicate with your customers in a way that makes them naturally want to ascend your ladder of offerings and give you more money as you provide them more value.

Once you know the foundational concepts behind these DotCom Secrets, we'll dive into the phases of a sales funnel and explore the building blocks you will need to use in each phase.

Finally, I will give you the 10 core sales funnels I use in all my companies, plus all the sales scripts I use to convert people at each stage in those funnels. You can choose to model my proven funnels and scripts as is, or you can tweak them to better fit your specific business.

When you implement each of these secrets, you will transform your business and your website from a flat, two-dimensional company into a three-dimensional sales and marketing machine that allows you to outspend your competitors, acquire an almost unlimited number of new customers, make (and keep) more money, and most importantly, serve more people.

That is what this book is about.

NOTE TO
THE READER

THE SECRETS TRILOGY

I wrote this book and designed the original funnel frameworks while we were working on a new startup idea for a software platform that would make it simple for entrepreneurs to create funnels like I was teaching about in this book. The idea eventually became the software platform found at ClickFunnels.com and this book became the playbook for how to build sales funnels online.

Over the next five years that I served as the CEO of ClickFunnels, we started to see a gap between the funnel builders who were making a lot of money with their funnels and those who struggled. People had mastered funnel structure and framework because of *DotCom Secrets* (and they could quickly build those funnels inside of ClickFunnels), but some people weren't making any money because they lacked the basic understanding of how to convert their funnels visitors into customers. They didn't understand the fundamentals of persuasion, story-selling, building a tribe, becoming a leader, and communicating with the people who entered into their funnels.

And so I began a second book with a goal of helping its readers to learn and master the persuasion secrets that are necessary to convert people at each stage of your funnel. It is called *Expert Secrets: The Underground Playbook for Converting Your Online Visitors into Lifelong Customers*. While *DotCom Secrets* was the "science" or structure of funnel-building, *Expert Secrets* became the "art" of what you say inside your funnels.

Then, over the next few years, as we watched members of ClickFunnels growing their companies with funnels (using the structure from *DotCom Secrets* and the persuasion skills they learned in *Expert Secrets*), many people were still struggling because they didn't know how to get consistent traffic or people into their funnels. Because of that, I wrote my third and final book in this series called *Traffic Secrets: The Underground Playbook for Filling Your Websites and Funnels with Your Dream Customers*.

Each of these books was written as a stand-alone playbook, but mastering the skills from all three is essential for long-term growth of your company. Because of that, you'll see that the most recent versions of these three books refer to each other and tie in important concepts from each book.

I hope that you can use the books in this trilogy hand in hand to change the lives of the customers you have been called to serve. Everything written in these three books is evergreen and focuses on concepts that have worked yesterday, are working today, and will continue to work tomorrow and forever. If you don't have the other two books in this trilogy, I would encourage you to get a free copy at ExpertSecrets.com and TrafficSecrets.com.

If you are interested in the most up-to-date information, I invite you to listen to my podcast, *Marketing Secrets*. It's published twice a week and covers everything we're learning and discovering in real time. I share new secrets for free that build on the evergreen topics and frameworks that you are mastering in these books. You can subscribe to this podcast at MarketingSecrets.com.

INTRODUCTION

My junk mail addiction began when I was 12 years old. I remember the exact night my obsession with junk mail and direct response marketing started. My dad was up late watching TV while working on a project. Normally, he made me go to bed early, but that night he let me stay up late and watch TV with him. I was so excited—not because I was interested in watching the news so much as I was in spending more time with my dad.

When the news ended, I was waiting for him to send me to bed, but for some reason he didn't, so I started watching the program that came on next. It was one of those late-night infomercials. This particular infomercial featured a guy named Don Lapre who was explaining how to make money with "tiny little classified ads."[3] I'm not sure why he grabbed my attention. Maybe, because I was so young, I didn't understand that making money fast "wasn't possible." Maybe my fascination grew because he was so charismatic. Whatever the reason, as soon as he started talking, I was hooked.

During this infomercial, he told stories about how he started his first business. He explained how he came up with an idea for a product and then placed a classified ad in his local newspaper to sell this new product. The first week after his ad ran, he made enough money to pay for the ad and was left with about $30 in profit. While most people wouldn't consider that a big win, Don knew that he could take that same winning ad, run it in other newspapers, and make a profit from each paper.

He ended up running that ad in thousands of newspapers and made tens of thousands of dollars a month doing it!

I didn't realize it at the time, but Don was teaching me (and everyone else who was watching) the basics of direct response marketing, which could be applied to any company.

Well, as you can guess, my 12-year-old eyes opened wide, and my heart started racing. I remember getting so excited that I couldn't sleep that night—or the rest of the week. All I could think about was buying Don's system so I could start making money. I asked my dad if he would help me pay for it, but as any good father should, he made me go out and work for the money. I mowed lawns, weeded gardens, and worked really hard for three or four weeks to earn the money to buy the system.

I still remember calling the 1-800 number to order. When the box showed up, my heart was racing as I ripped it open. I started reading the pages as Don explained to me the basics of direct response marketing through classified ads.

And that is where this journey began for me.

After that, I started to search for classified ads inside of our newspaper to see if other people were actually placing ads and selling things. As I looked, I found hundreds of ads from people who were making a living doing exactly what Don was teaching!

One day my mom took me to the grocery store and I saw a magazine on the shelf called *Small Business Opportunities* that had quotes on the front cover about making money. I grabbed a copy and started flipping through the pages and instantly saw the same types of ads that I had seen in the newspapers. I had my mom buy me a copy of that magazine, and when I got home, I called every phone number I could find, requesting the free "info kits" that the ads were promoting.

Within three or four weeks, I started getting "junk mail." (I put "junk mail" in quotation marks because studying that junk mail has literally made me millions of dollars.) I started getting so much mail that the mailman couldn't physically fit it all into the mailbox. I would come home from junior high school and I would have a huge stack of my very own mail on the countertop. I'd take it all into my bedroom and read through every letter. I didn't know it at the time, but I was reading long-form sales letters from some of the greatest direct response marketers of all time. I saw what they were doing and how they were doing it, and it was fascinating to me.

Whatever they were selling, the process was the same. They would place a small ad asking people to contact their company for a free report. After you contacted them, they would send you a sales letter disguised as a free report, selling a low-ticket information product. When I purchased the product, they would send me their "system"—along with another sales letter selling me a high-ticket product.

Figure 0.1:

The offline sales funnels brought prospects through a predictable series of steps.

This was my first exposure to sales funnels. I didn't know it at the time, but this process I was seeing over and over again offline would become the exact *same* system that I would use to grow hundreds of companies online.

Now, while funnels often get much more advanced than this, look at this diagram to see what offline funnels look like, and note how similar they are to the online funnels I will be showing you throughout this book.

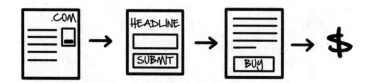

Figure 0.2:

Today's online sales funnels are practically identical to the offline direct response marketing funnels I studied as a kid.

Looking back, I think it's funny that while most kids my age were collecting baseball cards, I was studying junk mail and learning marketing funnels. When I left for college, my mom made me throw my junk mail in the garbage, but I got this one last picture with the best marketing and sales education I could have ever received.

Figure 0.3:

My love for direct response marketing gave me a huge collection of junk mail.

Unfortunately, I was never able to afford to sell stuff through classified ads and direct mail when I was 12. But I understood the concept. It wasn't until 10 years later, during my sophomore year in college, that I rediscovered direct response marketing and saw how I could use it on the internet.

MY FIRST ONLINE BUSINESS

One late night during my sophomore year in college, I was lying in bed—way too tired to turn off the TV. So instead, I flipped through the channels, and one commercial caught my eye. It explained how people were "making money online with a website." I knew I needed to learn more. I dialed the number, got a ticket for a local event, and the next night I was at a seminar in a local Holiday Inn. That little seminar reignited my interest in business and direct response marketing. I remember hearing the speakers talk about how people were using the internet to make money in a way that was almost identical to what I learned when I was a kid. But instead of using mail, they were using email; instead of using magazines, they had blogs; and instead of the radio, they were using podcasts. It was fascinating, and I was hooked from day one.

Figure 0.4:

Blogs, podcasts, and online video are simply newer versions of the old-school offline media channels.

I started looking at other people's websites, studying how these businesses were making money. I decided to model what I saw. After all, if it worked for them, it could work for me. So I created similar products and services to what others were selling online. My websites looked similar and the copy on the pages was similar, but for some reason, my efforts made very little (if any) money. I was frustrated because I could see others making money successfully. What was I doing wrong?

It took almost two full years of studying, researching, and interviewing successful marketers before I realized that what I was seeing online wasn't the full business. The people who were making money were doing it through steps and processes invisible to the naked eye.

While I had modeled the part of their businesses that I could see, there were multiple things happening behind the scenes that made the magic work. I found that the difference between a $10,000 website and a $10 million company was all the things happening *after* a buyer came into the initial sales funnel.

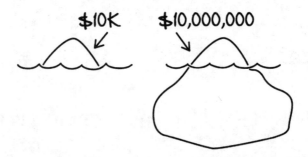

Figure 0.5:

I was modeling what I could see happening on the surface, but the real money was made in ways I couldn't see.

It took me years to discover and master these DotCom Secrets—but when I did, my company quickly went from a few hundred dollars a month to millions of dollars a year in revenue.

I wanted to write this book because I know there are people like me who have been trying to be successful online yet are not having success. So many people try to model the surface level of what others are doing and are frustrated that they aren't getting similar results. This book is the culmination of a decade spent analyzing thousands of companies and their successful sales funnels. I have built hundreds of sales funnels of my own and have worked with tens of thousands of students and clients to build funnels in every market you can dream of—both online and offline.

I hope that after reading this book you will realize your dreams of success are a lot closer than you think. You will soon see that by providing a ton of value, communicating effectively with your audience, and building out your sales processes and funnels in a very strategic way, you can get your product, service, or message out to the world. And you can get paid what you're worth while doing it.

THREE WAYS THIS BOOK IS DIFFERENT

By purchasing this book, you have put your trust in me as your coach. I know that you're busy; I fully understand and respect that. It's important for you to know that I will not waste your time. You have many choices in business and success training, and I'm honored that you've decided to spend your valuable time with me. Here's how this book is different from other business books you may have read:

1. Everything I show you in this book is evergreen: If you've tried to learn how to grow your company online in the past, you've probably purchased books and courses with systems that worked when they were created, but became outdated, oftentimes before they even got to the publisher. When Google changes an algorithm or Facebook introduces a new layout, many tactics suddenly become obsolete.

This book, on the other hand, is a playbook for creating sales and marketing funnels that will exponentially increase your sales online. It is an evergreen guide and will be just as useful 10 years from now as it is today. I only focus on strategies and concepts that will remain the same—even when technology changes.

2. I don't just teach this stuff; I actually do it: There are a ton of people teaching internet marketing, and the vast majority of them make money by teaching other people the internet marketing strategies they learned about online. Dan Kennedy calls those people "shovel sellers" because during the gold rush, the people who made the most money were the ones selling the shovels. Today's shovel sellers are selling you internet marketing strategies without actually using any of the strategies themselves.

The difference between me and most of my competitors is that *I actually do this for real.* That's right. I use every one of the secrets I'm about to reveal to you. And I've tried them in dozens of different markets—from physical products to services to coaching and software. I also work directly with hundreds of other businesses, advising them and increasing their profitability in almost every niche and every industry you can dream of.

About seven or eight years ago, I had the good fortune to work with direct marketing legends Dan Kennedy and Bill Glazer. They work with entrepreneurs all around the world, and I was their main internet marketing trainer for almost six years. This was a very unique situation, and I was able to work with hundreds of offline businesses, teaching them to implement the same concepts I'm about to share with you.

I've also had a chance to teach these DotCom Secrets at Tony Robbins's Business Mastery seminar. I can tell you from experience that these strategies work for both online and offline businesses in just about any industry you can think of. Throughout the book, I'll share examples of these different types of businesses so you can see how each strategy could work in any market.

The book is divided into several sections. Section One gives you the core strategies and concepts that you MUST understand before you can create your first marketing funnel. Once you understand the secrets behind what makes online selling work, then you'll learn in Section Two how to build the main 10 sales funnels we use in our companies every day.

Section Three gives you the sales scripts you need to move people through your marketing funnel so they will purchase from you. Section Four will show you some of the easier ways to implement all the technology involved. I see people get tripped up by the tech all the time, so I want you to skip the hard stuff and make it easy on yourself.

Once you know how funnels work, implementing them is a simple matter of picking which one you want to use and setting it up. Please don't skip ahead to Section Two until you've read the earlier chapters, or you will miss learning the core strategies that make those funnels and scripts work. I want everything to make total sense to you, so make sure you follow the process in order.

3. The doodles are engineered for instant recall: Throughout the book, you're going to notice tons of simple little doodles to illustrate each concept. The reason the pictures are so basic is because I want you to be able to look at the image and immediately recall the concepts. At some point in the future, if you need to remember how to structure an upsell sales letter or how to set up your "cart funnel," you'll be able to pull out the picture and instantly recall how to do it. When you need that image recall, you can flip through the book to find the pictures, if you like, or you can go to DotComSecrets.com/resources and print them out. I like to keep a notebook of all the pictures of funnels and scripts I develop so I can always find the one I need. I even have some students who have certain images taped to their office walls as memory aids.

I recommend reading through the entire book once from beginning to the very end. You're uncovering the rest of the iceberg, and you need to understand the concepts in order. Once you've gone through all the material, then you can go back to the chapters you know will make a big difference right away.

I'm excited for you to dive in and have some fun with this. So, let's get started!

SALES FUNNEL SECRETS

I had just gotten married earlier that year, which meant I was one of just two married guys on the Boise State wrestling team. It was spring break and all our friends had jumped into their cars to make the six-hour drive to Vegas to celebrate. But Nate Ploehn and I were stuck at home because the beautiful women we had married earlier that year were working hard to support their jobless, wrestling husbands.

I was a sophomore, and I had been studying marketing and learning how to sell things online. But at that point, almost everything I tried had failed. I tried selling things on eBay, but never made enough profit to cover my shipping and listing fees. I then tried dropshipping and selling things on Craigslist, and eventually I tried becoming an affiliate selling other people's products online. Yet nothing I tried seemed to work.

By the third day of spring break, Nate and I were bored. We needed a project . . . something fun to do while we were waiting for our wives to get home from their jobs. And that's when Nate had "the idea."

"Hey, Russell, do you want to try to make a potato gun?" he asked.

I had heard of potato guns before, but I'd never actually seen one. He told me you could make them by gluing PVC pipes together. When they're dry, you jam a potato down the barrel, spray hairspray into the chamber, create a little spark, and shoot them a few hundred yards! I was so excited I could barely contain myself!

There was only one problem—we didn't know how to make one.

So we found some websites that had free potato gun plans. During our research, we found out a bunch of interesting things.

We learned you had to have the correct barrel-to-chamber volume ratio or your potatoes wouldn't shoot very far. We found out the right propellant to use, the correct pressure for the pipes, and lots of other important details. We also learned how to keep ourselves safe (meaning which kinds of pipes and propellants would blow up and which ones wouldn't). It didn't take long before we knew a *lot* about potato guns.

Armed with this information, we were ready to make our first gun. We went to Home Depot and bought the things we needed, including pipes, glue, and barbecue igniters. We spent the next few days making the gun, and when it was finished, we found a secluded location and started shooting it. We had one of the best times of our lives. It was so much fun!

We spent the rest of that week making more guns, trying out other plans, and even creating some designs of our own. During that week, we learned more about potato guns than 95 percent of the world would ever know. In fact, you might say we became experts.

The next Monday when school started back up again, I remember sitting in a finance class wishing I was out shooting potato guns, and then I had a flash of inspiration. I thought, *Has anyone else besides me searched for information on how to make potato gun plans?* Online, you can find websites that tell you how many searches in Google are happening each month. So I went to one of those websites, typed in the keyword "potato gun," and found that over 18,000 people that month had searched for the phrase "potato gun"!

At that time, there were no products, no paid plans, and no other experts out there teaching people about potato guns. There was a lot of free stuff, but nothing for sale. It occurred to me that this was my chance. This was my opportunity to become an expert in potato guns and to sell my advice. I figured I knew about as much as any other "potato gun expert" out there, so all I needed to do was create a product and sell it. I called Nate and convinced him to help me record a demo of us making potato guns. We borrowed a little video camera and drove up to Home Depot to start filming our first product.

When we got there and started filming, someone asked us what we were doing. We told them we were recording a video about making potato guns. Apparently, Home Depot didn't want that type of liability, so they threw us out. Then we drove to another Home Depot in town, and this time we went into stealth mode. I hid the camera under my jacket, then pulled it out and started recording what we were buying as we picked up the supplies.

We returned home and filmed ourselves assembling the guns. We described each step as we did it, shared the secret barrel-to-chamber volume ratios we'd discovered, told them about our favorite propellants, and instructed them how to keep safe. Eventually, we had a video explaining the whole process. Then we turned our homemade video into a DVD to sell online.

I remember being so excited that I was going to have my own product selling online. We burned a bunch of copies of our new DVD, got my website set up, added an Add to Cart button, connected it to a shopping cart, and then went to Google to start buying some ads.

At first it was easy—almost too easy. I told Google that anytime someone typed in "potato gun" or "spud gun" or "potato gun plans" to show my ad, and then they would charge me on average about $0.25 every time someone would click on my ad. On an average day, I would spend about $10 on ads, and from those $10, I would average about one sale of our DVD per day! When you do the quick math, I was averaging about $27 per day in profit from my little potato gun website (not bad for a couple of college wrestlers!).

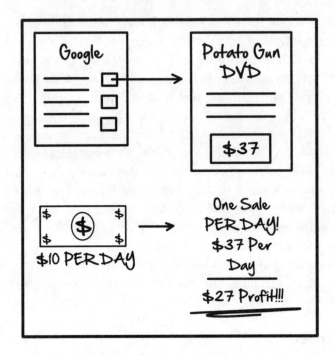

Figure 1.1:

On average, each day I spent $10 in ads to sell one $37 DVD, so I was able to make a profit of $27 every day.

But then it happened. I didn't understand it at the time, but I experienced the first "Google slap," where Google decided, literally overnight, to change everything. I woke up one morning to find out that my costs went from $0.25 to almost $3.00 per click! I was sick to my stomach knowing that if this stayed the same, I would be out of business in just a few days. By the end of the week, I started to look at the damage. The stats showed me that it was now costing me almost $50 per day in ads to sell one DVD per day.

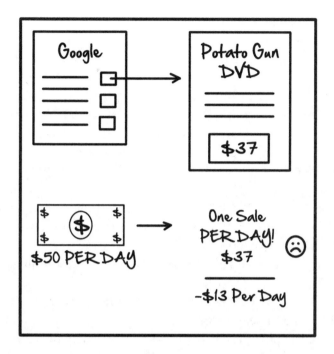

Figure 1.2:

After the Google slap, I realized that I spent on average
$50 per day to sell one $37 DVD, so I lost $13 every day!

I was devastated. I turned off my ads that morning thinking that I had missed the opportunity of the internet. It was no longer for little guys like me. I spent the next few weeks feeling sorry for myself, and then one day I got a call from one of my friends, Mike Filsaime. He had a similar business to mine, selling information products online.

"Hey, man. Have you recovered from the slap yet?" he asked.

"No, I turned off all my ads. I'm not sure what to do now," I responded.

I could then hear him smiling from the other end of the line. "Dude, we figured it out. I know how to make your ads work again!"

"What?! How?" I asked.

"Did you know that when you go to McDonald's, they spend $1.91 in advertising to get people into the drive-through? That means that when they sell you a burger for $2.09, they only make $0.18."

"No," I responded. "But what does that have to do with my website?"

"Well, after you order your burger, they have their cashiers ask this magic question: 'Do you want fries and a Coke with that?' They charge $1.77 more for this upsell, but they make—and more importantly they keep—$1.32 profit from everyone who takes this upsell! That's eight times the profit of the initial sale!"

I could tell he was excited, but I still didn't understand what this had to do with me. He went on to tell me that after he got hit with the Google slap, he decided he needed to have his own upsells like McDonald's. His ad costs had gone up, so if he could get his profits to go up eight times, then he could still buy ads and be profitable.

He showed me a few of his sites, and he set them up in a way that I had never seen before. After someone purchased one of his products, the next page had an upsell page, where he made people a special "One-Time Offer," or OTO, asking them to upgrade their order.

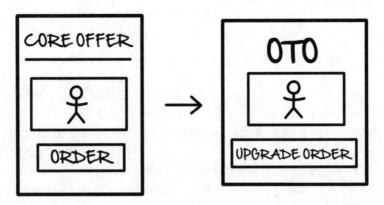

Figure 1.3:

By adding OTOs after your core offer, you'll be able to increase your customer's total order so you can still buy ads and remain profitable.

He told me that one out of three people who saw this upsell offer were buying it, and because he was making so much more money from each sale, he was able to turn his ads back on!

I could barely control my excitement. "But wait . . . What would I sell for my OTO?" I asked. "I only have a potato gun DVD."

"What other value could you give them, Russell?" he asked. "After they have the DVD, what else could you do to serve them?"

After thinking for a minute, I said, "Well, the biggest complaint I get from my customers is that they have to go and buy the pipes, barbecue ignitors, and all the supplies to make the guns."

"*YES!*" he shouted. "That's perfect. After they buy your DVD, then make them a special offer to have you ship them a kit with everything they need to make their potato guns."

After I got off the call, I searched online for someone who was selling potato gun kits. Eventually I found someone in northern Idaho who made these kits, and I set up a partnership with them where they shipped out the kits I sold online. I then added this one simple upsell page to my sales process, turned back on the ads, and what happened next changed everything for me.

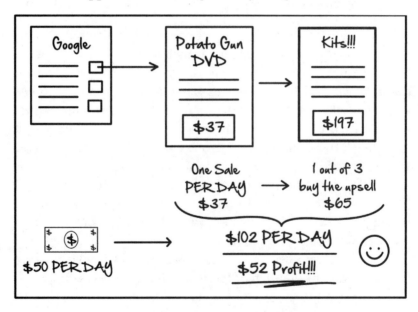

Figure 1.4:

After adding a potato gun kit as my OTO, I was able to increase my customer's average order from $37 to $102. Instead of losing money with $50 per day ad costs, I was able to make a higher profit than I did before the Google slap.

Google kept charging me $50 a day in ads, but now one out of three people started to buy my upsell for the $197 potato gun kit! That means I made an extra $65 on average for each person who purchased a DVD from me! I was now spending $50 a day on ads, but because I generated an average of $102 revenue from each order, I was able to make a $52 profit on every DVD that I sold. I was making more money than before the Google slap ever happened!

Without even knowing it, I had built my first sales funnel, and by doing it, I was able to do two amazing things:

- **Give my customers a better experience.** By making the special offer for the potato gun kits, I was able to serve them at a much higher level than I had before.

- **Spend a lot more money to acquire a customer.** Even when spending $3.00 or more per click, I was able to remain profitable.

Although I didn't have any competitors in the potato gun market, I had learned a valuable principle. Dan Kennedy said it best: *"Ultimately, the business that can spend the most to acquire a customer wins. A business beats its competition by making the same prospect worth more to his business than to that of his competition."* Because each of my customers was worth more, I could spend more to get those customers. Anyone else who was in that market with me would have gone out of business with the increased cost in ads, but I was able to flourish and take all the traffic for myself!

After seeing how this simple funnel changed my business overnight, I knew that I could apply it to *any* company and dramatically increase how much money they would make from each of their customers. I became slightly obsessed and started launching funnels in dozens of different industries. I had funnels selling:

- Speed-reading courses
- Baby sign-language books
- Couponing classes

- Dating courses
- Supplements
- Physical products
- Weight-loss training
- Network marketing
- Apps
- And more . . .

During that time, we were innovating and trying to come up with crazy ideas for other types of funnels besides the basic one I just showed you. We tested hundreds of ideas and found dozens of types of funnels that can be used for different situations. In Section Two, I will show you the main 10 funnels that I use daily in my companies and the companies I consult. Each one has a different purpose for acquiring customers, ascending them, and monetizing them, and using each can help you geometrically grow your company.

Outside of my own companies, I started to share these funnels with other types of businesses in every category that you can dream of, from information to physical product sellers to service-based businesses, including local brick-and-mortar-style companies. People often ask me, "Russell, does my business need a funnel?" to which I always respond, "Only if your company needs leads or sales." If you want to generate leads, there are funnels for that. If you want to sell products, there are funnels for that. Funnels will grow any company. Your goal is to figure out which funnels are right for your specific situation. Most people start with one funnel to acquire new customers and then build other funnels to help them make more money on autopilot from each new lead they get.

WHAT IS A SALES FUNNEL?

The question that I get asked daily is: What is a sales funnel? And no matter how hard I try, I've never been able to figure out a one-sentence answer that quickly describes it. The thing that I've found to be most helpful is to contrast a funnel with a website. Many people think they are the same thing, but when you see them side by side, it quickly becomes apparent why a funnel is superior.

When websites first came into existence, people didn't really know what they were or how they were supposed to use them. There was little strategy involved, and the people who were selling the websites to business owners (the designers) just wanted to make something that looked pretty and made the business owner feel good about themselves. Because of that, most websites for the first decade or two of the internet looked a lot like a glorified brochure: they looked awesome and had links to everything that the business could potentially do for a customer.

The problem was there was no strategy or process behind the website. It was similar to hiring a salesperson, having them stand outside your store and hand out brochures to people who were walking by, with the only sales strategy being the hope that they'd look at the brochure, find something they liked, and then come back to buy something. If I had a salesperson who just handed out brochures and only waited for people to come and buy, I'd fire them immediately, yet this is what most people are doing with a website.

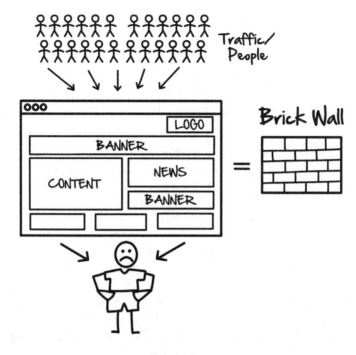

Figure 1.5:

A traditional website is a lot like a brochure, where it shows everything about a business. With so many options, though, sales usually suffer because visitors are confused about what their first step should be.

One of the fundamental rules of marketing is that "a confused mind always says no." Most websites have so many buttons, so many calls to action, and so many menus leading to hundreds of different pages that the only thing the website really does well is to confuse people.

A funnel, on the other hand, is created to be simple. From the outside, it may look like a website, but you'll notice that each page and each step only has *one* call to action. There is strategy behind what page someone sees first, and then the journey you take them on. It's similar to hiring the best salesperson, putting them outside of your store, and then as each person walks buy, they ask them for their name and contact information. After they have that, then they ask the person what it is they are looking for. When they find out, they take the person into the store, bypassing the dozen things that could distract them, and helping them find the exact thing they are looking for. After the salesperson gives them exactly what they are looking for, they can upsell them on other products or services that perfectly complement the original purchase and will help serve that customer at a higher level. When a salesperson takes someone through a funnel like this, two things happen:

- **The customer has a better user experience.** They aren't confused, and they can find exactly what they're looking for.

- **You as the store owner actually make more money.** Because you don't confuse your customers, you upsell them on the right things that will help them on their journey.

That same process is what happens in a funnel. I take someone to a page that only has one goal: to get their name and contact information. From there, I take those people who became leads into a sales process to sell the one product or service they are looking for. After they make that purchase, I help to customize the order for them through an upsell process, and later I use other funnels to help ascend those customers to other things I have to sell.

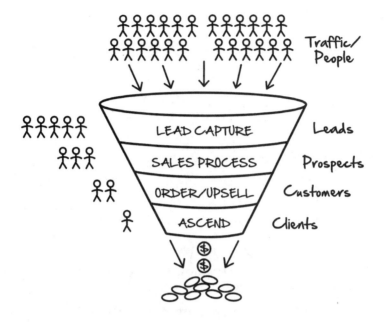

Figure 1.6:

A sales funnel is similar to cloning your best salesperson and having them guide your prospect through the entire sales process until they reach your desired destination.

Each type of funnel that you will learn about in this book will do this in a different way, but the process is always the same. Each page is simple, has a hook that will grab your attention, tells a story to create value, and makes you an offer that will move you to the next page of the funnel.

THE SECRET FORMULA

Now that you understand the basics behind what a funnel is, I want to walk you through a framework that I call "the Secret Formula." Inside each of the chapters in Section One, I am going to go deeper into each piece of this process, but I wanted to introduce it to you now so you know where we are heading in this section. The secret formula asks four simple questions that serve as the guide for everything we'll be doing inside this book.

Figure 1.7:

If you were to hire me for a $100,000 consultation day, we would work on answering these four questions in the secret formula for your company.

Question #1: *Who* is your dream customer? If you could pick your dream customer, the type of person who would make you wake up every morning on fire because you're so excited to work with them, what would they look like? The better you can identify this person, the easier it will be for you to find them.

Question #2: *Where* are they congregating? After we know *who* we are looking for, the next step is to find out *where* they are hiding. Where are they spending their time online? When I can identify exactly where they are online, getting them into my funnels becomes easy.

Question #3: What is the *bait* that you can use to attract them to you? Now that I know where they are, my job is to throw out *hooks* to try to grab their attention. After I have their attention, I tell them a *story* to build a relationship and increase the perceived value of what I have to offer, and then I need to make them an actual *offer* to get them into my world.

Question #4: What is the unique *result* that you can create for them? After they have come into my world, what other things can I do to help give them the results they are looking for? People don't come to you because they want your product, they come to you because they want a specific result. So what is the process you will take them through to give them more value so you can serve them at a higher level and give them a result that will truly change their life?

Those four simple questions will not only be the framework for Section One, but everything else you learn inside of this book will fit somewhere inside of that structure. These are the same four questions that I ask anyone who hires me for personal consultations. At the time of writing, companies pay me $100,000 per day to help them understand and implement this formula, as well as the funnels and scripts that move people through the value ladder.

Now while I know you didn't pay anywhere near that to learn this information and go through this process, I recommend you treat this and all the exercises in this book as if you did invest the full amount. If you do, you will get a lot more out of the process I'm going to take you through, and this book will become like a private $100,000 consultation with me. Let me now walk you deeper through the process we call the secret formula.

THE SECRET FORMULA

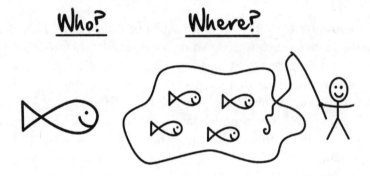

Figure 1.8:

First, you must ask yourself, *Who is my dream customer?*
Then go find where your dream customers are congregating.

It was 11:27 A.M. on a Monday morning, and no matter what I told myself, I just couldn't get out of bed. The muscles in my body ached, although it didn't make sense. I knew I wasn't sore from exercise because I hadn't worked out. I had a sick feeling in my stomach that felt like the flu, but I knew I wasn't sick. In my head, I was *wishing* that I had a boss, so that he or she could fire me and end this nightmare that I knew I had to face as soon as I finally stumbled out of bed.

How had I gotten here? Just a few years earlier, I had "officially" become an entrepreneur and launched my own company. And despite a lot of mistakes along the way, I was having some moderate success. The company I started was profitable. We were serving people and making a difference, but for some reason, I was miserable.

I thought back and tried to figure out where I had made the wrong turn. The more I thought about it, the more I started to realize that I didn't love the customers I was serving. But why? Was something wrong with me? Or was it something different?

A few weeks later, I was having a conversation with one of my entrepreneur friends, and I told him how I was feeling. He smiled at me and said, "If you don't like your customers, that's your fault, not theirs. You attract your customers based on the content and offers that you put into the marketplace." And then he said the line that I'll never forget, *"If you change your bait, you'll change your customer."*

Immediately I had one of those mind-blowing moments where I realized that when I got started, I never knew who I wanted to serve. Instead, I got excited about a product idea, threw it into the market, and waited for whoever was attracted to it to come. Unfortunately, the people who came with the offers I put into the marketplace were not the people that I enjoyed being with.

I then asked myself a powerful question that changed everything for me, *"Who* is the person I really want to serve?" Up to that point in my business, I had never asked myself that question. I had been trying to sell to anyone and everyone I could. I had focused all my efforts on creating a good product without any thought about who I actually wanted to serve. While focusing on the product sounded smart at first, it left me tired, frustrated, and empty inside. If I were to pick my dream customers, who were they, what did they look like, and what were the offers I could create that would attract them? This is also the first question you need to ask yourself when starting your new company or making the shift to truly grow your existing company.

Question #1: Who is your dream customer? The first question you have to ask yourself is, *Who do I actually want to work with?* Most of us start with a product idea, never thinking about who we want as clients or customers, yet these are the people you will be interacting with day in and day out. You'll oftentimes spend more time with these people than your own friends and family.

You choose your significant other carefully, so why wouldn't you take the same time and care in deciding who your dream client or customer will be? If you're just getting started, this may not seem important. But I promise you that if you don't consciously choose your dream client, one day you will wake up like I did, working with people who exhaust you and wishing that someone could fire you from the business you created.

After I had successfully launched my first software company, a lot of people took notice of my success online and began asking me how I started my company. Because I saw the demand, I thought it would be fun to teach others how to start their own businesses online.

The good thing was there were a *lot* of people who wanted to start businesses, and we made a lot of money teaching them. But the downside was that most of them didn't have any money (and couldn't invest in the higher-ticket things I wanted to sell). Many had no business experience, so I had to spend tons of time on the fundamentals, and that drove me crazy (which is one of the many reasons why I didn't want to get out of bed in the mornings). I had so much value *I wanted* to provide people—showing how I had scaled my companies, teaching conversion secrets and how we structure our funnels—but 99 percent of my time was spent showing them how to buy a domain and set up hosting.

I literally spent years serving these customers, and it made me miserable. My family suffered, and no matter how much money we made, I wasn't happy. It took years before I sat back and actually thought about the *who*. I realized I had overlooked some pretty important questions such as:

- Who are my dream clients? What do they look like?
- What are they passionate about?
- What are their goals, dreams, and desires?
- What are the offers I could create that would attract them and repel everyone else?

After about a week of thinking about the *who* question, I sat down and created two customer avatars: one for the men I wanted to work with and one for the women I wanted to work with.

For the women, I picked a name and wrote it down: Julie. Then I listed out the things I knew about the Julie that I wanted to serve. She is successful and driven; she has a message to share; she values her personal growth over money; and she's already started a business and had some success, but wants to learn how to grow it.

Next, I wrote down the name Mike. Next to Mike's name, I wrote out the things I knew about him. He is a former athlete. At some point, he has helped to change someone's life in a small way and wants to learn how to help more people. He values growth over money, and he's already built his business, but wants more impact and feels a need to learn how to grow it.

Then I went to Google images and typed in *Julie* and the characteristics I had written out. Within minutes, I found a picture that looked like the woman in my mind. I did the same for Mike, and within minutes, I had both pictures of my dream customers printed and hanging on my wall.

At the time this seemed like a silly exercise, but just last month I hosted a private event here in my office in Boise, Idaho, with 100 of my top entrepreneurs that I serve. Each of them paid me $50K to be in that meeting, each of them had businesses that made a minimum of $1 million per year, and each of them were my dream clients. I stood up and told them that I had written something about one of them, and I wanted to see if they could guess who I was talking about. I read aloud the characteristics for both Mike and Julie. When I asked them to raise their hands if they thought I was talking about them, almost every hand in the group went up.

I told them that six years earlier I had written out my dream customer avatar and had focused on creating offers and producing content that would attract that exact person. Six years later I was sitting in a room with 100 of the exact people that I had set out to attract just a few short years earlier.

As I said, this may seem like a silly exercise, but it's important that you do it anyway. It will change your business, and for most of you reading, it will likely change your life. Really spend some time thinking about who you want to work with. Write out their characteristics and then go find an actual picture to represent them. It's amazing how your perspective changes when you have a physical picture of your ideal customer—instead of a hazy, half-formed image in your head.

John Lee Dumas from the *Entrepreneur on Fire* podcast recently shared at one of our events how he crafted his "dream listener" when he first launched his podcast:

> When I was trying to figure out what I wanted *Entrepreneur on Fire* to be, I was overwhelmed because it was hard for me to find the path that I wanted to take my listeners on.
>
> When I really sat down and said, okay, my listener (or my avatar) is Jimmy. He's 37 years old, and he has a wife and two kids, ages three to five. He drives by himself to work every single day. It's a 25-minute commute to work. He gets to a cubicle at a job he hates for nine hours. He gets done with his job, drives home, and it's a 35-minute commute home. He gets stuck in a little bit of traffic. He gets home and hangs out with his kids, has dinner with his family, puts his kids to bed, hangs out with his wife, and then he has a little Jimmy pity party at the end of every single night because he's sitting on the couch asking himself, *Why do I spend 90 percent of my waking hours doing things that I don't enjoy doing? Commuting to a job I don't like, being at a job I don't like, commuting home, and only 10 percent of my waking hours doing things that I love, like spending time with my kids and my family.*
>
> Jimmy is my avatar. He's the person that, as he's driving to work, should be listening to *Entrepreneur on Fire* so that when my guest is sharing their worst entrepreneurial moments, he can understand that it's okay to fail, that you can learn lessons from failure. And that when he's driving home and my guest talks about their aha moment, he can talk about how you take an aha moment and turn it into success. And then instead of having that pity party at

night by himself on a couch, he can listen to the lightning round where my guest is sharing their best advice they've ever had, their favorite book, or their favorite resource, so he can start to put together the pieces of the puzzle.

So for me, whenever I come up to any question I have about the direction of my podcast, I go to my avatar and say, "WWJD: What would Jimmy do?" And I know from that one answer that that's the way I gotta go. So if you sit down and really say, "Hey, this really is the one perfect listener of my podcast," then you're going to know that person inside and out. You're going to know where that person hangs out, what Facebook groups they're in, what LinkedIn groups they're in, how to advertise to them, and what lead or ad is going to be appealing to them on Facebook that's going to get them to download it.

And again, this is your ideal, perfect client. You can probably picture right now this person, that whenever he sits down in front of you, you're just like, "Dude, you're like my favorite client." And he's like, "I know I'm your favorite client." That's the person that you want to be drawing in. So if you sit down and really just figure out who your perfect one ideal listener is, everything changes from that point forward and all the decisions you make are based off that. So every piece of content you make for your podcast is speaking to that avatar, that one person. Every call to action you give, every intro, and every outro is for a specific purpose.

A few years ago, two members of my Inner Circle high-end coaching program, Dean and Robyn Holland, had launched a makeup cosmetic brush company in the UK. They had developed these special brushes because Robyn suffers from a condition called polycystic ovarian syndrome (PCOS), and the brushes she created helped her to apply makeup and feel more confident about herself.

So they did what any good entrepreneur would do and found someone to create the brushes, spent a small fortune in inventory, built out a funnel, and started selling them to women around the world who would need cosmetic brushes.

After two years of selling these brushes, almost nothing happened. They had no momentum and almost no sales. Then one day they had a big epiphany. As Robyn was looking in the mirror, she realized that her dream customer was staring back at her. Her avatar wasn't all women who use makeup; that was too broad. Her market was women like her who were suffering from PCOS. What if instead of trying to sell their brushes to all women, they changed their customer avatar to look just like the person who was looking back at her in the mirror?

So they changed their dream customer avatar, which caused them to change the words on their landing pages in their funnel to speak specifically to this person, and then they changed the ads to be bait that would hook their dream person. They rebuilt their company to focus on their dream customer first, and it changed everything. Their makeup company went from making about $34K the entire previous year to making over $100K in the first 60 days after changing and focusing on their dream customer. Honestly, they would have done a lot more than $100K, but they blew through an entire year's worth of inventory in those two short months and had to shut off their ads while they rush-ordered new products to keep up with the demand.

The change didn't come from changing their products; it came from changing *who* their dream customers were, and then speaking directly to and attracting them. That is the first question you need to ask inside of the secret formula: *Who is your dream customer?*

Question #2: Where are your dream customers congregating?
The next question in the secret formula is *where* can you find your dream customer? Where are they already congregating online?

The real power of the internet is the power of congregations. Groups of people gathering in little corners of the internet make it possible for people like you and me to get into business quickly and be successful without all the barriers and expensive hurdles of traditional media.

When I say the word *congregation*, what's the first thing that pops into your head? For most people, the word *congregation* brings to mind a church. A church is really nothing more than a group of people who gather based on similar interests. For example, each week, the Baptists all congregate based on their similar beliefs and values. The Catholics also congregate and so do the Mormons, Seventh Day Adventists, Muslims, and Jews, right? So if I were selling a perfect product for Mormons, where would I go to sell it? Of course, I would go to the Mormon church. My dream customers would all be there together. All I'd have to do is put my message out in front of them, and if I made a good offer, some of them would buy.

I want to stop here before this analogy goes any deeper, because my point is not to teach you how to sell things to churches. I just want you to understand the power of a congregation because it's one of the main reasons the internet is such an amazing tool for businesses. Prior to the internet, it was hard for people around the world to congregate. We were limited by location and ability to communicate. But now it's possible for anyone and everyone to congregate and discuss almost anything with groups of people who have similar interests.

When I was in high school, there were five or six kids who would get together every day at lunch and play card games. One of the games was called *Magic: The Gathering*. They could congregate every day at lunch and play the game they loved. I'm sure there were a handful of kids in high schools all over the country doing the same thing, unaware of one another. Before the internet, that was how things worked. You were kind of limited based on geography; you might not be close to other people in your congregation. As a marketer, I would have found it difficult to reach five kids at one high school and three at another school and six or seven at yet another. It would have cost too much money to be successful. Yet now, thanks to the internet, those five or six kids in my high school can congregate with others all over the world to play *Magic: The Gathering* online. They can hang out on forums and play games with people halfway across the world. Now if I have a product to sell to a congregation of people who love *Magic: The Gathering*, it's easy and economical to go online, find where they are, and get my message in front of them.

Here's another example: I was a wrestler in college, and every night all the student athletes had to spend two hours in study hall to make sure we got our homework done. Naturally, I would sit next to my wrestling buddies, and we'd goof off online. I remember looking over one day and noticing that all my friends were looking at the exact same website I was. It was called TheMat. com—a website for wrestlers. We were all chatting about what had happened that month in the wrestling world and commenting on the big matches we were excited to see.

Every single person on my college wrestling team was in that study lab for two hours every night, hanging out on TheMat.com and talking about wrestling—rather than doing our homework.

Interestingly, this was likely happening in every single university around the country. Add in all the high school wrestlers, as well as their parents and other wrestling fans and fanatics, and you can see that almost anyone in the world who cared about wrestling were all in this same spot online, congregating and talking about the sport we love. Now, if I had a wrestling product, what would I do to sell it? I would find the existing congregation of wrestling fans, and I would put my bait out in front of them. Simple!

There are congregations online for *everything* you can dream up. What are the online congregations that you participate in? My guess is there are at least a dozen or more things that you're interested in, and you have a special place on the internet to go be with your people and talk about what's important to you.

I want you to now start thinking about congregations as they relate back to your dream customer. What are the congregations that they are already participating in? Start asking yourself these questions:

- What are the top websites that my dream customers already go to?

- What forums or message boards do they participate in?

- What are the Facebook groups they participate in?

- Who are the influencers they follow on Facebook and Instagram?

- What podcasts do they listen to?

- What are the email newsletters they are subscribed to?

- What blogs do they read?

- What channels are they following on YouTube?

- What keywords are they searching for in Google to find information?

Once you understand the core concept of congregations, driving traffic becomes incredibly easy. My job as a marketer is to figure out *who* it is I want to serve, and then figure out *where* they are already congregating.

Question #3: What is the bait (hook, story, and offer) you'll use to attract your dream customers? Once we know *where* the dream customers are, we have to create the right hook to grab their attention. The hooks are the ads that will grab the attention of your dream customers just long enough for you to tell them a story. The goal of the story is to build rapport with them as well as break the false beliefs they have that would keep them from taking you up on your offer. The offer is the thing you've created for your dream customer so you can give them the results they desire. If you do this step correctly, it will repel the customers you don't want to serve and attract the right customers to you.

As my company moved away from selling to beginners and toward attracting our dream customers, our first step was to create new offers that would attract a Mike or Julie.

The first new offer I created was called *DotCom Secrets Labs: 108 Proven Split Test Winners*. This offer worked great for us because most beginners don't know what a split test is. But we *knew* that Julie and Mike (our *dream* customers) would know what those terms meant and they would be hungry to get their hands on that information. Within days of launching this new offer, we had thousands of dream clients lining up to work with us. When you find out what your dream clients want, it becomes very easy to attract them. Throughout this book, we're going to talk more about creating the right offers. Right now, just realize the offer has to match what your dream customer wants.

Because this step in the formula has its own framework (called "Hook, Story, Offer"), I dedicated all of the next chapter, Secret #2, to going deep into that framework.

Question #4: What is the unique result or value that you can create for your dream customers? Once you've hooked your dream customers with the perfect offer, the last question is what *result* or *value* do you want to give them? I'm not talking about what product or service you want to sell them. A business is *not* about products and services. A business is about what *result* you can get for your clients. Once you (and they) understand that concept, the price is no longer a barrier.

For me, I know that the *best* way I can serve my dream client is to give them a funnel that works for them that gives them consistent leads or sales (whatever result they want), and the best way for me to deliver that to them is for me to just do it all for them. That is how I can have the deepest impact and serve the client at the highest level. Ideally, it's where I would like to take all my customers. That type of service is *not* cheap, but the results I can deliver at that level are amazing. To put it in perspective, for that service, my company used to charge $1 million up front plus a large percentage of sales.

I understand that many of my customers won't be able to pay me for that level of service (which is why we develop other products and services), but understanding where you ultimately want to take the dream client is the key to this step.

Imagine that your clients could pay you anything to get a desired result. What, then, would you do to help guarantee their success? Where would you lead them? What does that place look like? Keep that place in your mind; it's the pinnacle of success for your clients. It's where you want to take them.

The framework for this step of the secret formula is called "the Value Ladder." It will be broken down in greater detail in Secret #3 and will show you how to ascend your customers so you can make more money and they can receive more value.

Figure 1.9:

Mastering the secret formula is the foundation for business success.

That's it. The four questions to the secret formula, again, are as follows:

1. *Who* is your dream customer?

2. *Where* are they congregating?

3. What is the *bait* that you can use to attract them to you?

4. What is the unique *result* that you can create for them?

HOOK, STORY, OFFER

I was standing on stage in front of over 2,000 men, all dressed in black. I don't normally dress up when I speak, but for this event it was required, so I had on a black suit, black shirt, and black tie. As I started my presentation, I was nervous, because the men in this room had come not only to learn how to grow their companies, but also how to "have it all" and be successful in business, in life, and in relationships.

The person who had invited me to speak was named Garrett J. White, and his men were part of a movement called Wake Up Warrior. As I sat there looking at all these high achievers, I knew that the most valuable thing I could share in that moment was my Hook, Story, Offer framework because this was not only the key to getting what you want in business, but it's also the key to getting anything you want in life.

To illustrate my point, I pulled my iPhone out of my pocket and told all the Warriors that I was going to show them a magic trick. "I just purchased this new iPhone for $600 last week, but in the next ten minutes, someone here will be willing to give me at least $100,000 for this phone." I smiled and asked, "Is there anyone here who would be willing to give me $100,000 for this phone right now?" Not a single hand went up.

"Last week when I bought this phone," I said, "I decided to not just have the person who sold me the phone transfer everything over. I wanted this phone to be a clean start, so I went home and just manually copied over the things that I really wanted on it. As I was transferring everything, I got really excited about some of the gold that I moved over."

I went on to explain a few of the things that I had moved onto this new phone. I told them that if they were to buy this phone from me, these are all the things that were already installed on it that they would get immediate access to.

1. **Apple's Books app:** I told them, "Over the past ten years that I have been online, I have purchased well over $750,000 in courses. I have purchased every marketing, sales, investing, and personal development course that has ever come out. As soon as I get the big box of DVDs in the mail, I always have my brother rip the audio and turn them into an audiobook file that I then add to the Books app so I can listen to them over and over again. If the courses aren't good, I delete them, and I've left the ones that had the answers to the most important questions I had." I started reading a list of every course that was on the phone; most of them were super rare and not available online anywhere.

2. **My contacts list:** I showed the Warriors the names of some of the people who were inside my address book. I told them that I had been networking at hundreds of events over the past decade, and I had the personal cell phones and email addresses for some of the most influential people in the world. I said, "Many of these names have been worth millions of dollars to me alone. If you had my contact list, you could tell them that you know me and that I referred you, and I guarantee that they'll at least take your call." I then started to read the names of the people in my address book to them.

3. **Voxer:** I said, "My highest-end coaching clients pay me $100K per year to have access to my private Voxer channel. They have the ability to ask me any question at any time. I'll review their funnels, tweak their copy, and make connections and introductions to the people inside my network; they just have to message me. If you had this phone, you would have lifetime access to my private Voxer channel."

4. **Other apps:** I showed them the Google Drive app and how it had all the standard operating procedures

(SOPs) for every division in my company and my spreadsheets that listed all my investments, their rate of return, and the projections from the top financial analysts in the world, all updated in real time.

I went on and on telling the Warriors stories about each of the apps and how it's added to my network and my net worth. After about 10 minutes, I started a live auction.

"Who here would now give me $600 for this phone?" Every hand shot up. "This is a real auction, so don't lie. If your hand is up, you need to be ready to pay the actual price."

"$1,000," I said, and all hands stayed up.

"$5,000," I said, and not a single hand dropped.

"$10,000. $20,000," I said, and at each price increase a few hands would drop.

"$50,000. $75,000. $100,000," I said, and I still had over 50 hands raised.

"$250,000. $500,000," I said, and at this time, even I was a little shocked a few hands were raised.

Then I said, "If you're willing to pay $750,000 for my phone right now, come up on stage with me."

I watched in amazement as three people walked across the room and onto the stage with me. I asked them the question that all of us were thinking: "Why would you pay $750,000 for this phone?"

One of the guys said, "After hearing everything that is on that phone, $750,000 actually seems like a really good deal. Just one contact from your address book alone could more than pay for the investment immediately. I would have paid more."

I looked back at the audience and said, "You have to understand there are two ways to have the lowest price product in your market. The first is to *decrease the price* of what you sell (and cut out your margins and profit). The second is to *increase the value* so much that when you sell it for what it's worth, it seems inexpensive."

I quickly explained how I had used this Hook, Story, Offer framework on them. "I started with a *hook* to grab your attention: 'In the next ten minutes, someone here will be willing to give me at least $100,000 for this phone.' I then told *stories* about what was on my phone to increase the perceived value, and then I made an *offer*, and within minutes the value of this phone went from $600 to over $750,000."

HOOK, STORY, OFFER

I've just shown you a glimpse of how quickly we can change the value of a product by changing it into an offer and dramatically increasing its value by using stories and a hook to grab attention, but I want to go deeper so you can master this concept for your own business.

Figure 2.1:

Each piece of bait you put out (such as ads, emails, landing pages, upsells, webinars, and phone calls) should include a hook, a story, and an offer.

At this point in the secret formula, you should know exactly who you want to serve, and you should have started to identify the places that your dream customers are congregating online. Now it's our job to create bait that will bring those dream customers into your world. The way we do that is through a framework that we call Hook, Story, Offer.

Every step of your funnel will have a hook, a story, and an offer. The ads you place online, the emails you send, the landing pages you create, as well as any upsells, webinars, or phone calls you make, will all have a hook, a story, and an offer. If something isn't working in your funnel, it's always either the hook, the story, or the offer.

This framework is the key to your success online, so I want to dive deep into how to create hooks that will grab your dream customers, how to tell stories that will increase the value of your offer, and how to create and present an offer in a way that people have to say yes. Even though it's called Hook, Story, Offer, I want to actually start with the offer first. After we talk about how we create an irresistible offer, then we'll talk about how to craft a story that will increase the value of that offer, and lastly we'll talk about the hooks we will create to grab someone's attention long enough that they will listen to your story.

YOUR IRRESISTIBLE OFFER

If you're reading this book, then you likely already have a product or a service that you are selling or would like to sell online and you want to figure out how you can sell a *lot* more. If you don't have a business yet, and you are trying to figure out what you should sell to be successful online, then these are the three core categories that almost every business online falls into:

- **You're selling a physical product:** This could be anything from supplements to flashlights to RVs or more. Any type of physical product that you would ship out to someone after they order.

- **You're selling an information product:** These are my authors, speakers, coaches or consultants (or affiliates selling these products for others). These products often include digital courses, membership sites, live events and training.

- **You're selling a service:** Many of my local brick-and-mortar companies like restaurants, dentists, chiropractors, Realtors, and financial planners would

put themselves in this bucket, but it's also true for
online services like software, design work, etc. . . .

If you currently fall into any of these three categories, you
are likely selling what I call a "commodity." My definition of a
commodity is something that someone can also buy somewhere
else. You may have your own unique spin or twist on the product,
but the reality is that there are other ways for someone to get the
same result you are offering from someone else. That is the same
problem that I had in my iPhone example I shared earlier. If I was
trying to sell iPhones, I was competing against Apple, Best Buy,
and Amazon, and the only way for me to get an advantage over
these other sellers would be to lower my prices and cut into my
own margins.

Dan Kennedy once said, "There is no strategic advantage of
being the second lowest price leader in town, but there is a huge
strategic advantage of being the most expensive," and I believe
this is so true. If you fight on price, you lose your margins, you
can't pay for advertising, you can't pay for and hire the best team,
and you can't provide the value your dream customers deserve.
On the other hand, when you build an offer that is perceived as
inexpensive to those customers because you've created so much
value, then you are able to serve them at the highest level. This is
a big mindset shift that most entrepreneurs need to make to really
become successful.

The solution to selling a commodity is to restructure what you
are selling and turn it into an offer. When you add more value
than anyone else, you are no longer needing to compete on price.
For my physical product owners, my information product owners,
and my service-based entrepreneurs, the first step is to increase
the value of what you're selling by creating an actual offer.

The goal of an offer in its most simple form is to:

- Increase the *perceived value* of what is being sold.

- Make the thing being sold unique to you and only
  available within this special offer.

When I created the iPhone offer for those at the Wake Up Warrior event, I increased the perceived value by showing everything that they got inside of the offer, and I made it unique because no other phone on earth had that information inside it. The offer stack that I created for it would have looked like this:

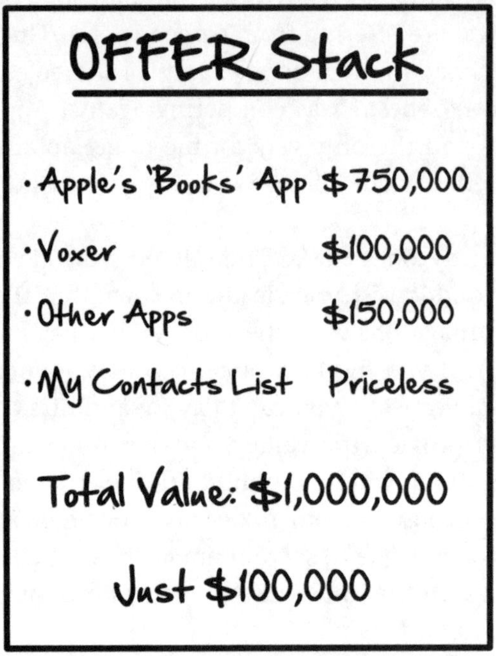

OFFER Stack

- Apple's 'Books' App $750,000

- Voxer $100,000

- Other Apps $150,000

- My Contacts List   Priceless

Total Value: $1,000,000

Just $100,000

Figure 2.2:

To overcome price resistance, increase the value of your offer so it's worth 10 times more than what you're selling it for.

My goal for any offer is to make the total value of it 10 times as much as what I am actually charging. So if I'm selling something for $100, I want to add enough value that the entire offer is worth over $1,000, and then I can easily sell it for $100. If I want to sell something for $1,000, then I need to create enough value that it is actually worth $10,000, and then $1,000 will seem like a bargain.

If you have price resistance when trying to sell your offer, the problem is not that your customers don't have money, it's that you haven't increased the value to a point where what you are selling becomes inexpensive. For example, if I'm trying to sell you a pair of shoes for $10,000, you will probably tell me that it's too expensive and that you don't have the money, right? Because it "seems" expensive. But if I told you that I had a brand-new Ferrari outside for sale and it only cost $10,000, you would find the money quickly, because you know the value of a Ferrari is much more than that, and the $10K "seems" inexpensive.

What are the things you could create to include inside of your offer? The first step to creating your offer is to look at the product or service that you are currently selling and to try to figure out what the other things are that you could include in an offer that would help your dream customers get better results from what they are buying from you.

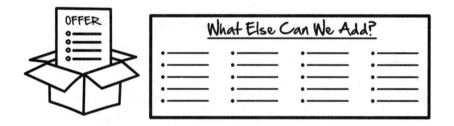

Figure 2.3:

Write down all the products and services that you can add
to increase the value of your core offer.

When creating a new offer, I'll often sit in front of a whiteboard with my team and start a brainstorming session by asking, "What else could we give them that would help to guarantee their success?" We write down every idea, no matter how crazy it gets. In one recent brainstorming meeting, while trying to figure out what else we could add to the offer to get people to create a free trial account at ClickFunnels, the team threw out ideas like:

- "Russell could fly to their house and build their funnel for them!"

- "We could give them our SOP documents that we use to launch each funnel!"

- "Let's give them 100 new funnel templates!"

- "What if we gave them access to the recordings from one of our big events?"

- "What if we gave them the contracts we use when people hire us to build funnels? That way they could start selling funnel design services to other people!"

The list started to grow bigger and bigger, and within an hour we had a whole whiteboard filled with ideas. We then looked at them and said, "Okay, what are our nonnegotiables? What are we not willing to do for this offer?"

I quickly raised my hand and said that I wasn't willing to fly to their home and build their funnel if they got a free trial account, so we crossed that one off the board. Then we went through the others on the list, added dozens of amazing things, and built a truly irresistible offer. Prior to that, our offer for someone joining ClickFunnels was that they could try our software for free for 14 days, which wasn't a horrible offer, but it wasn't irresistible. By adding in all these elements, we created an offer that became truly irresistible and added tens of thousands of new members to our platform.

Each year, I run an event called Unlock the Secrets, where I let entrepreneurs and their kids come and learn how to build companies online. I taught everyone how to create offers, but many of the adults seemed a little bit confused, so I pulled one of the kids on stage to help teach the adults how simple it was to create an offer. The person I pulled on stage was the 12-year-old daughter of one of my Inner Circle members, Ryan Lee. His daughter's name is Kiana.

"Kiana, what is your business?" I asked.

"I am a babysitter," she said.

"Cool. So how many other babysitters are there in your neighborhood, and how much do they all charge?"

"All of my friends are babysitters," she said. "There are a lot of us, and most of us charge around $5 an hour."

I paused and looked at the audience. "Right now Kiana is selling a commodity. Everyone is selling the same service for about the same price. My guess is when most parents want to go on a date night, they look at the list of babysitters in their area, start calling them one by one, and then hire the first babysitter who's available." I wrote *babysitting* on the whiteboard as the core offer that she was creating.

Figure 2.4:

By adding more products and services to your core offer, you can make it irresistible by seeming less expensive than what your competition is offering.

I asked Kiana what other things she could add to her offer to increase the value of her babysitting for the parents. Within minutes, she came up with an amazing list that we added to the board.

She said, "I could wash the dishes after dinner and make sure the house is clean. I could make sure the kids don't play video games; instead I would bring fun activities that we could play outside together. I could bring my favorite books and read them to the kids, and help them with their homework, too!"

"That's awesome," I said, "What else could you add to your offer?"

She continued, "I could make sure the kids are in bed and asleep before the parents get home. I could bring snacks for the kids and cook treats for the parents for when they get home! I could take pictures of the kids when they do cool things and print out collages with the pictures showing all our activities."

She kept going on and on with idea after idea, and about three minutes into the exercise, I stopped her and told her that I would literally pay her $20 per hour if she would babysit my kids that night!

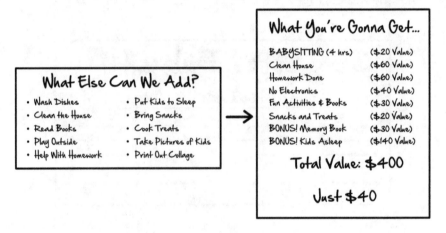

Figure 2.5:

Instead of offering just babysitting, Kiana was able to increase the value of her offer so that parents would be more likely to choose her over (and pay her more than) her competition.

Can you imagine how different it would be if one of the babysitters in your neighborhood gave you a babysitter offer stack like that? On date night, would you still randomly call babysitters trying to find someone who wasn't busy, or would you call weeks in advance to reserve the babysitter who made you that irresistible offer? My guess is that you'd probably choose the latter, and that you'd also probably pay that babysitter two to three times more money than the other babysitters in the area, simply because she offers more value.

Get good at making offers. The first key to having success with funnels is learning how to make offers. Each ad you post will be making an offer such as: "Click here to see a video that will show you how to _____." Each step in your funnels will also have an offer such as: "Give me your email address and I'll send you a free _____." Each level of your value ladder will have a new offer, and every email you send your list will contain some type of offer. Creating offers will not be a one-time exercise, but something that you do over and over again. It's one, if not the most important, role you have as a business owner.

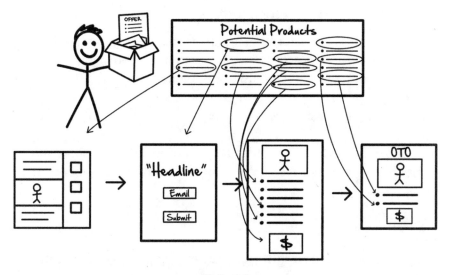

Figure 2.6:

You'll put out offers everywhere in the marketplace, including in your ads, emails, and funnels.

To increase the value of this role for you I want to tell you a story about Claude Hopkins, who is considered by many to be the father of modern advertising.[4] He was famous for taking Schlitz beer from number five in sales to tying with the powerhouse Anheuser-Busch in the early 1900s. Back then, the early advertising agencies called people like him "scheme men." Their job was to come up with the most important part of the advertising puzzle: the offer. In 1907, Claude was paid $52,000 per year (the equivalent of $1,396,471 in today's dollars) to come up with offers that would sell. That's how valuable it is to become a master at creating offers for your company.

Your first assignment right now is to figure out what elements you could add to your current product to increase its value by turning it into an offer.

Step #1: Brainstorm as many different ideas that you can come up with for other things that you could give your dream customer to help guarantee their success.

Step #2: From those ideas, what elements could you take to create an irresistible offer?

Spend time brainstorming and figure out something that is so irresistible that your dream customers would be certifiably insane if they didn't give you the amount of money you were asking for in exchange for that offer. The more you can increase the value of the offer, the easier it will be to get them to say yes to the price you are asking.

Now that you have created your first offer, I want to show you the secret that will increase the value of your offer even more!

STORY-SELLING

Drew Manning had recently started a new company to teach people about how to live a ketogenic lifestyle. He started by creating an offer that he knew would be irresistible for his audience. The offer was called the "Keto Jumpstart," and inside of that offer he included:[5]

- The Keto Jumpstart Meal Plan

    • Eight weeks of keto meal plans

    • Eight weeks of grocery lists

    • 35 keto recipes

- Keto Food List: over 80 foods you *can* eat
- Keto Challenge Workouts: eight weeks of bodyweight workouts
- Keto Friends Restaurant Guide
- Keeping It Keto Facebook Community

While the offer was good, Drew had a silver bullet that would be the key to getting people to take him up on this special offer: his story. You see, just offering someone a list of stuff isn't necessarily going to move the needle. It's you telling them the story behind the offer that increases the perceived value of each element that makes the offer truly irresistible.

Instead of just telling people that he could help them, he told the story behind why he was uniquely qualified to make this offer to them. Drew's story of weight loss is different than most personal trainers. He had an idea a few years ago that if he was to gain weight and then lose it again, he felt he would have a better perspective on what his clients were going through, and that he could serve them at a higher level, so that's exactly what he did! He gained 75 pounds in six months, then lost the weight during the next six months. This journey helped him to learn more than just the mechanics of weight loss, but to truly understand the emotional and psychological journey that people must go on.

This story of Drew's journey from being fit, to becoming fat, to getting fit again is the story that Drew tells in his ads, as well as on the landing page before he makes them the offer. After they hear his story, they build a relationship with Drew, trust him, and feel he is uniquely qualified to help them with their problems. His story is what increases the perceived value of what he has to offer.

Figure 2.7:

A great offer is usually not enough on its own to produce a sale. You also need a story that helps your dream customers trust you enough to buy from you.

Within a few months of Drew launching this offer and telling his story, he qualified for one of our Two Comma Club awards (meaning he had made over $1 million inside of this funnel) and within a few years he won our Two Comma Club X award for making over $10 million! That is the power of creating the right offer and telling a powerful story.

There will be stories that you tell at every step in your funnel. There will be a story in the ad that will get people to click on your ad. There will be a story on the landing page that will convince someone to take advantage of your first offer. There will be stories in the upsell pages, the webinar presentations you give, and more.

I wish I could spend the next 200 pages going deep into story structure and how to use stories to break false beliefs, but that actually became the work of my second book in this trilogy, *Expert Secrets*. Reading and mastering that book will help you to find and tell the stories you need for each element inside of your funnel. In the meantime, I will give you many different story frameworks and scripts that you can use inside of your funnels in Section Three: Funnel Scripts.

THE HOOK

Every day, as you're scrolling through your Facebook newsfeed, checking your email, or searching to find something on Google, there are hundreds of business owners who are throwing out "hooks" with a goal to grab your attention long enough that they can tell you their story.

The hooks are the headlines, images, and videos that we put in front of our dream customers wherever they are congregating, with a goal to capture their attention just long enough that we can tell them our story.

In the first edition of *DotCom Secrets*, I called these hooks "Enquirer Interrupts" because they reminded me of being at the grocery store and walking through the checkout stand, where one of the headlines from the tabloids grabs my attention. Your job online is almost the same. You are going to the busiest places online, where your dream customers are congregating and throwing out dozens of hooks, with a goal to capture the attention of those people, just long enough that you can tell them a story, and then make them a special offer.

Figure 2.8:

Though we presented these in reverse order, the hook is the first step, as it grabs your dream customers' attention.

The hook doesn't provide any value by itself, but it grabs attention for the story, and each story could have dozens of different hooks. For example, Drew has his story about him going from "fit to fat to fit," and within that story here are a few of the hooks he could easily use:

- Video of him on Jay Leno telling the story
- Before and after pics from the journey
- Picture of him with his product
- Pictures of him with people he's helped
- Videos of him telling the story
- Pictures of food that will grab people's attention
- Headlines about his weight loss
- Headlines about his weight gain

This list could go on and on. Every story we put into the market has dozens of potential hooks that we could be throwing out. We never know which ones will grab our market's attention, so it's important that we keep throwing out hooks until we find the ones that effectively hook our dream customers.

THE SECRET FORMULA

Figure 2.9:

The last step, after identifying your dream customers, finding where they're congregating, and putting out bait to attract them, is defining the result you can create for them.

Hook, Story, Offer. After we know who our dream customer is, and we've identified where they are congregating, this is the bait that will get them to come into your world so you can serve them and change their lives with the business that you've built. This leads us to the last step in the secret formula, which is the result. What is the big result that you are trying to get for them? In the next chapter, we will be talking about the value ladder, which will give you the ability to serve these dream customers at a higher level while you make more money doing it.

THE VALUE LADDER

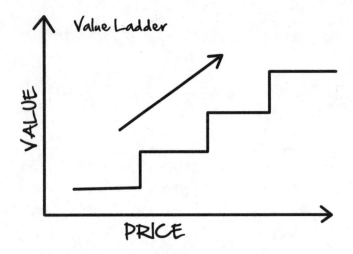

Figure 3.1:

As customers ascend your value ladder, your offers will increase in value and price.

"Russell, are you a smoker?"

"What?" I responded. "No, I've never smoked in my life. Why do you ask?"

"Well, I noticed that your teeth are turning a little yellow, and I wasn't sure if you were a smoker or maybe you drink coffee?" he asked.

"No, I don't drink coffee either," I said. "My teeth look that yellow?"

Those were the first words my new dentist said to me about 10 minutes into our first appointment.

When I started my new business a few years earlier, my wife and I had no insurance of any kind because I didn't have a job and I was just hustling to sell things online to try and put food on the table.

Then about five years into my business, I started hiring employees. What I didn't realize when I first hired them was most "real" companies give their employees benefits. Because I had never had a real job before, I wasn't sure what benefits were (besides hanging out with me all day, which I assumed was the best benefit ever!). No, they wanted health insurance and dental insurance. So I had to learn how to set up a benefits package for our new team. Within days of getting our new dental insurance, I got a postcard in the mail offering a free teeth cleaning from a local dentist.

I thought, *Sweet! We've got insurance. It's a free cleaning. I'm in!* And that's where it all started.

Within minutes after looking at my teeth, the dentist commented on their color. "Are they really yellow?" I asked.

"Yeah, they are. But don't worry. If you want, I can make some custom teeth-whitening trays for you. You'll have to use them for a few weeks, but if you follow the system, your teeth will be white again soon."

Well, I'm sure you know what my response was: "Yes, please! I don't want yellow teeth."

The dentist kept working on my teeth, and a little while later, he said, "So, did you have braces when you were a kid?"

"Yeah, I did. How can you tell?"

"Your two bottom teeth are shifting pretty bad, and that usually happens to people who had braces."

"My teeth are shifting? Seriously? What can you do about that?"

"If you want, I can build a retainer for you, which will help keep your teeth in place, or we can try Invisalign and get them straight again."

"Yes, please!"

When I walked into the dentist office that morning, I had come in for a *free* teeth cleaning. And in less than an hour, I walked out paying over $2,000 for my whitening kit and my new retainers. This dentist had strategically taken me through a powerful process that I call a value ladder.

First, he had created bait (free teeth cleaning) that would attract his dream client (me).

Second, he provided value to me by cleaning my teeth, and while he was helping me, he noticed that my teeth had become yellow. Because I had received value from him at this point, I naturally wanted to move forward and get additional value from him.

He then found another way that he could provide value to me—the retainers—and again, I naturally took him up on that offer as well.

Now, for many dentists, they make the most money and provide the most value for their patients by offering cosmetic surgery. Luckily, I didn't need any cosmetic surgery on that visit, or I could have been out $10,000 or more.

On my way out the door, the secretary scheduled me for another appointment six months later, adding me to their "continuity" program. Continuity is where you continue paying on a weekly, monthly, or yearly basis until you decide to cancel. This dentist had a perfectly executed value ladder.

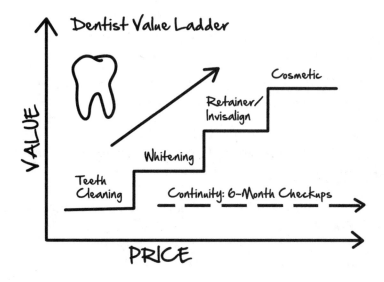

Figure 3.2:

Dentists put out free offers for teeth cleaning in the hopes they will ascend those customers up their value ladder and get them on a regular teeth cleaning continuity program.

YOUR VALUE LADDER MISSION STATEMENT (VLMS)

Whenever I start a new company or start working with someone on their business, the first thing I always do is map out the customer's value ladder. It helps to give you a vision of how you plan on serving your dream customers and where you want to take them. It helps you figure out the real purpose for your company: the main goal or result that you are trying to help them achieve.

Two of my Inner Circle members, Stacey and Paul Martino, call their value ladder their customers' yellow brick road. They say that when anyone comes into your world, they have an "Oz," or a result that they want to achieve when they are going to start working with you. Your value ladder becomes the brick-by-brick road of solutions that is designed to get them to their Oz.

But it starts with defining the result (or Oz) that your dream customers will be coming to you to achieve. I call this your "value ladder mission statement," or VLMS, and I break it down like this:

We help (insert who) to (insert result they want to achieve) through (insert your new opportunity).

Who is the person you want to serve? We have talked a lot about your dream customers so far in this section. We build everything inside of this value ladder to attract and serve them.

What is the result that you can provide for your dream customers? What is it that they have been unsuccessfully trying to accomplish before entering your world that you know you can solve when you have a chance to serve them?

What is your new opportunity that you want to offer them? What is the offer that you are providing them that is different from the things they have tried in the past when attempting to achieve this same result?

If I was a dentist, my value ladder mission statement would read something like this:

We help families in our community to increase their confidence through creating a beautiful smile they are proud to share.

After you've defined that for your value ladder, everything you create will be moving people toward that Oz. Every offer you create at each step of the value ladder will be helping to achieve that core goal. My dentist had an offer for free teeth cleaning that fulfilled his VLMS. For people like me who received value at that tier of his value ladder, he ascended me and offered me teeth whitening. This was a new offer that achieved the same VLMS for those patients who were able to purchase it. The same is true for every offer inside of the value ladder; they're just different ways to fulfill the same mission statement.

The value ladder mission statement we have for ClickFunnels is:

We help visionary entrepreneurs to grow
their companies through sales funnels.

It's simple, but it defines exactly who my dream customers are (visionary entrepreneurs), shows the result or Oz that I provide them (growing their companies), and shares my unique vehicle that I teach (sales funnels). Now when I create anything inside of my value ladder, it's all focused on getting that result, to those people, through this process.

We fulfill this VLMS though our books, online courses, live events, software, coaching, and mastermind groups. Each is a separate offer in the value ladder, all helping to fulfill on the same VLMS.

Take a minute now to write out your value ladder mission statement, and then we will dive in and actually work on your value ladder!

THE VALUE LADDER, AKA YOUR BUSINESS PLAN

Now that you have the big result that you want to offer, it's time to create an offer that will deliver on your big promise. When I first launched my coaching company, I knew that my end result was to help people to create a funnel, get it integrated into their companies, and set up the traffic systems they needed to make sure they had a consistent stream of new leads coming into their businesses.

I created an offer that was so irresistible; I assumed that everyone would say yes. It included me flying to them with my team and working with their team to build the funnels and the processes for them. It would take over a week of my time, and then a few months of time from my core team. It was amazing, but my costs to fulfill on it were close to $250,000. I also knew that the opportunity costs of me doing their project instead of just working on my own funnels was huge, so I decided to price this offer at $1 million down, plus a percentage of equity in the company.

Now, I want you to see that I did create an offer and it did fulfill on the value ladder mission statement, right? But the problem is that it was priced so high, the majority of the people that I would want to serve wouldn't be able to pay for it. On top of that, the people who I did want to pay for it probably wouldn't take me serious enough to actually wire me the funds. Just think about it. If I were to walk up to you on the street today and say, "Give me $1 million plus a percentage of your company, and I'll help you to grow your company with a sales funnel," you would either laugh in my face or run away.

Why is that?

It's because we just met. I honestly look like I'm about 14 years old, and so far, I haven't provided you any value yet, and it "seems" expensive.

The other day I was at a live event with over 1,000 of my dream customers sitting in the room. I had spoken for a few days and had built a lot of value with the audience. I asked them, who in this room would take me up on the million-dollar offer right now if I made it available? Instantly over 50 hands shot up from people who would have written me a check and given me equity, had I been willing to take it. How is that possible? It's because of the value ladder.

If you're reading this book right now, then you're currently inside my value ladder. I spent an insane amount of time writing this book for you, hoping that it will provide you so much value that you will come looking for more. The price to get this book was low, so your resistance to buy was low. You read the book, you receive value, and you will naturally want more. You'll want to ascend my value ladder and see if there are other ways I can provide value for you.

You may buy one of my home study courses or attend one of my live events. If you receive value from that, you may decide to sign up for my high-end coaching programs or mastermind groups, and if I provide awesome value there, then you will naturally want to keep ascending . . . and *that* is how we sell our million-dollar packages. We provide insane amounts of value at each step of our value ladder, so our clients naturally want to ascend, get more value, and pay us more money. It's how we're wired as humans: to seek more value from the places that we've already received it from.

Think about it. It's the same way most of us picked (or will pick) our spouses. You see someone who you think is cute, and you ask them out on a date. If you have a good time and receive value, you will naturally want more and will likely ask them out on a second date. If that date goes well and you receive value, you'll keep moving up their value ladder. "First comes love, then comes marriage, then comes a baby in the baby carriage." Even that nursery rhyme pushes you naturally up the value ladder. It's a human tendency that works on all of us. When we receive value, we naturally want more, and the same is true here inside your business.

Your value ladder is your actual business plan. It shows how you are going to acquire your customers, where you will make money as the business owner, and the result you are going to help your dream customers achieve. If someone doesn't have an actual value ladder, they don't really have a business; they are just selling a product.

If you look at how we structure the value ladder, you'll see that on the left-hand axis we have value, and on the bottom axis we show the price. As you move up the value ladder, you will be providing more value to your dream customer as well as charging them more money.

Each tier in the value ladder is a new offer that is created to fulfill your value ladder mission statement.

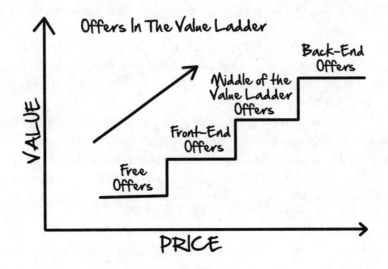

Figure 3.3:

As you provide value at each step of your value ladder, your customers will naturally want to receive more value from the person they received it from: you!

If you look at a traditional author, speaker, coach, or consultant, their value ladder usually looks like Figure 3.4. On the bottom of their value ladder, they typically have an offer for a book or a report or something they can give away or sell inexpensively to provide value to their dream customers. From there they will usually ascend people into their online courses, and then their live events, and eventually their mastermind groups.

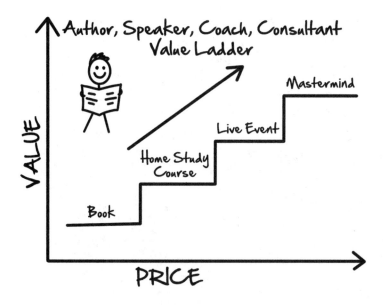

Figure 3.4:

The value ladders for authors, speakers, coaches, and consultants often look similar to this, as they're able to work more closely with their dream customers as they ascend their value ladder.

Stacey and Paul Martino took this basic framework and tweaked it to fit the products and services that they wanted to offer to help get their dream customers to their Oz.

At the bottom of their value ladder, they use lead funnels to generate leads and get people to listen to their free *Relationship Transformer* podcast. They create value for their customers there and invite them to their "14-Day Boost" program that they sell for $47 through a challenge funnel (one of our "unboxing funnels"). At the end of their challenge, they ascend their customers into their "Quick Start" home study program that they sell for $997 through a webinar funnel (one of our presentation funnels).

Those who receive value from the Quick Start program naturally want more, so they attend their three-day "Relationship Breakthrough Retreat" live immersion event for $1,997. There, they serve their clients at an even higher level, and at the end of that event, they make an offer for their RelationshipU year-long coaching program (tuition is $14,997 through an application funnel). Their value ladder has helped them to save thousands of marriages (their RelationshipU program has a one percent divorce rate), transform countless people's lives, and to win multiple Two Comma Club awards in a very short period of time.

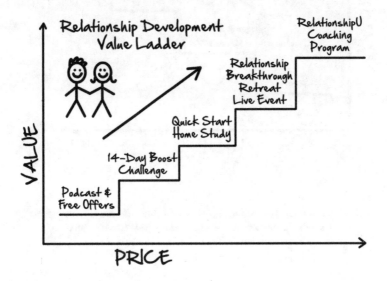

Figure 3.5:

Stacey and Paul Martino are able to help their dream customers find more success in all their relationships as they ascend their value ladder.

When we launched ClickFunnels, the first step was to sketch out our value ladder and then plug in offers to each tier. At the bottom of our value ladder, we have lots of free books and reports that educate people on why they need funnels and how they can use them inside their companies. By seeing that we provide massive value, they will want to start using funnels to grow their companies. From there, they start using ClickFunnels at $97 per month. When they receive value at that level, they ascend to our $297 per month Platinum level. Eventually, they ascend to our Collective level where we offer live support, group coaching, and events. Each tier of this value ladder helps to fulfill on the VLMS we wrote out when we first launched this company.

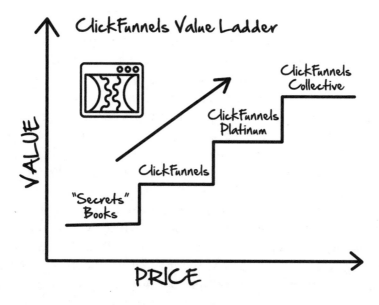

Figure 3.6:

As our customers receive value at every level of our company, they naturally want to ascend to the next level to receive more value.

WHAT DOES YOUR VALUE LADDER LOOK LIKE?

Now I'm aware that everyone reading this has a different type of company. At this point, you're probably trying to figure out how the value ladder applies to your business. I want to share with you a story that will show you how we were able to create a value ladder for a business that didn't seem to have any type of ascending products or services.

I have a chiropractor friend, Dr. Chad Woolner, whom I've known for a long time. In fact, it was his urging that got me to create this book. Like most chiropractors, he makes his living doing adjustments for about $50 each. After he runs ads, patients come in, get adjusted in about 10 minutes, pay him $50, and leave. Sometimes, if the person has a more serious condition, Dr. Woolner may put the client on a continuity plan and have them come in a few times a week over the next few months. But that's about it.

One day Dr. Woolner and I were talking, and he wanted to know what I would do differently in his business if I were him. I thought it over for a few days when a funny thing happened. At the time, I was working with a group of wrestlers who were training for the Olympics. Each week a chiropractor came in and adjusted all the wrestlers. One week, the regular doc couldn't make it in. So instead of waiting for a week, one of the athletes jumped on YouTube, typed in "how to give a chiropractic adjustment," and watched a few videos until he felt like an expert. Then he walked into the other room and quickly adjusted everyone on the team.

Now, before I move on, I feel like I should give a disclaimer or a warning or something. Don't get me wrong. The point of this story is *not* to say you should go watch YouTube videos and start practicing medicine! (And don't send me emails telling me that's illegal or crazy . . . okay?) The point is that in about 30 minutes, someone with no formal training at all learned to do what we were paying the chiropractor for. I started laughing, called my chiropractor friend immediately, and told him the story.

Naturally, he wasn't as amused as I was. He launched into a long rant about why that was dangerous and why he shouldn't have done it. I stopped him and said, "Look, I wasn't just calling to be a jerk. I want to teach you something really powerful. You went to college for years to learn how to be a chiropractor—yet, within thirty minutes, one wrestler was able to learn *everything* that you currently do in your clinic."

Silence.

I continued, "I'm curious, while you were going to school, did you learn anything else besides adjustments?"

Defensively, he started to tell me about all sorts of other things he had learned and knew how to do. He said, "I spent years learning nutrition and natural healing. I can help stop fibromyalgia, carpal tunnel syndrome, and—"

And that's where I stopped him. "Have you ever provided *any* of these services to your clients, or do you stop giving them value after the fifty-dollar adjustments?" I asked.

Now I want to pause here, because most companies I work with, even if they think they have a value ladder, really only have *part* of one. Almost always, I spend my time working on adding products and services to the front of their value ladders, as well as to the back.

After that discussion, I sat down with Dr. Woolner and we mapped out his current value ladder.

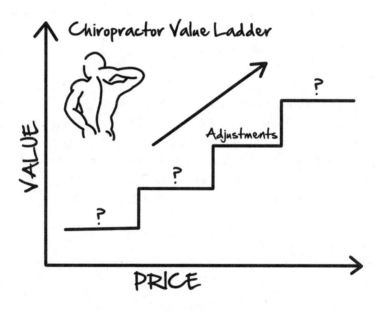

Figure 3.7:

Dr. Woolner's business was struggling because he only offered one basic service.

Then we looked at other ways he could provide more value to his clients. We figured out where he really wanted to take them. Ultimately, he created a new wellness program, for which he could charge $5,000 or more. The clients who participated would get 10 times more value from each visit to his clinic. That was the back end—the highest point—of his value ladder.

After we built out his back-end value ladder, we still had to find an attractive front-end offer to get people through the door. A chiropractic adjustment just isn't that sexy. It's not like a massage that people enjoy getting, and it's not like going to a traditional medical doctor where you think you're going to die and need some medicine fast. People usually wait until they're in great pain before they'll come in for an adjustment.

If you have a boring front-end offer, your business will always struggle.

So Dr. Woolner worked to make his offer more sexy. Instead of just giving people a "free exam," he decided to create an offer where he gave away a free massage, some supplements, and a meditation CD when people booked their first appointment. Armed with this new offer, he went out and started advertising. Within months he had filled his clinic to capacity with new people coming into the front of his value ladder and a percentage of them upgraded to longer-term care, his wellness packages, and more! He was now getting more people in the front door, making more money from each person who became a client *and* serving his dream customers at a level he never was able to do before.

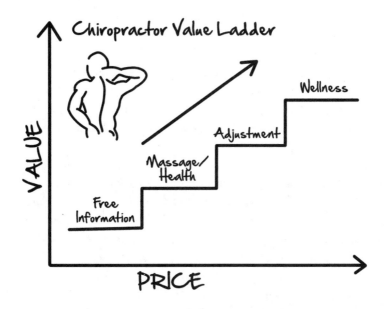

Figure 3.8:

**Once Dr. Woolner had a fully developed value ladder,
his business completely turned around.**

Oftentimes, it's hard for companies to figure out how to add more offers to their value ladders. Typically, the process is very easy for someone selling information products because that ascension path has already been created and proven in thousands of different information-based companies. But what if you're selling something else? What if you're selling physical products or professional services where the path isn't quite as clear? Sometimes it just takes a little thought and creativity.

If you already have a product or service that you sell in the middle of your value ladder, what type of "bait" could you create to attract your dream customer? One of my friends owns a company that makes custom suits for people. He was stuck selling a high-end service but unable to see how to construct a solid value ladder (probably because the "front" at the time was $2,000). After a while, my friend tried giving away free cufflinks online. He put the offer up, started to advertise, and within days, he had generated hundreds of perfectly qualified leads. He then took these people through his funnels to get them to purchase their own custom suits.

Oftentimes, companies have a front-end product but nothing more to sell on the back end. For that, I love to look at what else they could bundle together. Could they offer a coaching program? How about a live event? What other results or value could they give their clients?

Most businesses I look at have one or two pieces of the ladder, but they rarely have a full value ladder. Once we add in the missing pieces, the business can start to expand dramatically. There's no end to the level of back-end services and experiences you can add. If you keep providing more and more value, people will spend more and more money to keep working with you.

I remember paying $25,000 to be a part of the Bill Glazer/Dan Kennedy Titanium Mastermind program. At the time, my highest back-end offer was $5,000. Someone in that program asked me, "So, Russell, what do you sell *next* to the people who paid $5,000?" I told him that I didn't have anything else to offer, and he responded, "Russell, that's a $5,000 buyer lead—you need to sell them something else!"

Interestingly, later that night the group (yes, the *same* group that had already paid $25,000 to be in the room) was offered a chance to be in the movie *Phenomenon* with Dan Kennedy for an additional $30,000. And 9 out of 18 people in our group bought the offer! That was when I realized that there really is no end to your value ladder. It's one of the reasons why we created our million-dollar program. Imagine my shock and excitement the first time someone said yes! A percentage of your audience will always want to pay you the premium to get more value.

The only limit to your value offerings is your imagination. Keep thinking of higher and higher levels of service, and you can keep charging more and more money. There's always something else you can offer.

I told you earlier that FitLife.tv's core issue was not a traffic or conversion problem. The only real problem was that they had no value ladder. Because of that, they couldn't build out a true sales funnel. They brought people into their funnel, but then the relationship ended. People wanted to give them money, but there was no clear path for them to follow. As soon as they added those things into their business, customers naturally started to ascend the ladder, ultimately paying Drew and his team what they were worth.

While it's not always obvious what you can add to the front end or the back end of your company, I promise that the solutions are there. I also know that if you want to succeed and beat out your competition, you need to have this value ladder in place.

DIFFERENT TYPES OF FUNNELS FOR EACH STEP OF THE VALUE LADDER

Just like we have different offers on each tier of the value ladder, there is a different type of sales funnel that is specifically designed to sell each type of offer. For example, at the first tier of most value ladders, you are creating free offers that will get people to come into your value ladder, receive value, and give them a desire to want to start ascending to your paid offers. There are specific types of funnels that we call "lead funnels" that are designed to get your dream customers to join your lists and become leads.

In Section Two, I will show you the exact lead funnels we use and how you can model them inside of your company.

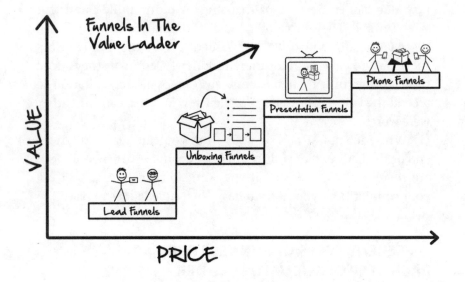

Figure 3.9:

Because the price points are different at each step of the value ladder, you need to use different types of funnels at each step to sell them.

As you move up the value ladder to the lower priced products, the types of funnels we use at this tier are called unboxing funnels. Typically, products from $1–$100 are sold in an unboxing funnel. There are three types of unboxing funnels we use, and I will also break them down in detail in Section Two.

From there, we ascend our dream customers to the next tier, where products are typically priced between $100–$2,000. Offers priced this high generally require a different type of funnel to sell them. We call these funnels "presentation funnels," and I'll show you my favorites in Section Two.

Finally, for the back-end funnels where we sell high-ticket offers priced over $2,000 (like my million-dollar offer), we traditionally take people offline and onto the phones. I'll show you this application funnel and the scripts we use to close high-ticket sales as well.

Even though we haven't gotten to any funnels yet, I wanted you to be able to see where they fit into the value ladder now so they will make more sense when we get to that section.

THE FIRST FUNNEL IN YOUR VALUE LADDER

I get nervous the first time I share the concept of the value ladder with someone, because they'll often sketch out their value ladder, spend the next few months or years trying to create all the offers for each level, and never actually sell anything.

You don't have to have the value ladder finished to launch your company. In fact, when someone joins my Inner Circle, I first have them sketch out what their value ladder will become, and then I have them pick one level of the value ladder and commit to me that they will only focus on that one offer, that one funnel, until they've made it into the Two Comma Club (meaning they've made at least $1,000,000 gross in that funnel).

Traditionally, I tell them to pick an offer in the middle or the back-end of the value ladder (typically a presentation or a phone funnel), because the price at that level is usually high enough that you can cover your ad costs and still make a profit.

Liz Benny was one of the first people to join my Inner Circle a few years back. She had seen all my funnels online, and she assumed that I was going to have her first write a book, and then maybe launch a coaching program and so on. I told her that those things would come, but that her only focus for the next 90 days was to create a webinar funnel (one of the presentation funnels) and to sell a $1,000 course that she would need to also create.

Liz put in the work, built the course, wrote the "Perfect Webinar" script, created the funnel, and started buying ads. Within a few weeks, it started to sell. Almost immediately, she did what all great entrepreneurs that work with me do and said, "Now that this funnel is selling well, what offer should I create next?" I think my answer surprised her when I told her that she wasn't allowed to create the next tier of her value ladder until she had passed the million-dollar mark. She needed to sell at least 1,000 copies of her $1,000 course (1,000 x $1,000 = $1,000,000). Liz put her focus back into the webinar, and within a year she had passed the $1 million mark! She had 1,000 dream customers who loved her and who wanted more from her.

After she passed the million-dollar mark, I messaged her on Voxer and said, "Okay, they're ready." I could hear Liz grin on the other end of the phone, because she knew that her people were ready for more. She created the next tier of her value ladder—a high-ticket coaching program—created the funnel, sent out an email to her customer list, and within days had filled up her coaching program!

For many people, this simple two-tier value ladder is enough to make them a lot of money and give them the number of clients they need to feel fulfilled. After we had launched ClickFunnels, I did a very similar thing. I had a $1,000 offer that sold an online course as well as access to ClickFunnels. The first year I sold over 2,500 people into that program, and 100 had joined my Inner Circle program. After we passed about 10,000 copies of our $1,000 course sold, it got harder to continue to advertise this product because so many people had already purchased it.

That's when I decided to launch the first version of this book. We created a book funnel (one of our unboxing funnels) and launched this book. It was able to attract a whole new audience of people who didn't know what funnels were. They received value from this book, and then they naturally ascended and watched the webinar where I sold the $1,000 course.

I share those stories to help you understand that the goal after you sketch out your value ladder isn't to build all the tiers, but to focus on one. After you have figured out how to sell that offer, and you have built up pressure from your customers for more, then open the back end of your value ladder and start serving your true fans at a higher level.

When your ads stop working as well for your core offers, that's when you start to build out new front-end offers to get new people into your value ladder so you can then ascend them to the offers you've already created.

THE VALUE LADDER VS. THE SALES FUNNEL

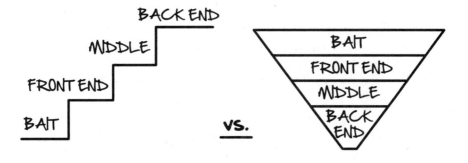

Figure 3.10:

As your dream customers ascend your value ladder (left), your offers will increase in price. Because of this, the number of your dream customers will decrease (right) until you're finally left with your true fans, eager to be served at your highest level.

The secret formula was created to help you figure out who you want to serve, how to find them, what kind of bait you should use to attract them, and where you want to take them.

The value ladder was created to help you figure out what products and services you need to add so that your dream clients move from your bait to your high-end services.

Now it's time to bridge the gap between a value ladder and a sales funnel. In Sections One and Two, we will go into a lot of detail about the strategy, psychology, and tactics you need to build out your own sales funnels. But first, I need you to understand what a sales funnel is and how that relates to everything we've discussed so far, as it's critical to your success.

In a perfect world, I would immediately be able to talk my dream client into purchasing my best, most expensive service. But as we discussed earlier, that's almost impossible because I haven't provided value yet. Besides, my highest-level service might not be the best fit for all people. So instead of trying to convince someone to buy the most expensive offering right away, we build a funnel that will help us to do two things:

- Provide value to each customer at the unique level of service that he or she can afford.

- Make money and be profitable while identifying our dream clients who can afford our highest offer.

The best way to show you how this works is to draw a funnel.

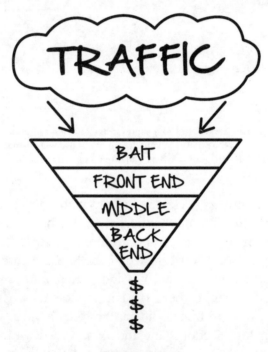

Figure 3.11:

A funnel moves people through the sales process. They enter as prospective customers (traffic), and your job is to convert as many as possible into repeat customers by selling to them at the front end, middle, and back end of your funnel.

Above the funnel is a cloud that represents all my potential customers. At the top of my funnel is the "bait" that will attract my dream customers. Notice that this bait is also the first rung of the value ladder. As I start to place ads featuring my bait, potential customers will start raising their hands, and a certain percentage of these people will purchase my front-end offer.

Then I will move to the next step in my funnel. Here I will introduce the next product or service in my value ladder. This will, of course, be something offering *more* value, while also costing more money. Unfortunately, not everyone who purchases my bait will also purchase this more expensive, high-value product, but a certain percentage of these people will.

From there, I move deeper into the funnel and introduce the next product or service on my value ladder. Again, not everyone will buy this product, but a percentage of the clients who initially took the bait will. I will continue to do this through all the levels of my value ladder, and at the bottom of this funnel, a handful of people will appear who can afford—and may be willing to purchase—my high-end services. These are my dream clients, the ones I want to work with at a more intimate level.

Now, before I "sell" you on why you need to be thinking about your company in terms of "funnels," I want you to understand that my approach wasn't always this detailed. When I first got started online over a decade ago, there was a lot less competition. I could have just a front-end product, and I'd spend $1 on ads and make $2 back in return. But as more people started businesses online and competition started to grow, ad costs went up, the consumer's buying resistance also went up, and it got harder to sell. People I know who were making millions of dollars a year are no longer in business because they didn't adapt and change with the times.

When I started to feel the pinch, I was lucky enough to have some amazing mentors who taught me the importance of building a deeper funnel with more offerings. The deeper your funnel is, and the more things you can offer your clients, the more each customer will be worth to you. And the more they are worth to you, the more you can spend to acquire them. Remember this truth by Dan Kennedy:

> *"Ultimately, the business that can spend the*
> *most to acquire a customer wins."*

Every product I sell online has a sales funnel that I take people through. In fact, immediately after the customer buys something, they are offered an upsell or two before they even leave the page. This is one type of sales funnel. But after they have purchased something from me, I use other types of communication and "follow-up funnels" to build a relationship and encourage them to purchase other products and services that we sell. You'll learn about these special communication follow-up funnels at the end of this section. Every product we sell has its own sales funnel to provide value and convert the buyer into a higher-end customer. You'll see all 10 of these funnels in Section Two.

The fact that you picked up this book and are reading it now is proof that this concept works. I already know that a percentage of everyone who buys this book will upgrade to one of my more expensive products. I also know that from there, a percentage of those people will upgrade and come to some of my events or join my Inner Circle program. And a few, the ones who are the right fit, will join my million-dollar program, and I'll be coming out to set up this whole system in their offices.

THE ATTRACTIVE CHARACTER

"I want to introduce you to our next speaker. He has a successful business online making millions of dollars a year teaching men how to get women to approach them," the emcee announced. "Let's stand up and put your hands together for John Alanis!"

I watched as John walked on stage and told us that he didn't normally teach internet marketers how to sell stuff online but that he knew the secret that almost all of us were missing. He said that we were missing the same thing that his men are lacking when they hire him to teach how to get women to approach them.

"Notice that I didn't say 'how to pick up women,'" he said. "I show them how to get women to come to them. Big difference. Now, how many of you here would like to have customers come to you?" he asked.

As a self-proclaimed introvert who is scared to death of starting a conversation with people, I quickly shot up my hand. I looked around to see that the majority of the people in the room had their hands up as well.

"When I start working with a guy, the first thing I teach them is a concept called the 'Attractive Character.' If you want to attract someone, you have to be attractive, and I'm not talking about your looks. I'm talking about your personality." He went on about some of the ways he helps his men to pull out the elements of their life and story to create an Attractive Character that women would be drawn to.

Then John stopped and said, "I bet most of you here are wondering what in the world this has to do with you. If you want to get people to be attracted to you and your brand, you need to design your own Attractive Character that your market will be attracted to." He gave some ideas on ways you could do this, and I started taking notes as fast as possible.

When I got home from this event, I wanted to start implementing everything I had learned as fast as possible, but this one concept of the Attractive Character was the thing that made me the most nervous. I wasn't quite sure how to do it, so I looked over my notes and started to blend elements of my own Attractive Character into the things I was doing online. I started to share the elements into my emails, and I'd tell the stories during podcast interviews and when I would speak onstage.

The first few times I spoke, I was still in school at Boise State University. I was a student athlete in the wrestling program, and when I spoke, I would tell that part of my story from the stage. I talked about wrestling and coaches and lessons I'd learned from the sport. When it was time to sell at the end of the presentation, I noticed that the people who came to the back to buy my product were mostly male athletes. They would say, "Hey, man, I played football in college," or "Hey, I'm a lacrosse player." I didn't realize it at the time, but my story was promoting the parts of my Attractive Character that other male athletes could relate to, and it was attracting them into my tribe.

A few years later, my wife and I were trying to start a family, but we had trouble getting pregnant. We went through a long process, but after months with a fertility doctor, we ended up getting pregnant with twins. I remember speaking at a seminar, and for some reason, I felt like I should tell that story. I was kind of nervous because I didn't usually share intimate, personal stories. But for whatever reason, I did share that story with the audience and tied it back to my presentation. Then I made an offer for them to buy one of my coaching packages like normal, but this time something different happened.

When I looked to the back of the room, the athletes were still there, but now there was a whole new group of people signing up that I had never seen before. There were wives, mothers, and families buying my products too. I thought, *How interesting! I shared something about my family, and suddenly there's a new segment of the audience attracted to that part of my Attractive Character.* This new audience segment suddenly felt they could relate to me, so they had enough trust to purchase from me. That had never happened before.

Over the past decade that I've been in this industry, I've shared aspects of my Attractive Character in all aspects of the business. It's in the content I post on all the social platforms. It's in the ads that we run online. It's woven into the sales videos and webinars that sell our products and the emails we send to our lists, as well as the fulfillment of everything we sell.

The Attractive Character is the thing that binds people to your value ladder. They come in looking for a result, but they stay because of their relationship with you. One of my favorite social influencers Jenna Kutcher once said, "A brand is the image and personality the business applies to its offers."[6] The value ladder contains all your offers, but the Attractive Character is the brand that you apply to the offers to increase their value even more.

I want to share this concept of the Attractive Character now because it will be woven into everything we do inside your funnels. You will be using it in the messages on each page of your funnels and inside the sales scripts and the email follow-up messages. You'll also see it used in your ads and the content you are publishing to get traffic into your funnels.

Inside of *Expert Secrets*, we go deeper into the Attractive Character. You learn how to use your character to tell stories that break people's false belief patterns so you can serve them at a higher level, how to become a leader, and so much more. This chapter is an introduction for you to understand the core frameworks, but I highly recommend reading *Expert Secrets* next to master communication between your market and your Attractive Character.

As you start thinking about things that you could incorporate into your Attractive Character, I want to share with you the highlights from my notes that I learned while hearing John Alanis talk, as well as the things I've discovered over the past decade as I've been developing my own Attractive Character. I will start with the elements of the Attractive Character.

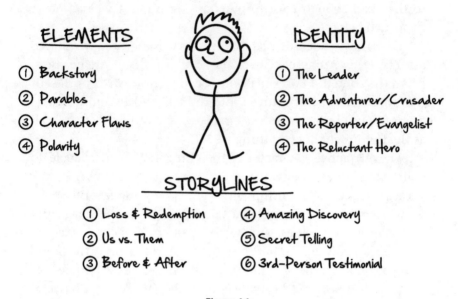

ELEMENTS

① Backstory
② Parables
③ Character Flaws
④ Polarity

IDENTITY

① The Leader
② The Adventurer/Crusader
③ The Reporter/Evangelist
④ The Reluctant Hero

STORYLINES

① Loss & Redemption
② Us vs. Them
③ Before & After
④ Amazing Discovery
⑤ Secret Telling
⑥ 3rd-Person Testimonial

Figure 4.1:

Your Attractive Character helps you build a relationship with your dream customers.

ATTRACTIVE CHARACTER ELEMENTS

Attractive Characters have a backstory and share it often: People won't care about any of the success you've had, and they won't follow you or your advice until they know that you've been where they are now. We mistakenly think that the key to leadership is to posture and show how great we are now, but the reality is that to build a following, they have to know that you've already walked the path that you are taking them on. You must become vulnerable and share the journey that got you to where you are today.

I remember when I first had a conversation with Dr. Woolner about building out his own personal Attractive Character. The first question I asked him was, "Why did you become a chiropractor?" He told me that it paid well and he got Fridays off.

I knew that there had to be more to his backstory than that, so I kept asking questions. Eventually we got past the surface-level reasons, and he told me the real story.

"I was actually going to dental school when my wife got into a car accident. She was in so much pain, and I didn't know how to help her. We tried painkillers, went to medical doctors, and nothing seemed to work. Finally, someone convinced us to go to a chiropractor. I still remember sitting in his office, very skeptical about the process until I watched him put his hands on my wife and get her out of pain. Within minutes we saw a very noticeable difference, and within a few weeks she was healed. After seeing what this man did for my wife, I realized that I wanted to have that type of impact on people as well. So I changed my major and spent the next few years of my life mastering this skill that changed our lives a few years earlier, and that is why I'm a chiropractor."

Do you see how powerful that is? If your chiropractor, dentist, or financial planner told you their origin story about why they were here to serve you, wouldn't that change your relationship with them? The same is true in every business. Sharing your backstory is one of the fastest ways to build rapport with people. Throughout this book, you've probably noticed that each chapter starts with the backstory about how I learned each secret. When I speak at events, I share my backstories; in my emails, ads, podcast episodes, sales letters, and more, I share my backstories. I tell my stories over and over again to the point I get tired of telling them, but you have to understand that you will get tired of hearing your backstory way before your market gets tired of it, so you need to start sharing it a *lot*.

So my question for you is, "What are the backstories that you can share that will build a better relationship between you, the Attractive Character, and your dream customers?"

Attractive Characters speak in parables: The best teachers in the world teach in parables. Regardless of your religious beliefs, if you've read the New Testament, then you've seen how the greatest teacher of all time, Jesus Christ, taught almost everything during his ministry in parables. As you're reading this book, or if you follow me anywhere else online, you'll notice that I try to teach every concept with some type of parable, or small story, to help my ideas and concepts stick in your mind.

For example, when I teach people about the fact that they can make money selling information products, I don't just tell them that they can; I tell them the story about how I first did it by selling a DVD teaching people how to make a potato gun. That parable now makes the concept real inside the listener's mind and helps them remember that concept forever.

I have other stories that I share when I have difficult concepts that I need my listeners to understand. One example of this is when I'm trying to sell something to people; I need them to understand the concept of investing versus buying. I could just tell them that buying my product is an investment that will help them, but that wouldn't stick for most people. So I pull out my parable I learned from my wrestling coach, Mark Schultz. That parable goes a little something like this:

> I had just moved into the dorms and gone to my first practice where I had an awesome time meeting my teammates and coaches. That night, there was a knock on my door. When I opened it, there stood Coach Schultz. He was an Olympic gold medalist as well as the winner of UFC 9 where he stepped into the Octagon with less than 24-hours' notice and no formal training and destroyed his opponent. As he walked in my dorm room, he handed me a videotape that was titled "Total Violence"; the footage held the highlights of his wrestling career.
>
> As I took the tape, he asked me to give him my wallet. A little surprised, but too afraid to say anything to the strongest man I had ever personally met, I pulled my wallet out of my pocket and gave it to him. He opened it, took all my money out, and handed me back an empty wallet. I was kind of confused but too nervous to say anything.

He then told me, "Russell, if I gave you that tape for free, you'd never watch it. But because you've paid for it, I know you're going to watch it and learn from it." And with that, he walked out the door. That night my coach taught me the power of investment, and he was right. Because I had made that investment, I did watch the tape over and over, and I became a better wrestler because of it.

Now I share that parable almost anytime I'm going to ask somebody to make an investment with me, because I know the potential customer wants success, but I know they can't have it unless they make that investment. Do you see how sharing that parable is so much more powerful than just telling someone they need to make a personal investment?

Look through your life and I promise that you'll start finding these little parables that can help illustrate important points. You can also draw parables from the lives of others. Just know that when you stop teaching only facts and start teaching through parables, your messages will stay with an audience longer. Start building out a Rolodex of parables that you can use again and again.

Attractive Characters share their character flaws: This next element is one that most people really struggle with sharing, but it's one of the most important ones to share because it makes you relatable and real. You need to understand that every believable, three-dimensional Attractive Character has flaws. Think about your favorite characters in movies, books, or TV shows. Every character that you bond with emotionally has flaws, right? One of my favorite examples is Superman. He's the Man of Steel. He's invincible. Nobody can kill him. As a storyline, though, that's not very exciting. But when you introduce kryptonite and his concern for the welfare of his family, suddenly he has vulnerabilities and flaws; he becomes an interesting character whom people care about.

If you follow the history of comic books, you'll know that the reason that the Marvel franchise has been able to dominate over DC—even though DC had a huge head start on them—is because of Stan Lee.[7] He knew that characters need to have flaws for people to relate to them. While initially all of DC's characters were similar to Superman, Stan Lee's characters almost all started as normal humans with flaws who received superpowers later (think Spider-Man, Iron Man, and the Hulk).

No one wants to hear about the perfect person—because you can't relate. Yet most of us try to put on a perfect facade for our audiences, thereby alienating the real men and women we are trying to reach. Conversely, as soon as you're vulnerable with your audience and show that you're not perfect because you have character flaws, they will start to empathize with you. They'll like you more because you are like them: not perfect.

Attractive Characters harness the power of polarity: Another challenge people face when communicating with an audience is trying not to offend anyone. So instead of being a relatable person, speakers become bland and stay neutral on many topics, only sharing safe things everyone will love.

Here's the problem: while that sounds like the logical thing to do—appeasing everyone—the problem is that being neutral is boring. When Attractive Characters try to win the votes of everyone, they end up reaching no one.

Instead, Attractive Characters are typically very polarizing. They share their opinions on hard matters, and they stick to their guns—no matter how many people disagree with them. They draw a line in the sand, and when they take a stand for what they believe in, they split the audience into three camps: those who agree with them, those who are neutral, and those who will disagree with them. As you start to create that polarization, it will change your fair-weather fans into die-hard fans who will follow what you say, share your message, and buy from you time after time.

One of the best examples of this concept is Howard Stern. He's very polarizing. People either love him or they hate him. But, as you can see from his following, people are listening. Think about the podcasts you listen to. Think about the blogs and books you read. Do the Attractive Characters you have bonded with and follow have a polarizing effect on you? Are there people you still follow and listen to—even though you can't stand them or their messages? It's very interesting that we will spend just as much time listening to, talking about, and sharing things from people that we despise as we do treasuring the wisdom from our favorite people. Yet if any of those characters weren't so polarizing, chances are you wouldn't even know who they were.

Being polarizing is kind of scary sometimes. It is scary knowing that once you start sharing your opinions, there will probably be a group of people who disagree with you and will voice their opinions online. If you search for me online, you're going to find out there are people who love me and people who hate me. That's just the way it is. If you're neutral, no one will hate you, but no one will know who you are either. As soon as you start taking sides on important issues, you'll develop haters, but you'll also develop a group of raving fans. Those raving fans are the people who will buy your products and services.

If nobody's talking about you, then nobody knows who you are. It's time to step out of that neutral space and start sharing your opinions. Bring the things you care about into the open.

ATTRACTIVE CHARACTER IDENTITY

Your Attractive Character will typically take on one of the following types of identities. You get to pick which one you want to be, and once we go over the choices, the right one will probably jump out at you. When you get your identity together, it's going to shape how you communicate and interact with your audience.

The Leader: The identity of the leader is usually assumed by people whose goal is to lead their audiences from one place to another. Most leaders have a similar backstory to that of their audiences and therefore know the hurdles and pitfalls their audience members will likely face on the journey to get ultimate results. Usually the desired result has already been achieved by the leader, and their audience has come looking for help along that same path. I am sure that there are leaders you follow in different aspects of your life, and this may be the role that will be the most comfortable for you when communicating with your audience.

The Adventurer: The adventurer is usually someone who is very curious, but they don't always have all the answers, so they set out on a journey to discover the ultimate truth. They bring back treasures from their journey and share them with their audience. This identity is very similar to the leader, but instead of leading their audience on a journey to find the result, they are more likely to bring back the answers to give them.

The Reporter: This identity is often one that people use when they have not yet blazed a trail to share with an audience, but they have a desire to. So they put on the hat of the reporter or evangelist and go out to discover the truth. Typically, people who use this identity interview dozens, hundreds, or even thousands of people and share those interviews and all they've learned along the way with their audience.

This is the identity I used when I got started. I didn't know a lot about marketing online myself, so I started interviewing people. I became a reporter, just like Larry King or Oprah. Because I started interviewing all these cool people and sharing their stories and lessons, I started building an audience of my own. People kept seeing me with these other high-profile people, and over time, I became associated with them. My status went up because I was constantly in the company of high-status people. The knowledge and credibility I gained from being a reporter naturally evolved into my coaching career. Becoming a reporter is a great way to start a business in a niche that you are excited to explore.

The Reluctant Hero: This is my personal identity now and typically the one that I try to share with my tribe. This is the humble hero who doesn't really want the spotlight or any fuss made over their discoveries, but they know the information or the secrets they have are so important that they must overcome their shyness and share them with the world. There's a moral duty that compels them to share all they know. Many of you may feel this way naturally; the spotlight is uncomfortable, but you know you need to be there. If that's you, the reluctant hero is the perfect identity for you. Play the part.

Leader, adventurer, reporter, or reluctant hero: you probably identify strongly with one of these four archetypes. Determine which type is a good fit and build out your Attractive Character using the traits for that identity. If you're an adventurer, tell stories of adventure. If you're a leader, tell stories about where you've been and where you are going. If you've chosen the right identity for you, it should be fairly easy to take on that role. If you're struggling to create your Attractive Character, perhaps you should take another look at your identity.

ATTRACTIVE CHARACTER STORYLINES

Becoming a master storyteller is one of the most important roles of the Attractive Character. Inside *Expert Secrets*, we go deep into story structure and how to build out your own inventory of stories that you can use, but for this section I wanted to give you six of the most basic story frameworks that you can use as you're communicating with your audience.

Loss and redemption: Loss and redemption stories are very powerful because they show the upside of going through hardship or meeting challenges. You start by telling about some level of success that you had accomplished, but then because of some trial, you lost it all. This storyline will relate to any of your fans or followers who are currently in a time of loss in their lives. As you tell your redemption journey, they will receive faith and hope that by following you they can experience something similar in their lives.

Us versus them: You want to use us-versus-them stories to polarize your audience. Who do you define as the "us" in your audience (people that do the types of things they need to be successful with what you are selling) versus the "them" (those who don't comply with what you need them to do)? Using these types of stories will draw your raving fans even closer and give them a rallying cry against what they don't want to become.

Before and after: These are stories of transformation, and they work great in any market. For example, in the weight-loss market, you may show your before and after pictures and tell the story of your journey. In financial markets, you could show your home before your success and then after. Every product or service promises a result, so the question is, "What was life like for you before you applied the result, and what does it look like now?"

Amazing discovery: Every day on your journey to help serve your dream customer, you should be discovering new things that can help them on *their* journey. Tell the stories about what you're discovering, how it's helped you, and how it can help them as well.

Secret-telling: You've probably noticed from the titles of my first three books that this is the one I go to a lot. What secrets do you know or have heard from other people that you can share with your audience? Even as a kid, when someone told me they had a secret, it would drive me crazy until I found out exactly what it was. The same is true online; a good secret can pull someone into your story better than almost anything else you can do.

Third-person testimonial: Sharing other people's successes with your products and services provides powerful social proof. Get as many third-person testimonials from your customers, clients, and students as you can. Then tell their stories over and over.

EXERCISE: THE ATTRACTIVE CHARACTER

Now that I've told you the elements, identity, and storylines for the Attractive Character, I want to show you some examples of people in our funnel-hacking community who have used this process to build out their own Attractive Characters. Read through their examples and spend some time in the following exercise defining your Attractive Character that you'll be sharing with your dream customers.

ATTRACTIVE CHARACTER FOR KAPOW

- **Name:** Liz (AKA The Queen of Kapow)

- **Dream Customers:** Her dream customers have a strong desire to build profitable businesses which, in turn, allow them to impact the world in a positive way. They believe they are called to do great things and they seek both financial freedom and personal fulfilment in the process.

ELEMENTS

- **Backstory**
Playing It Safe: One day, she found herself sitting in an office working on someone else's dream. She had the degree, the masters, and the "safe" job but was still deeply unfulfilled because she didn't feel connected to her purpose. She set off on a journey to finally fulfill her mission by doing something "big" in the world that made a difference (and a lot of money in the process).

- **Parables**
Systems Create Profit: After her first year in business, Liz sat at her table, heart broken, upon realizing that, despite all her hard work, she'd only made $25,000 that year. Desperate to find a solution, she read *The E-Myth Revisited*, and from that moment on she was addicted to systemizing her business. The following year, she made $181,932 *profit*. She teaches you how to implement her proven systems so you can bypass the pain she went through.

- **Character Flaws**
Dyslexia: Because Liz is dyslexic, she sometimes mispronounces, misspells, and misreads words on slides and presentations. She says, "I'm dyslexic" on her webinars to let her viewers know she's not perfect (and that you don't have to be perfect to be successful.)

Unfounded Fear of Not Knowing Enough: When she first started her social media management company, she feared she didn't know enough, and that her clients would "find her out" as not being an expert. She realized she just needed to be one step ahead of them, and she now shares this story on her webinar to let others know they don't need to be an "expert" to have success.

- **Polarity**
You Can Be 100% Yourself and Succeed: Others think that in order to be a success, you have to not "rock the boat" at home, at work, or with family, but her fans are sick of

being told who they can be. She shows them that they can be themselves in her KAPOW community by being *herself* (raw real and honest) thus showing them they are able to be themselves and *still* have success.

Scammers Suck: Having been scammed many times over the years (with courses being ripped off and people claiming they helped her in order to get clients), Liz stands for honesty and integrity loudly and proudly online. People flock to her who are sick of the scammers and want to be a part of something that's solid and not "smoke and mirrors."

IDENTITY

Her attractive character is the: Reluctant Hero because she feels called to help other business owners get faster and better results than she has, with less pain than she endured while creating her business success.

Figure 4.2:

The Attractive Character for Kapow is its creator Liz Benny.

ATTRACTIVE CHARACTERS FOR CASHFLOW TACTICS*

Note: If you have multiple founders in your business, this is one way you can have multiple attractive characters while still representing one brand.

- **Names:** Ryan (AKA Captain America)
  Brad (AKA Tony Stark)
  Jimmy (AKA Hulk)

- **Dream Customers:** Their dream customers have a deep-seated drive for personal freedom. They know they are meant for so much more, and they're stuck trading their most valuable resource (their time) for money, hoping that one day they'll have enough money to buy their freedom back.

ELEMENTS

- **Backstories**
Freedom Fighter: Ryan discovered the hard way that the conventional path of investing in your company-sponsored 401(k) and hoping that it would all work out "one day" was ultimately a path to being completely stuck. Through trial and error, he forged a path to finding financial freedom and living a purpose-driven life.

Mad Scientist: Brad sees the world through numbers (kinda like Neo from *The Matrix*). After calculating first hand that it was nearly mathematically impossible for people to ever be financially free using traditional, Wall Street strategies, he went on a quest to mathematically prove the only path to financial freedom in 10 years or less.

Drill Sergeant: Jimmy fought for freedom overseas only to come back home and realize he lost his freedom in the corporate rat race. He used his internal drive for freedom to discover the path to financial freedom.

- **Parables**
Stop Fighting Gravity: You can't see, touch, or feel gravity but when you put it to the test and take a step off of a ledge, you learn that gravity does indeed exist. Similarly, we believe that 97% of traditional financial advice is dangerous, misleading, or outright *wrong*. Like gravity, you can deny it, but you will find out the hard way that you will never be free as long as you follow this advice. Instead, they teach you to revolutionize the way you look at money by doing the exact opposite.

- **Character Flaws**
Constantly Chasing Goals: Ryan is constantly focused on personal expansion, so he has to remind himself that true freedom is found in the present moment while at the same time being blissfully dissatisfied.

Analysis Paralysis: Brad's biggest strength turns into his biggest weakness when he relies too much on the data and calculations rather than taking action toward getting results. Ryan and Jimmy help him to move forward without getting stuck on numbers.

Level 10 Quickstart: Jimmy rarely slows down to think and chases any shiny object that looks fun and exciting, so he has to double down on sticking to his own formula of freedom to gain the focus necessary to have success.

• **Polarity**
Do the Opposite: Everyone thinks that to be successful they have to do what everyone else is doing, just *better*. But if you do what everyone else does, you get what everyone else has. The only path to success is not doing the same thing better; instead, it's doing the exact opposite.

Goldfish Advice: Other well-intentioned advisers are incapable of helping you become financially free because they are not financially free themselves. You cannot lead what you don't live. Just as goldfish swim along, with no knowledge of what "water" is, traditional advisors can't teach you outside of their own knowledge: the traditional "goldfish" advice of Wall Street.

IDENTITIES

They each have a different identity in their brand, so their attractive characters are:
Adventurer because Ryan embodies the idea of freedom through intentional living and seeking adventure.

Reporter because Brad uses logic and math to make the unseen and confusing become logically sound and actionable.

Leader because Jimmy uses his drive for action and results to motivate others to get out of their heads and get into gear taking action.

Figure 4.3:

**The three Attractive Characters for CashFlow Tactics are founders
Ryan Lee, Brad Gibb, and Jimmy Vreeland.**

ATTRACTIVE CHARACTER

- **Name:** _____
- **Dream Customers:** _____

ELEMENTS

- **Backstory** (The journey that got your attractive character to where he/she is today)

  _____
  _____

- **Parables** (A story that helps your dream customers understand an important point)

  _____
  _____

- **Character Flaws** (The flaws that are shared to help your attractive character become more relatable to your dream customers)

  _____
  _____

- **Polarity** (The beliefs your attractive character holds to attract your dream customers and repel everyone else)

  _____
  _____

IDENTITY

- **Circle One:**   Leader | Adventurer | Reporter | Reluctant Hero
- **Why does your attractive character have that identity?**

  _____
  _____

Figure 4.4:

Before you start advertising, be sure to flesh out your own Attractive Character.

FUNNEL HACKING

"You can always tell who the pioneers are because they have arrows in their backs and are lying facedown in the dirt." I heard this quote for the first time when I was taking a college class; my professor explained that sometimes being a first mover in an industry wasn't necessarily an advantage. While it made sense, I didn't really understand the power behind this statement until I was sitting in a hotel room in Chicago at a Dan Kennedy event. The keynote speaker was Porter Stansberry, who at the time ran the largest division at the publishing company Agora called Stansberry Research.[8]

Agora is known in our industry as being the billion-dollar-per-year information marketing giant. As I sat in the back of the room that day, Porter talked about their sales funnel. He walked through how it worked, where they bought ads, and how they structured their pricing. As he talked, I was scribbling notes as fast as my hands would write. I couldn't believe he was sharing all the numbers behind his funnels. And then, in the middle of his explanation, he stopped.

"You know what's interesting?" he said. "Every year we have people who want to try to compete with us at Agora. They always come in thinking that they'll undercut us on price or sell through a different method or model than we do, and every year we watch as they try and fail. It always amazes me that they don't look at what we're doing now and just model it."

That message hit me like a ton of bricks. Agora had literally hundreds of people on staff testing every variable in their sales process. They have thousands of arrows in their backs. Why would you start down that same path and get the same arrows when you could just look at where Agora is now and start building your funnels modeling what they had proven was successful?

Before I build out any new sales funnel, the first thing I want to do is find other people who already have a successful funnel and are selling to my target market. If I can't find other businesses, then I won't continue to move forward. But if I *can* find others who are already successfully selling to the chosen market, then I can reverse engineer what they're doing. We call this process "funnel hacking," and it's the reason people inside our community call each other "funnel hackers."

The foundation for this concept came from a quote I heard from Tony Robbins, in which he said, "If you want to achieve success, all you need to do is find a way to model those who have already succeeded."[9] After hearing that, I thought about the things that I had been successful with. The first was my wrestling career. Like most kids, when I started I was really bad, but my dad would go to all the matches with his video camera and film the people that were winning. After the matches, we would watch the moves that the winners used, and we would practice them over and over. We did this at each level of competition. In high school, he would film the people who were the most successful, and then we would model the style and moves they would use. Within a short period of time, I went from being really bad to becoming a state champion, taking second place in the country during my senior year, becoming an All-American, and getting a college scholarship to wrestle at a Division I school.

The same thing happened when I started my business. I had no formal business training, but I saw the people who were having success and I modeled them. The first person I modeled was a guy named Armand Morin. He was selling software products online, so I decided to create my own software products. When I went to launch my sales funnel, I looked at what his looked like, and I modeled it.

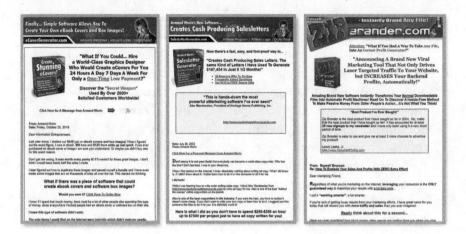

Figure 5.1:

I looked at Armand's two software funnels (on the left) and modeled his page structure, layout, and pricing strategy for my software funnel (on the right).

I modeled the look and the feel, the layout, and the pricing points. I did *not* copy anything. Oftentimes people confuse modeling with copying. I did not copy his product; it was my own product. I did *not* copy his sales letter; every word was mine. I modeled the page structure and layout and pricing strategy because he had proven that buyers in this market responded to that style. Where he had a headline, I had a headline. Where he placed his software box, I placed mine. Where he had a bulleted list of features and benefits, I added my own list with my features and my benefits. Copying is illegal and is not what I am talking about here. Funnel hacking is modeling a proven process or framework and then putting *your* product, *your* words, and *your* art into that framework.

Whenever I am going to create a new funnel, I first figure out what type of funnel I'm going to create (and I'll show you the 10 most common funnels in Section Two). Then I try to find as many examples of these types of funnels in my market and in other markets so I can see the framework. Finally, I create my own funnel inside of that framework.

I look for funnels to model in one of these three ways:

- **Direct competitors:** A direct competitor is a person or company selling something very similar to yours to the same people.

- **Indirect competitors:** These are people or companies selling something different than you but to the same demographic.

- **People selling through the same funnel type:** In many markets you will not be able to find someone who is successfully selling through a funnel, but that's okay. If you know that you are going to be using a webinar to sell your product, you can funnel hack anyone using a webinar. If you're selling through a free book funnel, you can model anyone using a free book funnel. Because we are not copying, but modeling the framework, matching the market is not essential.

After I've identified 10 or more funnels that I want to model, I act like a customer so I can see every part of their sales process. That means I actually go to each funnel and purchase their products so I can see everything that is working in real time.

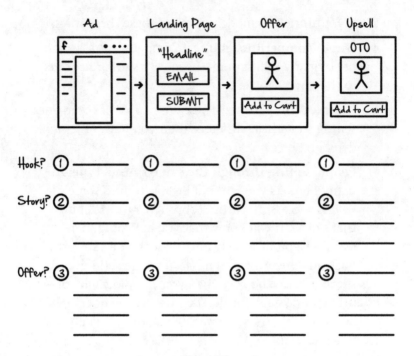

Figure 5.2:

To funnel hack someone, you'll need to go through their entire sales process to see their hooks, stories, and offers on all their ads and funnel pages.

I start by pretending I am a normal customer, and I go to Google and type in the keywords that I'd search for if I was looking for that product. I then start looking for paid ads that I can click on that will lead me to a funnel. I go to Facebook and start searching as well. I will "like" pages that are related, hoping that Facebook will start showing me ads with similar products. As soon as I start seeing ads, I make a note of what the hook, story, and offer are for that ad. Then I click on that ad and see where it takes me.

Sometimes it's a presell page, other times it's a landing page trying to get my email address, or it takes me directly to a video sales page. Regardless of where it takes me, I am watching (funnel hacking) the process. When I get to the landing page after the click, I write down the hook, story, and offer on that page. I then take whatever step they are asking me to do, and I move through the funnel.

I do the same thing on the sales pages, the order forms, and the upsell pages. What are the hooks, stories, and offers they are using for each page? This is my market research phase where I'm trying to figure out exactly how other people are having success. How are they using hooks to grab my attention? What are the stories they tell to get me interested and to create value? What is the offer and what things did they add to make it truly irresistible?

As you do this process, don't just do it to one funnel. Go through at least a half dozen or more so you can see the trends and figure out what's working now. This will give you a baseline that you now know you have to beat. You will need to make better hooks, better stories, and better offers so that your dream customers will come to you instead of your competitor.

Put on your marketing consultant hat. Start thinking about what things you would do differently or better if this was your funnel. How could you make that hook sexier? How could you tell your story differently to make them even more attractive? What things could you add to the offers and upsells to make them even more irresistible? As you start thinking like this, you will be working out your marketing brain, which will make it easier for you as you start building your own funnels.

Now that you understand the process of funnel hacking and how it works, I want to walk you through the seven phases of a funnel. As you are going through the funnel-hacking process, start to notice each phase as you experience them inside other people's funnels.

SEVEN PHASES
OF A FUNNEL

Growing up, one of my favorite stores was GNC. I loved supplements, and I loved going into the stores and reading the labels to see what each one could do for me. I would often spend hours in the store trying to decide, of all the supplements in there, which was the one that I wanted to try the most. I didn't have a lot of money, so I had to make sure that I got the perfect product for me on that trip.

The only thing that I hated about GNC is every time I would walk in the door, the person who worked there would run up to me and say, "Hi! Welcome to GNC. Can I help you with anything?" I never knew how to answer that question and it always made me feel uncomfortable. Oftentimes I would wait outside until the salesperson was talking to someone else and then I would sneak in and try my best to avoid eye contact.

I'm not sure if it's because I'm an introvert or just because I'm obsessed with marketing and sales processes, but I remember thinking that if the person working would just ask me a different question, I wouldn't have felt so uncomfortable and would have likely spent more time there.

As I grew older, I used to notice the process that different businesses would take me through and how I felt at each step. For instance, when I went to a hotel, how was I greeted? Where did they take me to get my hotel key? How did I get from the lobby to my hotel room? Did they have a bellhop take me on that journey? Were there clear instructions or did I get lost trying to find my room through the maze of the hotel? What was my experience at each step in the process? Some hotels made me feel special while others left me wishing for more.

I noticed the sales processes everywhere, such as how servers at restaurants would interact with me, how phone calls would go when I called to change my cable or phone providers, and even the people I met throughout each day. I became increasingly sensitive to how I felt at each step inside of any process that I stepped into.

When I started to buy things online, I was even more sensitive to how I felt. Sometimes the sales process or funnel they took me through was frictionless. Other times, I had to jump through so many hoops, I usually ended up just walking away from the purchase, even though I really wanted the thing I had come there to buy.

As I started to sell my own products and services online, I became obsessed with my customers' journey. What did they feel when they saw one of my ads, and what made them want to click on it? When they hit the landing page, what was that experience like, and what happened at each of the phases I took them through? The more aware I was of how someone was probably feeling at each step, the better I could craft messages and processes to help move them through the sale. The better you can make them feel at each step in the process, the more likely they will keep progressing with you through your funnels.

THE SEVEN PHASES OF A FUNNEL

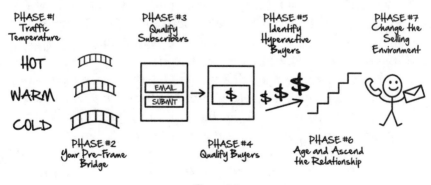

Figure 6.1:

From the moment your prospects are introduced to you, help them have a great experience at each step so they'll continue moving through your sales process.

After more than a decade of building funnels, I've identified that there are seven core phases we take every visitor through when they come into our world. The better you understand each of these phases and focus on how your customers will feel when they are in each step, the more success you will have.

Earlier we talked about the difference between a website and a funnel, and I told you that one of the rules of direct response marketing is "a confused mind always says no." As you are looking at each of these phases, notice that on each step, I am only asking them to do one thing. Each step will typically have its own hook to grab their attention, its own story to build perceived value, and its own offer (one call to action). If you try to get them to do more than one thing at each step, you'll essentially be putting up a brick wall in your funnel that will stop most people from progressing. My goal is to make this customer journey through the seven phases of a funnel as frictionless as possible, and it all starts with thinking about what your goal is for each step in the funnel. Then craft your hook, story, and offer around that one thing.

IT'S ALL ABOUT THE PRE-FRAME

In the book *Sway: The Irresistible Pull of Irrational Behavior* by Ori and Rom Brafman, I read about a fascinating study that took place at MIT, demonstrating the pre-frame principle in action.[10] They tell a story about a class of 70 economics students who were told they would have a substitute professor for the day. Since this professor was new, each student was to read a short biography of the teacher. The bios that were handed out to all the students were identical—except for one phrase. All the bios praised this teacher's graduate work in economics and listed various fabulous accomplishments. Then half the bios described the professor as "a very warm person," while the other half described him as "rather cold." That was the only difference—one phrase.

After the lecture, each student was asked to fill out a survey to see how they liked the teacher. The ones who received the "warm" bio said they loved him. They said he was good-natured, considerate of others, and sociable. The students who received the "cold" bio didn't like him at all. They said he was self-centered, formal, irritable, and ruthless. These students all sat through the same lecture, but the pre-frame changed their perception of what they witnessed. This study is such a cool example of the pre-frame principle at work.

Before we talk about the seven phases of a funnel, you need to understand the concept of a pre-frame because each step in a funnel is a pre-frame for the next step. It's essential to optimize these steps—not only for monetization, but also to build relationships and get visitors to continue to buy from you, someone they know and trust. One big mistake many marketers make is focusing 100 percent on short-term conversions or monetization. They sell so aggressively, focused on the sale at hand, that they lose the respect of their customers. This mistake will cost you the long-term relationship that can be worth 10 times as much as the money made through the initial point of contact.

A pre-frame is simply the state you place someone in as they enter the next step in your sales funnel. Changing the frame you take someone through can profoundly change the answer to a question or the experience they will have on the next step.

My first internet marketing mentor was a guy named Mark Joyner. I remember him saying that "not all clicks are created equal." That struck me as odd because business owners always talk about traffic and how to get more clicks to their websites—not a certain type of click. Wasn't a click just a click? But Mark made me understand that what really matters most is the frame that someone goes through before they actually get to your funnel. He even went so far as to say that often the frame people enter your website through is usually more important than what you actually say on that page when they get there.

He used me as an example: "Consider a person came from a website that said 'Russell Brunson is a scam artist. He stole my money. He's unethical. He's a liar, and I don't trust him. Click here to see his new product.' What do you think will happen when they click through to see the product?" The pre-frame was terrible.

That visitor would probably not like me, and I would have a hard time getting them to buy anything.

On the other hand, what if the person came from a site that said "Russell is an amazing person. I had a chance to meet him; we talked for an hour, and what he taught me changed my business and my life. My company was able to go from nothing to $1 million in revenue a year. Click here to see his new product."? The chances of converting that potential customer on my site are much, much higher. I can sell more if the visitor enters my website through a good pre-frame. The frame through which he enters my website completely changes what can happen on the page. So the trick is to figure out how to control the frame that your traffic is coming through.

The first time I really understood this principle was a few minutes before I got on stage to speak at Armand Morin's "Big Seminar." I was backstage talking to Armand and he told me that after speaking at hundreds of events, he noticed that the number one thing that would affect his sales after his presentation was tied directly into how the event promoters introduced him before he came on stage. We joked about how bad most emcees were and how they would read our name and a bio off a card and then we'd have to come up and speak. He told me that if you take control of your introduction, your pre-frame before people hear you speak, it will change everything.

As this was Armand's event, he told me, "Watch how I introduce you, and then let's see what percentage of the room buys your products when you're done." Typically, I would close about 15 percent of the room on my $1,997 course I would sell at the end of my presentation. During this event, after Armand introduced me and I delivered my presentation, I ended up closing over 42 percent of the people who were in the room. Same presentation, same offer, same price point, different pre-frame.

I became so obsessed with my pre-frame that I actually made a video that was crafted to give me the perfect pre-frame and I made all emcees introduce the video, and then I'd let the video deliver the perfect pre-frame every time. I rarely ever closed less than 40 percent of a room from that point forward.

I now use this lesson of pre-framing on every step of my funnel. Each page has its own hook, story, and offer, but it's also serving as the pre-frame for the next step. That's why it's so essential to really understand this concept and master it in your funnels. As you go through my funnels and other people's, notice how the good funnels successfully create a pre-frame that makes you more likely to say yes in the next step.

Phase #1—Determine traffic temperature: When most people build a funnel, they start with the landing page, but I've found there are critical steps *before* the visitor even gets to the landing page that have a huge effect on how well your funnels perform. The first phase to examine is what we call traffic temperature. There are three levels of traffic that come to your website: hot, warm, and cold. Each group needs special treatment and individualized communication. Each needs to come across a different bridge to arrive at your landing page. Yes, that means you may even need three different landing pages, depending on how you're driving traffic. Trust me, it's worth taking the extra time to set this up correctly.

Here is a quote from Eugene Schwartz that helped me to understand the different traffic temperatures and how you must communicate differently with each type:

> "If your prospect is aware of your product and has realized it can satisfy his desire, your headline starts with the product.
>
> "If he is not aware of your product, but only of the desire itself, your headline starts with the desire.
>
> "If he is not yet aware of what he really seeks, but is concerned with the general problem, your headline starts with the problem and crystallizes it into a specific need."[11]

Figure 6.2:

Start your copy wherever your prospect is at the time.

You have to figure out where your prospect is along the product-awareness continuum: problem aware, solution aware, or product aware. Where they are determines the temperature of the traffic.

Hot traffic is made up of people who already know who you are and what products you sell. They know what their problem is, they're aware of all possible solutions, and they're also aware of the products you offer to help them solve their problems. They are on your email list, subscribe to your podcast, read your blog, follow you on Facebook and Instagram, and subscribe to your You-Tube channel. Because you have an established relationship with them, you're going to talk to these people like they're your friends (because they are). You want to use personality-driven communication through the Attractive Character.

Warm traffic consists of people who don't know you yet, but they are aware of other potential solutions to their problems. When you read *Traffic Secrets*, I talk a lot about your "Dream 100," or the people who have already congregated your dream customers. They are your warm traffic. You just need to make them aware of your solution to their problems. These are usually the subscribers, fans, and followers of other people who are already in your market.

Cold traffic is made up of people who have a problem, but they aren't even aware yet of the potential solutions. These are typically the hardest to find and convert because they haven't yet congregated with the other "who"s in your market yet. Most of our traffic efforts will be to warm traffic, but as you grow, there will come a point where you will have to learn how to tap into cold traffic and create customers as opposed to moving them from another solution to yours like you do with warm traffic.

After you've identified what type of traffic you're going to focus on for this particular funnel, the next step is to set up the pre-frame bridge to capture and warm up that traffic before they get to your landing page.

Phase #2—Set up the pre-frame bridge: The second phase is your pre-frame bridge. This could be an ad, a video, an email, or an article. It's a bridge that pre-frames people before they get to your landing page. Different types of traffic need different bridges.

A *hot traffic bridge* is typically very short. You already have a relationship with these people, so you don't have to do a lot of credibility-building or pre-framing. You can probably just send out a quick email with a link to your landing page and that's about it. Or you can write a blog post or record a podcast encouraging people to check out your offer. These people will listen and do as you suggest simply because they already know, like, and trust you.

A *warm traffic bridge* is a little longer than a hot traffic bridge, but not much. If you are targeting your warm traffic on any of the social platforms, you can often use a video to bridge the gap between where they are (on someone else's fan page or watching a YouTube video) and where you want to take them. For example, if I have an ad that is targeting Tony Robbins's audience on Facebook, I may have a video talking about how I learned the concept of "growth and contribution" from Tony and that I have a book that will show you how you can take all the things you're learning and start contributing by creating a business. I would then guide them into the funnel where they could buy *Expert Secrets*. Do you see how that works? The pre-frame bridge speaks to them where they are now and gives them the context they need so they understand why they need your product or service.

A *cold traffic bridge* is the longest type of bridge. With warm traffic, I'm just showing them my solution to their problems;

with cold traffic, often I have to help them even know they have a problem. I'm not moving customers from one congregation to another; I'm creating a customer out of thin air.

For hot and warm traffic, the ad generally serves as the pre-frame. There's usually not much of a need for extra steps before those people understand your offer. But for cold traffic, you often need a whole separate page that they go through (we call this a bridge page) before they hit the landing page. As I just explained, this separate pre-frame page educates people, enabling them to better appreciate the offer and making them more likely to convert.

I used to own a company that sold supplements to help with neuropathy pain. We had our own customer list (hot traffic) that we would send emails to, and they would reorder just by us reminding them that they should. We would then target people who suffered from neuropathy (warm traffic) on all the social channels to let them know about our new, groundbreaking product that was the answer to their problems. It was easy to get this warm traffic to at least give us a try and become a customer.

But then we bought ads to people who didn't know they had neuropathy. Many people know they have nerve pain but have never heard the word *neuropathy*. So our cold traffic offer helps people with *nerve pain*, a simpler, more relatable term. My pre-frame page states that "if you have nerve pain, it's probably caused by neuropathy." The page goes on to explain a bit about the unfamiliar term. Then when the visitor gets to the funnel's landing page, all the language suddenly makes sense. They now understand that the nerve pain is due to neuropathy, and our supplements can help. What happens when we do that? Our universe of potential customers expands exponentially! If you can create a cold traffic bridge that will take cold traffic and warm it up for you, your potential to grow your company dramatically goes up.

Whatever product you're selling, it's critical that you match your message to your traffic's temperature and knowledge. This awareness will help you determine the kind of bridge required to take them to the landing page.

Phase #3—Qualify subscribers: The whole goal here is to take all the traffic—hot, warm, and cold—and find out who is willing to give us an email address in exchange for more information. (This is known as subscribing to a list.) If people aren't willing to give their email addresses at this point, they are highly unlikely to give me money later. Qualifying subscribers is done through an opt-in or squeeze page that offers something of value in return for contact information. This is typically the very front end of your value ladder. For my companies, it's usually a free report or a free video showing the visitor one thing they would really want to know. Let's say I have 1,000 visitors who come to my site each day. If I have a 30 percent conversion rate, then I know I have about 300 people who will be interested in my information. Now I have a list of warm leads and I can continue to move them through the rest of my funnel.

Phase #4—Qualify buyers: Immediately after you qualify your subscribers, you want to find out who among them is a buyer. How many of those 300 people who were interested in getting free information are willing to pull out their credit cards and make a purchase? Notice I said you must find your potential buyers *immediately* after you qualify subscribers. Don't wait a day or a week. Qualify buyers right away. My early mentor, Dan Kennedy, taught me this golden principle: *a buyer is a buyer is a buyer.* If someone is willing to buy from you once, they'll continue to buy from you as long as you keep offering value. So as soon as someone fills out their name and email address and clicks the Submit button, they should land on a sales page that offers them your first premium offer.

I typically sell very low-ticket products here that range from being free (they just cover the shipping and handling costs) to somewhere in the $7–$10 range. I like the offer to be extremely inexpensive so I can find out who all my buyers are. Who is willing to pull out a credit card in exchange for something I am selling? I want to know who those people are, because if they are willing to buy something, then I'm willing to spend more money to market to them. I might be willing to call those buyers on the phone, send them a postcard or a letter in the mail, or make them special offers that I don't send to just my subscriber lists. At this point, I have two lists: subscribers and buyers. Each list is unique and gets treated differently.

Phase #5—Identify hyperactive buyers: After you've identified the buyers, you want to identify the *hyperactive* buyers. These are your dream customers who are willing to pay more money to solve their problems now.

I'm a self-proclaimed hyperactive buyer in the markets that I'm passionate about. Let me tell you a quick story to illustrate how many of the people who come into your funnels work.

A little while ago, I decided to take some of my employees bowling. Now, bowling happens to be my third favorite sport (behind wrestling and jiu-jitsu). All three are markets that I spend time congregating in. I'm a pretty good bowler, but for some reason that day, I was off. Even though I brought my own ball and my own glove and shoes, no matter how hard I tried, I couldn't close out a frame. Normally that would be okay, but one of my other employees was having the night of his life. Strike after strike, he taunted me in front of my team. While we all had a good time at my expense, that night I went home and I was in pain; I wanted out of that pain as fast as possible. I started searching online for help. Within minutes I bought a new ball from one site and new shoes from another. I purchased books, videos, and more. During that moment I was a hyperactive buyer and I wanted to buy everything I could get to make me feel better.

You want to be able to identify these people as quickly as possible and help them. If you don't, they will go to your competitor and give them money instead. When they're in pain and want relief, they will spend money to solve that problem now.

There is a funny ending to this story. Within a few days I was out of pain and no longer thinking about bowling. The things I ordered showed up in the mail, and for years I've received emails from these companies trying to get me to buy more things, but I've never been in enough pain to buy anything again from them. The window for them closed. I want to make sure that I give people the ability to buy when they want to buy. That is why having upsells and cross sells inside your funnel is so important, because if they don't get their itch scratched by you in the moment, they will keep searching and spend their money somewhere else instead. If you honestly believe that you have the best products and services to help your dream customers, then you owe it to yourself and to them to offer upsells inside your funnel.

Now that I've identified who my hyperactive buyers are, I will also put them on a separate sublist and I will market to them differently. I will spend more money to market to someone who has spent $1,000 with me rather than someone who has only spent $10.

Phase #6—Age and ascend the relationship: At this point, the initial sales experience is pretty much over. Points one through five all happen during the "point of sale" within 5 or 10 minutes, and the next two phases are where the Attractive Character takes your new dream customer by the hand and helps to move them up the value ladder. You will be using follow-up funnels (Secret #7) to build a relationship with them and move them into the next funnel in your value ladder.

Phase #7—Change the selling environment: Typically, it's difficult to sell super-expensive products or services online. Not many people are going to read a sales letter and click the Add to Cart button for a fifteen- or a hundred-thousand-dollar product. Some might, but usually you have to change the selling environment if you want to sell high-ticket products. The most common ways to change the environment are to sell the pricier items over the phone, through direct mail, or at a live event or seminar.

The funnels in the back end of your value ladder typically are created in a way to sell people on an idea or a concept, but then you have them schedule an appointment to talk to you on the phone. There, you are able to customize what you offer and speak to them inside a completely different sales environment. People on the phone are more likely to listen closely to an offer. The salesperson has the benefit of live feedback. He or she can overcome objections and help people make up their minds on the fly. When we change the selling environment, we can communicate at a different level, and it becomes easier to move people up to the higher levels of the value ladder.

You've now had a chance to see the seven phases of a sales funnel, and I want to encourage you (as you are now a funnel hacker) to see what others are doing inside of each phase. Put on your "funnel consultant" hat as you do this and see what steps they are missing and what things they could do to make you feel better at each step in the process.

If I were to consult with a retail store on how to increase sales, I would look at everything that happens during a customer's experience with the store, including the moment a customer saw the ad, walked in the front door, and received a greeting from the employees. I would analyze what the customer saw that made them choose certain items, what products were point of sale, and how the cashier upsold them during checkout. I would then analyze the follow-up sequences already in place to bring that customer back.

Increasing online sales happens the same way. You need to break out and examine each of the phases your customer passes through in your sales funnels. After you are aware of the distinct steps and break out each into a separate experience, you can tweak each aspect to get more conversions. In this way, you can help people ascend to the next level of your value ladder.

If you're stuck in your business, it's probably because there's a problem somewhere inside of these seven phases. What's the temperature of the traffic you're driving? What's the pre-frame bridge you're taking potential buyers through? Are you qualifying subscribers on the landing page? Are you qualifying your buyers on the sales page and your hyperactives on the upsell pages? Are you aging and ascending the relationship to match the buyer with the offer they really need the most? Are you changing the selling environment for your high-ticket offers? Most importantly, how are you treating your different groups so that each receives a specially tailored experience?

I want to quickly recap the seven phases again:

- **Phase #1— Determine traffic temperature:** Are the people you are sending into this funnel hot, warm, or cold traffic?

- **Phase #2—Set up the pre-frame bridge:** Based on the type of traffic you're sending, what type of pre-frame bridge do you need to create?

- **Phase #3—Qualify subscribers:** Who of all your visitors are willing to give you their email address in exchange for your free offer?

- **Phase #4—Qualify buyers:** Who of all your subscribers are willing to give you their credit card in exchange for your first premium offer?

- **Phase #5—Identify hyperactive buyers:** Who are the people who are willing to spend more money now to solve their problems?

- **Phase #6—Age and ascend the relationship:** Now that I have their contact information, how do I build their relationship with the Attractive Character?

- **Phase #7—Change the selling environment:** How can I move them up my value ladder by taking them outside of just my online funnels?

Now that you've seen the overall strategy of how we take our customers through our funnels, I want to talk about a second type of funnel that we call a follow-up funnel.

FOLLOW-UP FUNNELS

In *Building a StoryBrand*, Donald Miller explains that your brand is *not* the hero.[12] He says that your customer is the hero, and your brand's role is to successfully guide the hero through the challenges they will face. Therefore, he explains that your brand should be like Yoda to Luke Skywalker.

When you look at your business through that lens, you will see that all we are really doing is looking for congregations of people or heroes who have challenges, throwing out hooks to grab their attention, and then you as the Attractive Character become a guide who will lead them through your value ladder, helping them through challenges so they can achieve the results they desire.

Figure 7.1:

Our customers are confused about how to reach their destination.
Once we become their guide, we can guide them to success.

As one of my friends, Jenna Kutcher, said, "A brand is the image and personality the business applies to its offers." You are the brand, you are the guide, and now it's time to apply *you* (the brand, the guide, the Attractive Character) to the offers in your value ladder.

In Section Three, I will be giving you the scripts that you will use on each page inside your funnel. These are the sales scripts that your Attractive Character will be using to guide your customers to the sale. During this chapter, I won't be focusing on how we use the Attractive Character on the funnel pages but instead on how we use the communication funnels (or follow-up funnels) that move people from step to step inside our value ladder.

There are two types of messages that we send out in our follow-up funnels. The first is what we call "Soap Opera Sequences," and their goal is to quickly build a relationship with your Attractive Character, pull your prospect through the initial funnel, and ascend them to the next funnel in your value ladder. The second type of message is what we call "Daily Seinfeld Emails," which you send out to people who are not currently in one of your follow-up funnels, with a goal to reengage them and get them back into your value ladder.

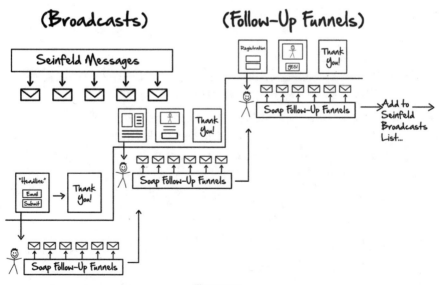

Figure 7.2:

Your prospects and customers go through a series of Soap Opera Sequences before eventually moving on to your Daily Seinfeld Emails.

THE THREE TYPES OF TRAFFIC

Before we get into exactly how to structure both these campaigns, I want to help you understand the power of follow-up funnels and the importance of building your list. Inside the "Seven Phases of a Funnel" chapter, we start to qualify our subscribers in Phase #3. At this point, we are able to start communicating with them through our Attractive Character.

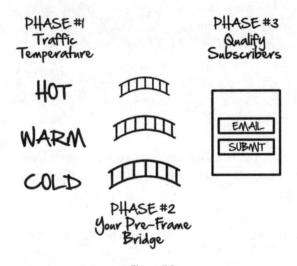

Figure 7.3:

Once people give you their email in Phase #3, you can continue the conversation with them and build their rapport with the Attractive Character.

So how do we get people into that step where they join our email list, become subscribers, and get added into our follow-up funnels? Inside *Traffic Secrets*, we go deep into helping you get traffic into your funnels, and one of the core concepts that you will learn when you read that book is that there are only three types of traffic.

1. Traffic that you control
2. Traffic that you earn
3. Traffic that you own

Once you understand how each type of traffic works and how they tie together, you will understand that your one and *only* goal is to *own* all the traffic you can.

Figure 7.4:

Your goal is to turn all your traffic into traffic that you own.

Traffic that you own: I want to begin our discussion with the third type of traffic listed because it's the most important. Traffic you own is the *best* kind of traffic. It's your email, Messenger, and customer lists. I call this the traffic that I "own" because I can send out an email or send a message to my followers to generate instant traffic. I don't have to buy it from Google or Facebook. I don't have to do any PR or SEO. This is my own distribution channel; I can send out messages anytime I want with no new marketing costs. I can sell things to these people repeatedly, and all that money comes back as pure profit.

I was lucky when I first got started online that my very first mentor, Mark Joyner, happened to be someone who had built his company and his wealth by focusing on building a huge list. As I was being distracted by all the shiny objects online, Mark's constant advice to me was "Russell, you have to focus on building a list." He ingrained that principle into my mind, and it became my only focus for years. As my list started to grow, so did my income.

About that time, another list-builder named Mike Filsaime told me that I should make, on average, about $1 per name for each name on my email list. I wasn't sure how that was possible at first, but I believed him and I started tracking my results.

The first month that I worked on building my list, I was able to get about 200 people to join. That month I also made a little over $200 in sales from the people who were on that list. Then I started to reinvest a lot of that money back into list-building. Within a few months, I had over 1,000 people on my list, and I was averaging over $1,000 in sales to those subscribers each month! When I hit 5,000 subscribers, I averaged over $5,000! As my lists grew, so did my influence and my sales. Within a year, I had over 100,000 people on my list; within five years, that list had grown to over one million people.

The best way to give yourself a raise every day is to spend time every day focusing on new ways that you can build your list. If you follow the processes in the Secrets trilogy, including becoming better at communicating with your audience, you should be able to average more than the $1 per month per name on your list. In fact, in most of the markets we're in, the profit is actually a lot higher than that. But as a rule of thumb, if you build a good relationship with your list, you should expect to see similar results. Once you understand that metric, suddenly list-building becomes a much higher priority!

That's why it's so important to convert the other two types of traffic (both traffic you control and traffic you earn) into subscribers and buyers (traffic that you own) as quickly as possible. The bigger your list, the more money you make.

Traffic that you control: The next type of traffic is traffic you control. You control traffic when you have the ability to tell it where to go. For example, if I purchase an ad on Google, I don't own that traffic (Google does), but I can control it by buying an ad and sending those who click on that ad anywhere I want. Any kind of paid traffic is traffic you control, including:

- Email ads (solo ads, banners, links, mentions)
- Pay-per-click ads (Facebook, Google, Yahoo, etc.)
- Banner ads
- Native ads
- Affiliates and joint ventures

Now, I personally *love* traffic that I can control, but my big problem is that every time I want more of it, I have to spend more money. So my goal is always to send any traffic that I am going to purchase over to a type of landing page that is often called a "squeeze page," because it will squeeze the email address out of the traffic you send to it.

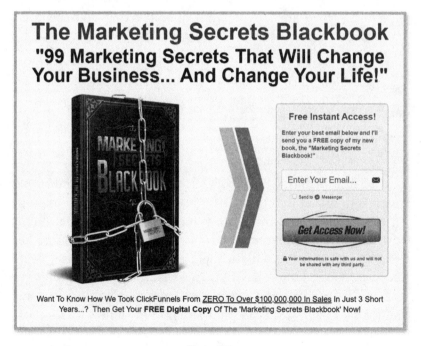

Figure 7.5:

Squeeze pages have one goal and no distractions. There is only one thing for the visitor to do on this page: join my list.

This squeeze page is a very simple page with *one* goal: to convert traffic that you control into traffic that you own. I send all my paid traffic to a squeeze page, and when the visitors get there, they only have *one* option: give me an email address or leave. Now, a certain percentage of people will leave, but the cool thing is that some of these people will give you a personal email address. After that, the traffic you control becomes traffic that you own, and you can start sending the new potential buyer through your Soap Opera Sequences inside your follow-up funnels.

Traffic that you earn: This last type of traffic you don't control but earn. For example, if you get interviewed on a podcast or someone mentions you on their blog or posts about you socially, their followers may search your name in Google, and they may land on some random page on your blog. Although you've earned that traffic, you don't have control over any part of that sequence of events. There are lots of types of traffic that you can earn, including:

- Social media (Facebook, Twitter, Instagram, Google+, LinkedIn, Pinterest, etc.)
- Search traffic (search engine optimization or SEO)
- Online PR
- Word of mouth

Just like the traffic that I control, my *only* goal with traffic that I earn is to turn it into traffic that I own. To do this, I try to guide all traffic that I earn back to my "funnel hub." A funnel hub is basically a website that has all my funnels, but it looks more like a traditional website. When people go there, the only real thing they can do is go into one of my funnels where they will have to give me their email addresses. After they do that, they become traffic that I own, and I can put them into my follow-up funnels.

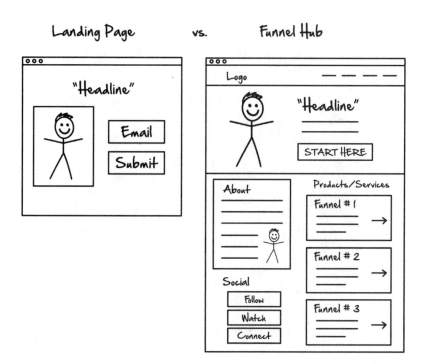

Figure 7.6:

The goal of a landing page and a funnel hub are the same:
convert all your traffic into traffic that you own.

Figure 7.7:

I created a funnel hub to capture as much traffic as I can
that I earn and turn it into traffic I own.

Now that someone has come to one of your funnel landing pages (either as traffic that you controlled or traffic that you earned), put in their email address, and qualified themselves as a subscriber, your Attractive Character will have a chance to start communicating with them through your follow-up funnels.

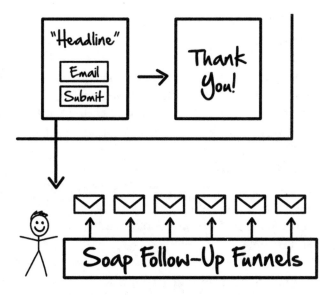

Figure 7.8:

You can continue the conversation with your prospects by
sending them emails after they've subscribed to your list.

THE SOAP OPERA SEQUENCE

When somebody joins your list for the first time, it's essential
that you quickly build a bond between them and the Attractive
Character. For years, I tried dozens of ways to build a quick
relationship with people after they joined my list, but I always
struggled until I learned about Soap Opera Sequences from one
of my friends, Andre Chaperon. The goal is to quickly create an
instant bond between you and the person reading the email. If
your first email is boring, you're done. They probably won't open
the next one. But if you give them something interesting and
hook them with an open storyline in the first email, they will look
forward to the next email, and the next, and the next.

If you've never watched a soap opera before, the stories rely on open-ended, high-drama episodes that hook in the viewers and keep them coming back every single weekday to find out what happens next. The programs are continuous narratives that never conclude. The characters are always either getting into trouble or getting out of trouble, falling in love or breaking up, heading to jail or escaping, or dying or miraculously coming back to life. If you relate to the characters, you can't help but get sucked into the drama, wanting to know what's coming next.

In the same way that the soap opera's open loop pulls you from episode to episode and season to season, we're going to use the same story structure and elements to get people to keep opening your emails and actually look forward to every message that you send!

There are many different story structures you can use to craft your Soap Opera Sequence, and I typically will use a different structure for each product inside the value ladder, but the key isn't so much which script you use as much as it is telling a compelling story that opens loops in each email that can only be closed by reading the next email.

Let me walk you through a very simple five-email Soap Opera Sequence that readers get when they join some of my lists. It's simple, and it works to build a relationship with the Attractive Character fast. In this example, someone just joined my list by filling out a form on a squeeze page requesting more information about becoming an expert, and the product I'm going to be selling them in this series is *Expert Secrets*.

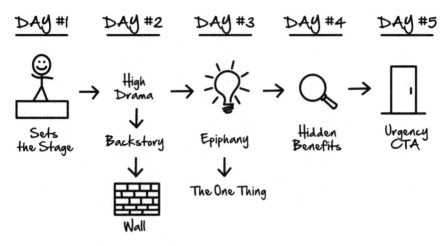

Figure 7.9:

In your Soap Opera Sequences, you'll send out one email each day for five days that pulls your reader through a narrative to sell your products and services.

Email #1—Set the stage: This is the first email I send people as soon as they subscribe to my list. It sets the stage for the emails to come, lets people know what to expect, and sets the initial "hook" that will get them to start reading my emails.

[EXPERT] Ch. 1 of 5

Hey, this is Russell, and I want to "officially" welcome you to my world.

About ten years ago, I started my first online business while I was in college (selling potato gun DVDs), and this little hobby became my obsession.

Over the past decade I've sold about everything you can think about online from supplements to weight loss and dating advice and about a dozen things in between.

But I'm not going to talk about those businesses here... Those are my playground where I test new ideas to see which ideas work the best, and then I report my marketing tests back to you here inside of my "Marketing Secrets" newsletter that you just joined.

My goal is always to give away better stuff in this newsletter for FREE than what other people charge for (that way you'll be sure to open every email as if you just paid me for it!)

In fact, tomorrow I'm gonna do just that. Yes, I'm going to ship you one of my BEST products for free—BUT only if you open the email when it comes . . .

Yes, you heard me right . . .

I want our relationship to start out great . . .

So, I'm going to WOW you with SO much value that you'll feel obligated to buy stuff from me in the future (just kidding... kinda).

Sound good?

Cool, then look for that email tomorrow.

Thanks,

Russell "Your New Marketing Buddy" Brunson

P.S. The subject line is "[EXPERT] Ch. 2 of 5: The day my education failed me" —so look for it!

Figure 7.10:

Your first email sets the stage of the emails that will follow.

Email #2—Open with high drama: If you did a good job opening a loop in Email #1, the reader will be anxiously waiting for your next email to come. For me, this is where the story "selling" process begins. I learned from my friend, Daegan Smith, that you *always* start any good story at the point of high drama. Most people mistakenly start their stories at the beginning, but usually stories don't get good until the middle, so it's better to start at the good part, and then you can go back and fill in the backstory after readers are hooked.

Backstory: Once you have their attention with emotional drama, you're going to go back and tell them the backstory. Tell them the events that led up to the high-drama moment. How in the world did you get yourself into such a predicament? Typically, your backstory is going to take you back to a similar spot the readers may be in now. If you're helping them to lose weight, you take them back to when you were overweight. If you're teaching them to achieve financial freedom, take them back to a time when you were broke. You want to bring them on a personal journey with you.

Wall: This backstory will lead up to a spot where you got stuck and hit a wall. Usually this is where the readers are in their lives right now. They're stuck, and that's why they're open to your answers. You explain to them how you hit that wall and then found the answer. But don't give them the answer yet. Just open the loop and promise to close it in Email #3.

[EXPERT] Ch. 2 of 5: The day my education failed me.

"How did I get here?"

I sat in the middle of a full auditorium, feeling a little confused that after everything, it would all end here… like this.

I had been blindly following the status quo for fifteen years, moving towards one goal, only to find out the whole thing was a lie…

I looked to my left… and I looked to my right… and I saw hundreds of others in the same situation as me. Only THEY had smiles on their faces.

Didn't they know what was about to happen to us?

It was Saturday, May 14th, 2005.

It was the day I was finally graduating from college, the day my parents had told me about for years.

"You need to get a college education so you can get a good job."

Sure, tonight there would be a lot of celebrating…

But what about the next morning?

That's when we all had a chance to meet the "Real World."

And as we quickly found out, it's not very nice or forgiving.

For most of the people who graduated with me, IF they were able to find jobs, they were going into entry-level jobs making thirty to forty thousand dollars a year, barely enough to cover the monthly payments for their student loans.

Loans which, by the way, are non-dismissible… EVEN if you declare bankruptcy.

The chains of debt and a job market that can't pay enough to cover the costs of our education is what we each inherited when we stepped into the "Real World."

So, when I looked around and saw them all smiling on graduation day, at first I was confused…

Not for me, but for them…

Because for me, I knew what my next step was. Just two years earlier, I had stumbled on a cool way to take the things I was good at in my life and turn those things into a business.

This was a business that had made me two hundred and fifty thousand dollars my senior year in college and would go on to make me over a MILLION dollars within just one year of graduation.

Would you like to know what I found out? Are you interested in how I was able to get my idea up and running with literally no money, while I was going to school, wrestling, and spending time with my new wife?

If so, then look for my email tomorrow. I'm gonna show you the epiphany I had, but more importantly, I'm going to explain how you can use it to get similar results in your life!

So, look for tomorrow's email. The subject line is [EXPERT] Ch. 3 of 5: Expert Secrets.

Thanks,

Russell "Wish I Had My Tuition Back" Brunson

P.S. I almost forgot. I told you yesterday that I was going to GIVE you my best product for free...

You can get it here (but please don't share it with anyone else)—this is for my faithful subscribers only:

www.ExpertSecrets.com <= my best product, just cover shipping and I'll send it to you for free!

This book has made more of my students independently wealthy than anything we've ever done in the past. So let me know where to ship your copy and let's see where it could take you!

Talk to you tomorrow!

Figure 7.11:

Your second email opens at the point of high drama.

Email #3—Epiphany: Today you get to reveal the big epiphany you had that will tie back to your product. It's the moment that everything turned around for you. By now the reader is hooked into the story, and they want to know what you discovered. An epiphany might start like:

- My epiphany was I needed to build a list, and that's when I learned about _____.

- I had to get a support system to help me get over my addiction, and that's when I found _____.

- I had to address the emotional roots of overeating, and that's when I found _____.

The epiphany ties into the solution you're selling (the One Thing). If you're selling someone else's product, it's enough to say your epiphany led to the discovery of the product.

[EXPERT] Ch. 3 of 5: Expert Secrets.

I was sitting in my college classroom, doing the math and trying to figure out how much my college professor was making per hour.

I assumed he was making about fifty thousand dollars per year. (My estimate may have been low or high; I have no idea.) If he was working forty-hour weeks, then he was probably making about twenty-five dollars an hour.

I then looked at a "how to" book I had bought the night before. I had paid fifty dollars for the book, and I thought it was awesome.

I knew the person who wrote the book had said that he sells, on average, one hundred copies of that book per day. One hundred copies!

I was doing the math, and at fifty dollars per book, he was making about five thousand dollars per day! Or $1,825,000 per year!

But the craziest part is the guy only spent a few days writing the book (it was 90% pictures and just 10% text), and when he was done, he NEVER had to write it again. The book did the teaching for him! He was able to create it once and then get paid for it over and over again!

That's when I realized I didn't want to sell my knowledge by the hour like my professor was doing... I wanted to sell it like this author!

And so that's what I did...

And by my senior year in college, I had made about two hundred and fifty thousand dollars!

And within a year of graduation, I had made over a million!

And I did this all by focusing on ONE thing...

Selling my knowledge the right way!

Would you like to know how I did that?

If so, I just posted a video online that will show you how I took twenty dollars and a simple idea and turned it into a million-dollar-a-year "how-to" business.

I posted the video here: www.ExpertSecrets.com

Go check it out, and let me know what you think.

Thanks,

Russell Brunson

P.S. Tomorrow I want to show you a few hidden benefits that being an "expert" will give you, benefits you probably don't even know exist. Look for that email tomorrow!

Figure 7.12:

Your third email shares the epiphany you had regarding your core product.

Email #4—Hidden benefits: If they haven't purchased your product, then they haven't seen how it's valuable to them yet, so in this email I'm going to point out other hidden benefits that they'll receive when they purchase this product from me.

[EXPERT] Ch. 4 of 5: The Hidden Benefits.

When I first became an "Expert," I was concerned because I didn't have any credentials, degrees or anything...

I just knew that what I showed people worked and I wanted to share it.

But what caught me off-guard was how helping people get what they want in life actually changed the quality of my own life.

Sure, I started to make a lot of money, BUT... more importantly, each person I helped opened up new doors for me. Through my "Expert" business, I've been able to travel around the world and meet cool people like Tony Robbins and Richard Branson...

But the REAL hidden benefit has been the fulfillment I get when I see someone else change his or her life. And that is what this business really is about for me. I'm guessing if you're here, then it's probably the same thing for you too—am I right?

If so, then you NEED to get a free copy of my new book called Expert Secrets. We normally charge $19.95 for it, but you'll get it for free if you let me know where to ship it this week.

Does that sound more than fair?

Cool—then go get your free copy here: www.ExpertSecrets.com

Thanks,

Russell Brunson

Figure 7.13:

**Your fourth email explains the hidden benefits
your reader may not have thought of before.**

Email #5—Urgency and CTA: This is usually the last email in my Soap Opera Sequence. The goal is to give the reader one last push to go take action right now. You do that by adding urgency into the equation and using a call to action (CTA). Up to this point, you've been casually using CTAs, but in this last email, you want to light a little fire under your readers. What legitimate reasons can you come up with that would make them need to take action right away?

- Your webinar starts tomorrow.

- You only have 10 seats left at your event.

- You only ordered 1,000 books, and most of them are gone.

- You're pulling the video offline.

Whatever the reason, your urgency needs to be real. Fake urgency will backfire on you, and you'll lose all credibility. Just think of a reason why you might "run out" of whatever you're selling. If it's an evergreen product, then create a special sale that ends soon or give readers a coupon that expires in 24 hours. Be creative! There's always some way to create real urgency.

[EXPERT] Ch. 5 of 5: Last Call.

I've been talking about my "Expert Secrets" book this week, and how you can get a copy for free...

But that special offer is going away TODAY...

Yes, if you read this email tomorrow, then I apologize, because it will be too late. If you want this book later, you'll have to pay the normal full price.

But—if you want to take me up on my special offer then go get your copy ASAP here:

www.ExpertSecrets.com

You've been warned—I don't want any emails tomorrow saying I didn't warn you.

So, go get your book, and I'll talk to you soon.

Thanks,

Russell Brunson

Figure 7.14:

Your fifth email adds urgency and scarcity with a strong CTA.

That's how the Soap Opera Sequence works: email #1 pushes the reader to email #2 . . . email #2 pushes the reader to email #3 . . . And so on.

Notice that the emails themselves are easy to read and fast to scan. I never write more than one or two sentences per line, and I add in lots of white space. Do not use long paragraphs because they slow people down and can look very overwhelming when they're trying to decide if they want to read it or not.

If this is my only funnel in my value ladder, I will move someone from this Soap Opera Sequence into my Daily Seinfeld Email list. If I have other funnels in my value ladder, I will move them from this Soap Opera Sequence into the next Soap Opera Sequence in the value ladder.

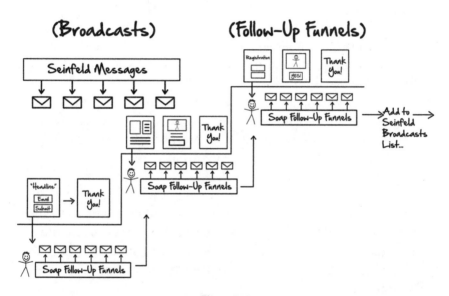

Figure 7.15:

After they finish each of the Soap Opera Sequences in the follow-up funnel, they will then be added into the daily Seinfeld email broadcast list.

DAILY SEINFELD EMAILS

One of my all-time favorite TV shows is *Seinfeld*, and I especially love the episode when George and Jerry are trying to pitch their idea to NBC about starting a show about nothing.[13] It was so funny because the show *Seinfeld* was literally a show about nothing.

When I first started growing my list, I really struggled to send emails. What did I have to say that was important enough that people would want to open and read them? So I started focusing on writing great, content-packed emails that often took days to write. I thought that was the answer. But I later discovered that after someone had gone through my Soap Opera Sequence and bonded with the Attractive Character, content wasn't what they responded to. What the readers responded to was . . . well, *nothing*.

My emails switched from 100 percent content to 90 percent entertainment with just 10 percent content, and my readership, opens, clicks, and sales all skyrocketed with the change.

You want your Attractive Character to be fun and entertaining. That's how you're going to write your Daily Seinfeld Emails. That's right; I recommend sending them *daily* after your initial Soap Opera Sequence is finished.

I know a *lot* of people get *very* nervous about how often they email their lists. I used to feel that way, too. I used to email once a month, and my response rates were horrible. Then I started emailing twice a month. And guess what? I more than doubled my income.

Then I decided to email once a week, then twice, then every other day, and what I've found now is that if I don't email my list every day, I lose money every day. I strongly recommend emailing every day, and if you do it with the Seinfeld style I'm going to show you, readers won't get annoyed because they will be so entertained.

The structure of a Seinfeld email is one that you've already started to master earlier in this book. By sending daily emails, you'll be able to flex this muscle over and over and get really good at it. As people are responding to your emails, you'll also be able to notice which emails are working best. The structure you will be using is Hook, Story, Offer.

Your email subject line hook gets them to open the email, the body story has a goal of entertaining them, and the ending body offer ties back into whatever your core offer is.

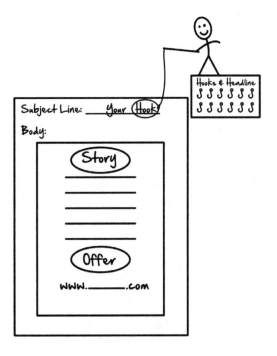

Figure 7.16:

Your Daily Seinfeld Emails will follow the Hook, Story, Offer framework to get them
to open the email, be entertained by your story, and take action on your core offer.

The Seinfeld emails I send are usually related to one of these
three styles of emails:

- **Episode style:** I tell a story about what happened
  today in my life, tell a story that ties back into my core
  offer, or share a controversial topic in my industry. My
  goal is to get people to go back into one of my funnels.

- **Epiphany style:** I talk about different ideas, such as
  inspirational or enlightening/thought-provoking ideas,
  or I can challenge existing beliefs. My goal is to help
  my readers have an epiphany that ties back into my
  core offers.

- **Educational style:** These may be checklists, how-tos, Q and A's, or FAQs that I can answer and use to direct people back into my core offers and funnels.

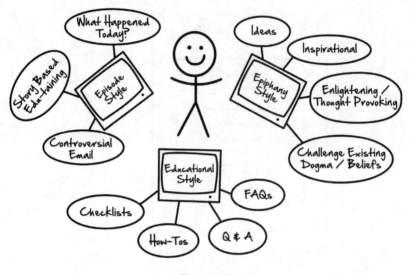

Figure 7.17:

With the wide variety of subjects you can discuss in your Seinfeld emails, you'll never run out of interesting things to entertain your audience with every day.

Unlike the Soap Opera Sequences, these Seinfeld emails have no sequence. Each day, they give you the ability to throw out a different hook, tell a different story, and get a different segment of the market to respond. The goal is to test a hook, tell a story, and lead people back to whatever you're selling (your core offer, some other product or service, or even someone else's product). Every story needs to relate back to something you're selling.

If you just send out entertaining emails and don't tie in your products or services, you won't make a dime (even if you're the best storyteller in the world!). *Every email* and every story must be tied back into some type of offer for your audience.

In the Seinfeld email examples to follow, notice how I tie the story back into the product I'm selling. Both these examples made over $100,000 each when they were sent out to my list, and they're great examples of emails about nothing.

[True Story] He FLUSHED $20 million down the toilet today...

So, yesterday we had a guy apply for my Inner Circle coaching program...

I saw his app come through, and I was actually really excited, because he is in the golf market.

Now, I'm no golfer, but I've got a lot of friends doing $20 million + in the golf market online.

I saw his product and KNEW it was a home run.

So, the coach who was going to call him back asked me for my opinion on his business before she called him, and I sat down for ten minutes and pulled up the following:

- His three major competitors
- Every site competitors were SUCCESSFULLY buying traffic from
- The top three converting ads for each of his competitors
- The sales funnels that WERE converting

And then I explained to her the main reason his was NOT currently working.

I then told her about the two media buyers I would use if I were in the golf market (both can send over one thousand sales a day, consistently).

Armed with this information, she called the guy up...

He was a little cocky (and rightfully so—he'd sold over 100,000 units of his product on TV). Yet, for some reason, he couldn't figure out this pesky Internet thing...

She started sharing some of my ideas with him, and then he stopped her...

"Look, I've read twenty books on internet marketing... there isn't a single thing Russell could teach me that I don't already know..."

So she tried to explain, "Look... you could read a million books on Jiu Jitsu, but that's not gonna help you in a street fight..."

I thought that was pretty funny, but what happened next was just sad.

He said, "Well, Russell doesn't know anything about golf..." and then he hung up.

Now, while he was right about me not knowing anything about golf...

I know EVERYTHING about SELLING golf stuff online.

I've been doing this for OVER ten years now. I've personally trained over 2,500 companies in my office here in Boise.

I've worked with a LOT of golf guys... (and one golf gal).

I've worked with people in just about every market I can think of (except bowling... I've never had someone teaching bowling come to me, which makes me sad, because bowling is my third favorite sport after wrestling and Jiu Jitsu).

Anyways...

For about everything else I can think of, I've mapped out a funnel, shown the client what they were doing wrong, introduced them to my media buyers, advised them on which sites to buy ads from, and instructed them on what they should be spending to acquire a customer in THEIR specific market.

I then usually introduce the client to the gurus I know in those areas. After speaking on Dan Kennedy's stage for six years, I have met most of the "gurus" in most industries, and my position makes it easy to find connections for others.

Those are the things you CAN'T learn in a book...

Those are the things we bring to the table for our Inner Circle people.

My goal for that group is not to teach them more stuff... it's to make them more money.

Anyway, if you've got a golf product, let me know, because I've got a killer twenty- million-dollar-a-year blueprint that this dude just flushed down the toilet because of his arrogance... or ignorance. Either way, he lost out.

You can just plug in and run with it...

Or if you sell, well, almost anything else, I'd love to help with that, too.

Our next Inner Circle meeting is here in Boise in May. If you'd like to come, you've got to act fast.

You can apply here:

www.InnerCircleForLife.com

Oh, and we only accept cool people. If you like to flush money down the toilet... PLEASE don't apply.

Thanks,

Russell Brunson

Figure 7.18:

In this email, I hooked the readers with the "FLUSHED $20 million down the toilet" subject line, told a story about how I created a $20 million/year blueprint for a man who was too arrogant to believe I could help him, and gave a call to action to join my Inner Circle so they could have my help on creating their own million-dollar blueprint for their business.

Jiu Jitsu is like wrestling for old, fat guys (and other marketing stuff)

So, tomorrow I'm fighting in a Jiu Jitsu tournament.

For those of you on my list who don't know what Jiu Jitsu is, it's kinda like wrestling for old, fat guys (which is GREAT for me because, while I still look like I'm thirteen, I am actually getting a lot older—34 yrs old now—and fatter—30 lbs. heavier than when I was wrestling).

Anyway, I have weigh-ins in a few hours, and as of right now, **I'm still seven pounds overweight...**

Good thing I'm a wrestler and have some awesome weight-cutting skillz. In fact, I just found my old weight-cutting clothes this morning.

Check them out:

Yes, they are a little tight, but my three-year-old Aiden told me I look like a ninja, so they can't be that bad... right?

Anyway, in about an hour, I'm gonna go to the wrestling room, and within thirty to forty minutes, I'll lose all 7 lbs. Then tomorrow, I get to step onto a mat with a bunch of younger, faster guys whose ONLY goal in life is to choke me out... (or to break my arm, whichever comes first).

I'm SO SO SO SO SO SO excited!

So, why do I tell you this?

Because this week, we did well over six figures in sales.

Not this month... **this WEEK.**

And we did it WITHOUT any product launches...

WITHOUT any affiliates...

And while that is a pretty normal week for us, this week was special because we also did it...

WITHOUT me actually being in the office...

Yup... You guessed it...

I spent most of this week in the wrestling room, getting ready for the tournament this weekend.

Yet, we still did six figures in sales while I was gone.

Would you like to learn how I did it?

Would you like to see how you build a business that can run just as well when you're gone as when you're there?

Are you ready to take your company to the next level?

If so, I've got good news for you...

As long as I don't end up in the hospital after my match this weekend, I'm gonna be coming into the office next week.

That gives me time to work personally with two more people to help build out their funnels... (the SAME type of funnel we use to pull in six figures a week like clockwork).

If you're ready to take your game to the next level and create a business that can truly give you time and freedom to do other things you love, then let's get on the phone and figure out how we can work together.

Sound good? If so, then you can apply here:

www.InnerCircleForLife.com

Oh, and if you're looking for a "get rich quick" scheme, this isn't it.

If you're looking for a **"work hard and build an awesome company"** scheme, then I'm your man!

Okay, I'm off to cut weight...

Wish me luck this weekend!

Thanks,

Russell Brunson

P.S. I already know that it's not healthy to cut seven pounds in under an hour... so no emailing me telling me it's not healthy.

I'm pretty sure that stepping onto a mat with someone 30 lbs. heavier is a lot less healthy than me losing 7 lbs. of water in an hour. Ha ha...

Figure 7.19:

In this email, I hooked the readers with the "Jiu Jitsu is like wrestling for old, fat guys" subject line, told a story about how I had spent the entire week training for a jiu-jitsu tournament yet still made over six figures, and gave a call to action to join my Inner Circle so they could learn how to create a business that produced money while they did things they loved.

Do you see how Seinfeld emails work, and how the story eventually ties into a product or a service you'll sell? That's how your Attractive Character is going to communicate with your list in every email you send after your Soap Opera Sequences. It's fun. And once you get the hang of it, the writing goes pretty fast. You can even dictate the email, record it on your phone, and have it transcribed online.

One thing I should note here. Seinfeld emails are broadcast emails, not a follow-up funnel sequence. Soap Opera Sequence emails are set up to be a follow-up funnel. That means after someone signs up, they get email one on the first day, then email two on the next day, etc. Please review Figure 7.15 to see how they work together.

Seinfeld emails are different, because after someone has completed your Soap Opera Sequence, they should be moved to a broadcast list where they will only get the Seinfeld email that you send out that day. Seinfeld emails are typically not lined up in a sequence that everyone has to go through. That doesn't mean you can't write them ahead of time and schedule the broadcasts in your email provider, but typically they are tied to relevant things happening in the life of the Attractive Character as they are happening in real time.

The Seinfeld emails push people into different funnels inside of your value ladder, typically based on what is happening in your company. If you're launching a new book or event, you can direct them to that funnel. If you have nothing new happening, then pick your best converting offer and guide people there each day until the next big event comes up.

I originally learned this concept from Ben Settle, who only has one core product (a $97-per-month print newsletter), and he has emailed about this same product every day for the 10 years that I have known him. Same product and same offer, yet with new hooks and new stories emailed every day.

The goal of Section One was to teach you the core foundational information so you can understand how to use funnels (the "vehicle") inside of your company. While Section One is the strategy of funnels, Section Two is the tactics of funnel building where you'll learn the 10 main funnels we use in our business.

SECTION TWO

THE FUNNELS IN THE VALUE LADDER

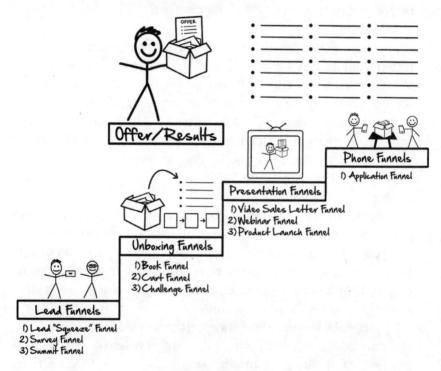

Figure 8.1:

Because each step of the value ladder has different goals, you'll use different types of funnels and scripts to achieve each step's goal.

The goal of Section One is to help us to create a common language that we could use to start building funnels together. You have now mastered the secret formula as well as how to use hooks, tell stories, and create offers. You understand how we ascend our dream customers through the value ladder and how we communicate with them through our Attractive Character. You've also learned the basic funnel phases as well as how we use follow-up funnels to move people up the value ladder.

This next section is going to look closely at each step of the value ladder and help you answer the following questions:

- What is the goal for that step in the value ladder?

- Which funnels are the best to use to achieve that goal?

- What offers do you have (or will you need to create) that plug in to that funnel?

- What sales or "funnel scripts" should you use for each page in the funnel?

I want to point out that each of these funnels, with their accompanying scripts found in Section Three, serve a different purpose. Both the sales funnels and the scripts are just a framework that form a starting point. You will need to plug in your offers and add in your personality (the elements of your Attractive Character) that will make these static funnels come to life. Use these funnels and scripts as the starting point, but don't be afraid to tweak them to fit your needs.

Front-End Lead Funnels

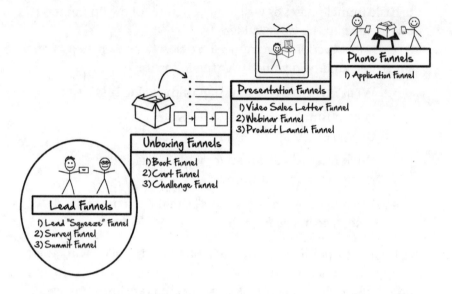

Figure 8.2:

The three best lead funnels we've used are: lead "squeeze", survey, and summit funnels.

Before entrepreneurs used funnels to generate leads and build email lists, we used to use something that you may remember was called a "pop-up" ad. When the internet first started, almost every page you visited had a big pop-up that would appear in front of the window telling you that you won a free prize or that you could download a new report or some other type of offer. I remember buying packages of pop-up ads where I'd pay a few hundred dollars to have my ad pop up in front of thousands of random websites.

As annoying as those pop-ups ads were for website visitors, they were great for marketers. People started to build huge email lists by using these pop-up ads. But, as often happens, the market complained, and so Internet Explorer and other browsers built pop-up blockers into their software so their users wouldn't be annoyed by these types of ads. Literally overnight most marketers lost the lifeblood and lead flow of their businesses.

Luckily, there were some brilliant marketers who suggested, "What if, instead of someone coming to our website being shown a pop-up to get their email address, we made the pop-up the page that people saw first? It would act like a gateway and it would force people to put in their email address to actually see what they wanted to see. If we created a good enough offer, it would literally 'squeeze' the email from them before they got to our website!" (That is why this type of page is often called a "squeeze page.")

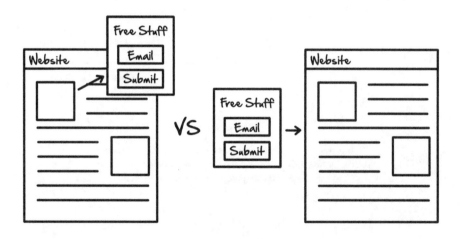

Figure 8.3:

Instead of using pop-ups, we turned the pop-up into the page that people saw first so they were forced to give us their email if they wanted to see more information.

Initially there was a lot of debate on if this concept would actually work. Would people give you their email address before they ever saw your website? Within months, we found that if we had a good enough offer (or lead magnet) on the squeeze page or landing page, we could get a huge percentage of people to give us their real email address. Even though less people saw our actual website, we were able to make more money because we had the ability to follow up with them!

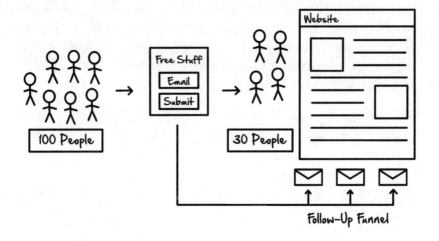

Figure 8.4:

With this new squeeze page process, less people saw our website, but we made more money because we were able to follow up with the ones who gave us their email address.

This brings us to the first types of funnels that we will be talking about in this section. We're going to start at the front of the value ladder with offers that cost almost nothing (just an email address) and start the relationship with your dream customer. We call these lead funnels because the main goal is to generate a lead and get them into your follow-up funnels communicating with the Attractive Character. There are lots of different types of lead funnels that you can create, but after funnel hacking thousands of lead funnels and testing hundreds of different variations, the three that have helped me to generate the most leads are:

- A simple lead "squeeze" funnel
- A survey funnel
- A summit funnel

As you will see, each has a similar goal (to generate a lead), but they do it through slightly different processes. We'll start with a very simple yet powerful funnel I like to call a lead "squeeze" funnel.

LEAD "SQUEEZE" FUNNELS

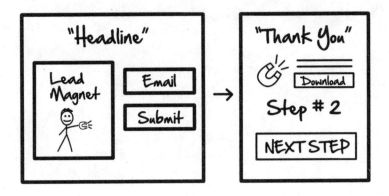

Figure 8.5:

Lead "squeeze" funnels have two pages: a squeeze page and a thank-you page where you offer the next step of your value ladder.

"You're About To Learn Secrets That Most Men Will Never Know About Women . . ." the headline read.

What was I looking at? This wasn't a website, but I wasn't really sure what it was.

"Yeah, they did twenty million dollars in sales online last year," one of the other attendees at the marketing seminar told me.

"With this page? I don't get it," I responded.

"It's called a squeeze page. He's using it to get people to join his list. They say his list has over a million people on it, and he sends out emails to that list selling his other products, but all his ads promote this one page."

This was the first time I had ever heard of, or even seen, a squeeze page before. It was from a company called Double Your Dating, which was owned by Eben Pagan at the time.[14]

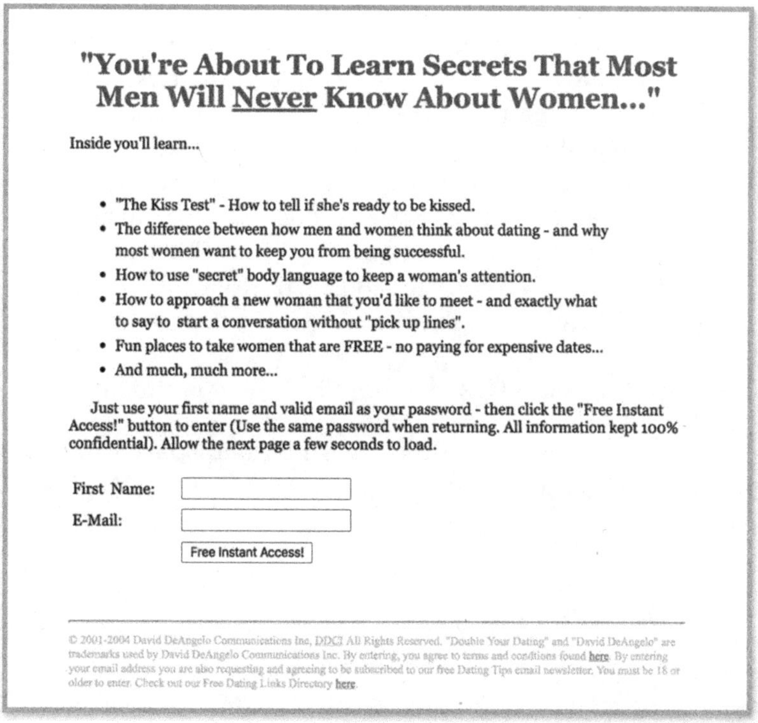

"You're About To Learn Secrets That Most Men Will Never Know About Women..."

Inside you'll learn...

- "The Kiss Test" - How to tell if she's ready to be kissed.
- The difference between how men and women think about dating - and why most women want to keep you from being successful.
- How to use "secret" body language to keep a woman's attention.
- How to approach a new woman that you'd like to meet - and exactly what to say to start a conversation without "pick up lines".
- Fun places to take women that are FREE - no paying for expensive dates...
- And much, much more...

Just use your first name and valid email as your password - then click the "Free Instant Access!" button to enter (Use the same password when returning. All information kept 100% confidential). Allow the next page a few seconds to load.

First Name:

E-Mail:

Free Instant Access!

© 2001-2004 David DeAngelo Communications Inc, DDC3 All Rights Reserved. "Double Your Dating" and "David DeAngelo" are trademarks used by David DeAngelo Communications Inc. By entering, you agree to terms and conditions found here. By entering your email address you are also requesting and agreeing to be subscribed to our free Dating Tips email newsletter. You must be 18 or older to enter. Check out our Free Dating Links Directory here.

Figure 8.6:

The very first squeeze page I ever saw was "The Kiss Test" lead magnet from Eben Pagan's Double Your Dating company.

As I kept reading down the page, he promised that if you gave him your email address, he would teach you "The Kiss Test." I had just gotten married earlier that year, and I was nervous that if I did give him my email address, my beautiful wife would think I was wandering, so I called her up and told her that I had to see behind this page, but it was for marketing purposes only. With her permission, I "opted" in and gave him my email address.

On the next page, he gave me what he promised on page one: the kiss test. It was just a few paragraphs long. On that page, he said:

> If I've been talking to a girl and want to know if she's ready to be kissed, I'll reach over and touch her hair while we're talking and make a comment about it. I'll say "your hair looks so soft" and just touch the tips of it. If I see that a woman is receptive to what I'm doing at this point, that she's responding positively by allowing this "innocent" physical contact, it's game on. If I see that she's smiling and drawing closer as I touch her hair instead of tensing, pulling away, I can take it as a SURE SIGN. She's "FEELING IT"—that irresistible, unstoppable emotion called ATTRACTION. But listen . . . if she does pull away at this point, or shows any sign that she's not into it, that is when I know to STOP and move on, and you should too.

That was it—the kiss test. It was short, but it gave value to the men who had been struggling to know if they should kiss a girl or not. After he gave them the kiss test for free, on that same page, he then said:

> Want to learn a ton more?
>
> There's a place you can go RIGHT NOW to do it . . .
>
> My e-book *Double Your Dating* is literally jam-packed with DOZENS and DOZENS of dating tips, tools, and techniques for moving FAST from "Does she like me?" to "She can't get enough of me". . .
>
> Downloading it is FAST AND EASY. You can be putting it to work for YOUR success with women in just a few minutes, so click here.

He provided value to the reader and invited them to move up the value ladder by showing them the next step. This simple lead "squeeze" funnel was the foundation for Eben's entire company. After I saw this framework, I quickly created simple lead "squeeze" funnels like this in each of the markets that I was in.

As I go through this funnel (and all the funnels inside this book), I will walk you through each page and help you to understand the strategy for the page, the sales scripts you use for the hooks and stories, as well as how to structure the offer for that specific page.

PAGE #1: THE "SQUEEZE" OR LANDING PAGE

Offer: The goal of the squeeze page is to make an offer, where you get someone to give you their email address in exchange for what is often called a "lead magnet." It's called a lead magnet because its goal is to attract your dream customers to you like a magnet. When I create lead magnets, I try to create things that the customer avatar I designed in Secret #1 will love, while at the same time will repel the types of people I don't want to work with.

In the Double Your Dating example above, the lead magnet wasn't complicated. The kiss test was a few paragraphs long, but it gave real value, and that is the key. If your lead magnet is awesome, and your audience gets real value, they will remember you, open your emails, and want to ascend up your value ladder. Your lead magnet could be an e-book, a coupon, a contest, a video, a membership site, or just about anything else you could dream of. How or what you deliver matters less than creating something that your people will truly want. The better the offer you create, the more likely they will be to give you their email address. Here are a few examples of lead magnets that I give away on a squeeze page:

Figure 8.7:

My lead "squeeze" funnel pages are short and simple because
I'm only asking for an email address.

Hook: You'll notice that these pages are all very simple. They all
have a headline that serves as the hook. The more curiosity you
can put into the headline, the more likely they will be to give
you their email address. If your conversion rates are low on your
squeeze page, it's usually because the lead magnet (offer) isn't
good enough or there isn't enough curiosity in the headline. In
Secret #18, you'll learn how to use "Curiosity-Based Headlines"
scripts for the squeeze page.

Story: On a traditional squeeze page, the story isn't long. For most
of my pages, the subheadline will tell a quick story. For example, in
the *Marketing Secrets Blackbook* squeeze page, the headline (hook)
is: "99 Secrets That Will Change Your Business . . . And Change
Your Life," and the subheadline (story) is: "Want to Know How
We Took ClickFunnels from ZERO to over $100,000,000 in Sales

in Just 3 Short Years . . . ? Then Get Your Free Digital Copy Of The Marketing Secrets Blackbook Now!"

I usually keep the story very short on the squeeze page because I don't want to distract from the offer. If the offer is strong and simple to understand, you don't need to spend as much time on the story. If your offer does need more explanation, you can use what we call a "reverse squeeze page," where you have a video (instead of an image) that tells the story and asks for the opt-in. You'll usually get a lower conversion rate on a reverse squeeze page, but the leads that come through are always more qualified. In Secret #19, you'll learn how to use the "Who, What, Why, How" script for the video on a reverse squeeze page.

Figure 8.8:

On a reverse squeeze page, you'll get less leads, but they'll be more qualified because they watched your video and still wanted more information.

PAGE #2: THE THANK-YOU PAGE

After someone has put in their email address to get your lead magnet, they'll land on your thank-you page, where you'll thank them for joining your list and give them the lead magnet you promised them.

If this is your first funnel, you may not have another funnel to direct them to on this page, and that's okay. Now is the time to start building a relationship with those people who just joined your list through your first Soap Opera Sequence. After you create your next funnel, you can go back and add a link to it on the thank-you page that guides them into the next funnel in your value ladder.

Figure 8.9

On the thank-you page, you give them what you promised and offer the next step in your value ladder (in this case: One Funnel Away Challenge).

SURVEY FUNNELS

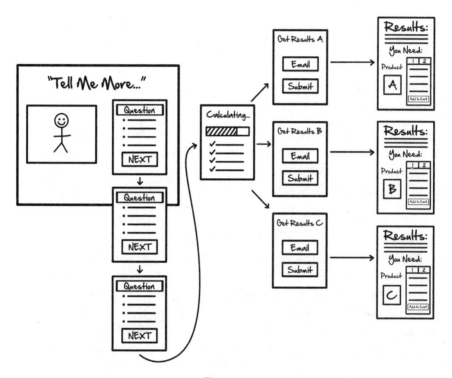

Figure 9.1:

Survey funnels have these pages: a survey page, a squeeze page for each group, and a results page for each type of person with a message tailored specifically for them.

I wasn't a tennis player, but as the original "funnel hacker," I looked at everyone's funnel that I heard was having any type of success. FuzzyYellowBalls.com was the domain, but hidden on their site, they were running a "quiz" for people who wanted to add speed to their tennis serve. I heard that this funnel was generating a ton of leads, and because of the ability to customize the message based on who was coming to the funnel, it had conversion rates that were unheard of.

I searched for a while, and then I found it! It was a simple quiz that asked me the question:

Can You Really Add 10–15 MPH To Your Tennis
Serve Overnight With This Trick?

(HINT: It All Has To Do With Eliminating Your #1 Serve Killer . . .)

The small quiz asked me a bunch of questions, and after the last question, it took me to a page where it "calculated" my responses. Finally, it took me to a page that said:

Based on your responses, we've pinpointed the Serve Killer which is costing you 10 to 15 miles per hour on your serve speed. Enter your name and email below and I'll send you a free video showing you how to fix your #1 Serve Killer.

I put in my email address and was immediately taken to a page that was talking specifically about *my* problem and how their program would help me to solve it. The sales message was perfectly customized based on what I had told them! I got so excited, I retook the quiz dozens of times, giving them different answers to see if it would take me to different pages—and sure enough, it did! It was selling the same program, but the sales message catered to my specific problems!

Since seeing this funnel, we've used the quiz (or survey) concept dozens of times for many different markets. It works best when there are many different types of people who would benefit from your offer. For example, inside ClickFunnels, we have many different types of business owners who could use our software, but they each use it differently. Our survey figures out what type of business they own, and then we give them a sales message that shows how their specific business can use ClickFunnels.

PAGE #1: THE SURVEY PAGE

For this type of funnel, the offer is simple: "Take this short quiz, and I will tell you _____." We ask our visitors to take a short quiz to find out which funnel will work the best for their specific business.

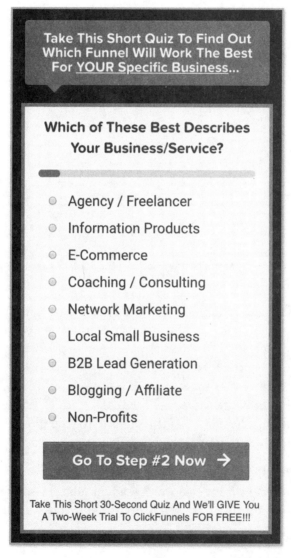

Figure 9.2:

The purpose of a survey is to separate your visitors into different "buckets" so you can speak directly to them.

My goal from this quiz is to ask my visitors some questions to get them engaged in the process. Out of all the questions, though, there is only one question that really matters. In the book *Ask*, Ryan Levesque calls this question the "bucket question."[15] How they answer this question will determine what landing page they end up on.

Figure 9.3:

While you may have many questions in your survey, only one question actually determines the "bucket" your visitor will land in.

In our survey, our first question was our bucket question. I wanted to find out what type of business they owned, and then I would redirect them to the sales pages that explained the benefits of using ClickFunnels to that specific type of business.

Often the bucket question will be buried a little deeper into the survey. In fact, when we originally funnel hacked several survey funnels, I found that the majority of the quizzes followed this general multiple-choice format:

1. Self-identifying questions (Gender; age; etc.)

2. Self-identifying question based on subject (Do you have a funnel?; Have you ever tried to lose weight in the past?; etc.)

3. Self-declare level of skill (How much money have you made with your business?; How much knowledge do you have on [topic]?; etc.)

4. Self-declare biggest challenge with subject (I struggle with traffic the most; I struggle with eating carbs; etc.)

5. Educate and clarify (Those with [#2 response] typically suffer from one of three [symptoms]. Tell me which issue you suffer from the most. [List 3 choices])

6. Surprise/random curiosity-based question (Wait . . . Are you drinking water first thing in the morning? Because that could matter . . . etc.)

One of these questions will become the bucket question that you will later assign different "results" pages to based on which answer they gave you.

PAGE #2: THE SQUEEZE PAGE

Once visitors complete the quiz, they're directed to a "calculating" pop-up that explains their results are being calculated. This page isn't essential, but we did see a lift in conversions by adding it.

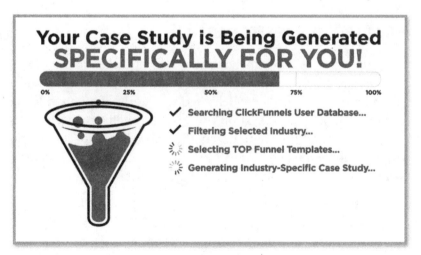

Figure 9.4:

The "calculating" pop-up shows your visitors that they're going to get information tailored to them.

Based on their answer to the bucket question, they'll see a case study from someone in their own industry. We have one case study for each of our nine options for our bucket question. We ask for their email address so we can send them the free case study.

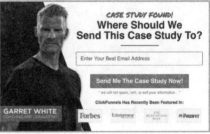

Figure 9.5:

Our squeeze pages feature different niche case studies that we send to our visitors after they enter their email address.

Prospects are also added to a specific Soap Opera Sequence follow-up funnel that talks more about their specific industry and how funnels will work uniquely for them.

PAGE #3: THE RESULTS PAGE(S)

After they give us their email address, they are taken to the results page where we show them the case study (story) and then make them an offer. Others have delivered the results through video, a custom PDF, or even in text on the page. The delivery mechanism matters less than the content you have customized for them. You can use the template below to show their specific results and offer your product as the solution to their problems.

Based on your answers, your #1 reason for [not succeeding/your self-declared pain] is likely because you don't have a [retail/coaching/author funnel—or other surprising result], which typically costs [subject] an average of [$/result] every [time], not to mention a lot of [other costs].

Figure 9.6:

Because our visitors went through a survey, they landed on a results page with messaging that spoke to their specific situation.

The more you customize each results page and follow-up funnel for each of your audience buckets, the higher your conversions will likely be.

SUMMIT FUNNELS

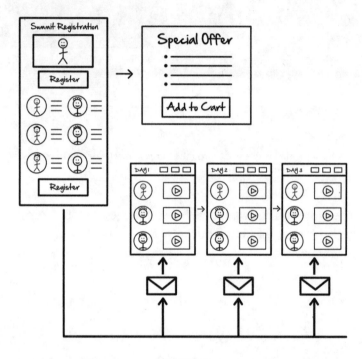

Figure 10.1:

A summit funnel has these pages: a registration page, a special offer page, and your broadcast page(s) to deliver the content to your registrant.

A summit funnel is another type of lead funnel, but one that is strategically designed to let you leverage other people's traffic and co-brand yourself to build your authority in a market. When I first started my company, summit funnels are how I built a list quickly and developed relationships with other influencers in my market.

About twice per year, we launch a summit funnel to get new types of people using ClickFunnels. Bailey Richert has been one of the key players on our team who has helped us to create and launch multiple summit funnels over the years. Because of her expertise with these types of funnels, I've asked her to teach this funnel to you in this chapter.

SUMMIT FUNNEL SECRETS BY BAILEY RICHERT

Hi, my name is Bailey Richert, and when I got started online just a few years ago, I had:

No email list.

No authority.

No credibility.

No "as seen on" media logos.

No stellar video testimonials.

No impressive profit reports.

This is the frustrating position in which I found myself several years ago when I was getting my coaching business started.

Like many who want to start a business, especially as a personal brand, I knew I had the life experience, knowledge, and passion in my subject matter to succeed. In my case, I had spent years in a previous online business learning to create, market, and sell information products and services, and I was ready to share (and monetize) that expertise in my new venture as a business coach.

The problem was that since I was "starting over" in a new niche, I lacked all the necessary components of a financially viable business with a new audience. And what was making it worse? I didn't have a huge marketing budget. The strategy of using paid ads to push visitors to my website simply wasn't a long-term feasible option at the time, so I had to rely on organic methods to drive traffic.

I was already doing all the marketing strategies a business owner is "supposed" to be doing (blogging, podcast interviews, posting on social media), but all those strategies for gaining leads were going too slowly for my liking.

That's when I decided to try something different: a virtual summit.

A virtual summit is a free online conference, and when organized and executed correctly, it can be an incredible business growth strategy which requires zero ad spend, making it an especially excellent funnel for beginners looking to propel their business quickly. Instead of spending time and money mastering paid traffic, a virtual summit allows you to partner with dozens of other established businesses in your niche, driving targeted traffic from *their* email lists to *your* funnel to grow your own subscriber list, all in a matter of weeks!

Additionally, by contacting and interviewing speakers for your summit, you begin to build a network of influencer colleagues with whom you will continue to do business for years if you work hard to maintain those positive relationships. (Plus, there is the added benefit of authority being given to you by viewers simply because your face appears alongside your guest speakers on your summit registration page, on promotional materials, and in your video interviews.)

In fact, it is because of the network I built through several launches of my own annual Infopreneur Summit that I even became connected with Russell Brunson. Being a ClickFunnels user since early 2015, I knew Russell's brand well and thought he could leverage a virtual summit to reach a wider audience online. However, having no prior relationship with him, I decided to first share my idea with a high-ranking ClickFunnels employee whom I knew because they had been a guest speaker on my own summit two years in a row before! Through this contact, I was able to meet Russell and convince him to host his own virtual summit, including appointing me as project manager.

This first summit we ran was the 30 Days Summit, where 30 Two Comma Club award winners shared how they would start their businesses again in just 30 days if they lost it all. That summit funnel brought in over $1 million in sales in just under two weeks, earning me my first Two Comma Club award and putting the power of virtual summits on full display. After that, I managed the Affiliate Bootcamp Summit and the Brick and Mortar Summit for ClickFunnels.

So let's take a look at how virtual summits work:

Invitations: First, a person who organizes the summit, known as the host, invites a group of colleagues in their niche to be interviewed. The ideal interviewee is a colleague in your niche who has their own email list of your ideal clients. A good-size summit has about 30 speakers, though you will likely find yourself approaching more people than that before you arrive at your final list of confirmed participants.

Interviews: Second, the host prerecords interviews with these guest speakers, which will be broadcast online for a limited period of time later during the summit event.

Promotions: Third, motivated by affiliate commissions and the prestige of being a featured speaker at an event, guest speakers join with the host to promote the virtual summit in advance of the interviews being broadcast. This is the key! By using a well-constructed virtual summit funnel, the host can collect the email addresses of everyone who opts in to watch the free summit event, as well as sell products to the summit registrants. When your guest speakers promote your summit to their email lists, a portion of their subscribers will become your subscribers, which is how your own targeted email list grows.

Now let's dive deeper into the process of hosting a summit by taking a closer look at the pages inside a virtual summit funnel.

Page #1: The Registration Page

The first page of a virtual summit funnel is known as a registration page, and its objective is simple: get the visitor to enter their email address and become a "registered summit attendee" in exchange for information about how to watch the free virtual summit event. One of the most important parts of your registration page is a good headline that hooks them with curiosity.

Figure 10.2:

The top section of the registration page features a hook (headline), story (video), and an offer (register for the free summit).

The registration page tends to be a long-form page, as it needs to detail the summit's name, topic (what will be spoken about on the summit), and dates it will be held. It should also feature the names, headshots, and basic information (website, interview topic) about each participating guest speaker. Your speakers will be promoting this registration page to their audience and they expect to be featured; it will help increase your conversions if their subscribers see their beloved influencers' faces on your registration page.

Figure 10.3:

More people will register for your summit if they recognize the leaders featured on the registration page. These are a few of the leaders featured in Affiliate Bootcamp Summit.

Page #2: The Special Offer Page

After registering for the free summit on the previous page, the lead is taken to the second page in the funnel, which presents a special offer. This type of page is usually an order form which has three main parts:

1. **Registration confirmation:** At the top of the page, the lead should be reassured that they have successfully registered for the free event, and an email with information about that will be sent to their inbox.

2. **All-access pass offer:** Next, an offer is introduced for the lead to purchase. A video featuring the summit host is usually included, which explains the offer, followed by text and images to provide further detail, just like a regular sales page would have.

3. **Order form:** Finally, the order form at the bottom of the page will allow leads to make a purchase.

What is the all-access pass offer? Remember, the lead magnet in a virtual summit funnel is the *free* pass to the summit itself where attendees can watch the interviews for a limited amount of time. By upgrading to the all-access pass, someone can get access to a membership area where they will have lifetime, unlimited access to all the summit interviews. This is attractive because then the summit registrant doesn't have to try to watch all the interviews in such a short period of time but instead at their own pace.

Additionally, the all-access pass might come with bonus materials, which are usually related to the summit content. These could include bonus interviews with speakers not shown during the free event, transcripts of the speakers' interviews, a PDF of compiled notes, or downloadable MP3 files of the interviews.

Alternatively, you could present another special offer that moves people up your value ladder, such as a challenge funnel, which could go to leads on this page instead of an all-access pass and could position the unrestricted summit interview access as a bonus to this offer. This is the approach taken by the ClickFunnels team during the 30 Days Summit.

Figure 10.4:

After someone signs up for one of ClickFunnels's summits, we offer special summit-only bonuses when you join the One Funnel Away Challenge.

In either case, the idea is to make this initial special offer low in price (approximately $100 or less). While the traffic coming through this funnel is largely warm since it originated from your guest speakers' email lists, you still need to impress leads with the value you're offering and initiate these first purchases with an incredible offer at a no-brainer price point.

Page #3: The Broadcast Page(s)

Finally, you will need to fulfill your promise of delivering a free virtual summit event to all registered attendees whether they upgraded to your special offer or not. These funnel pages are not shown immediately to the lead after they opt in on the registration page. Rather, the links to these pages are shared via email with the registrants on the dates when the "live" virtual summit is to be held. (The guest speakers' interviews are prerecorded, but the virtual summit itself is a limited-time event held on specific days.)

On the first day of the summit (Day 1), a certain number of speakers' interviews will be posted (embedded) on the first broadcast page alongside the guest speakers' photos and other details. You can use a timer on this page to show how much time is remaining for viewers to watch the interviews for free. I recommend a 24-hour viewing time for each day. This allows registrants in all time zones around the world to have an equal chance to watch.

Figure 10.5:

On each day of your summit, a few videos will be released live and taken away soon after. The CTA should be to get full access to all the recordings so they can watch it anytime at their pace.

At the start of Day 2 of the summit, Day 1's videos will be removed from the Day 1 broadcast page. The 24-hour viewing period for these videos is over, and the only way registrants can get access now is by purchasing your special offer. At the same time the Day 1 videos are removed, the Day 2 videos are posted on the Day 2 broadcast page. The link to the Day 2 page is sent to the attendees via email.

This process of posting and removing videos continues for every day of the summit until all the interviews have been broadcast. Typically, a summit of three to four days is all that is needed, as maintaining engagement for the event can be difficult over a longer period.

You are able to keep promoting your special offer where they can buy the replays throughout the summit and even when it's over. If you do buy ads to promote the summit, these sales should help cover all your ad costs and hopefully make you a profit. If you let the other speakers on the summit promote the event, you can pay them commissions on the sales they generate as well!

The summit funnel is a great funnel to quickly start building your list by leveraging the lists of other people. It provides a ton of value to new people joining your list, builds a relationship between your list and you, the host, and gives you the ability to start moving these new subscribers up your value ladder.

Unboxing Funnels

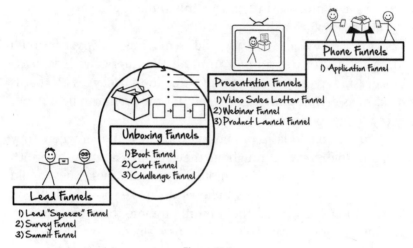

Figure 11.1:

The three best unboxing funnels we've used are cart, book, and challenge funnels.

As you learned earlier, the key to having successful funnels is moving away from creating a product (commodity) and creating an actual offer. After you've created an offer, there are different ways to sell it.

If you have an offer priced between $100–$2,000, you can use a presentation funnel to sell it higher on your value ladder. In an online presentation, you can spend anywhere from 20 minutes to three hours to sell someone on the perceived value of that higher-priced product. While we'll be discussing presentation funnels in detail later, I wanted to introduce them here so you can understand the purpose of an unboxing funnel.

The other way we sell an offer like this earlier in the value ladder is through something I like to call an unboxing funnel. In this funnel, we take the whole offer that may typically sell for $997, and instead of selling it as an entire package, we unbox that offer and sell a part of it on each page inside the funnel.

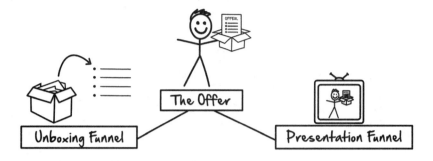

Figure 11.2:

When you're selling a higher-priced offer, you can sell the entire thing in a
presentation funnel or you can sell it in parts on each page of your unboxing funnel.

For example, when I was launching *Expert Secrets*, I could have
bundled up all the products I had to create a huge offer priced at $840.

Products I Could Sell:

Expert Secrets Book	$27
Expert Secrets Audiobook	$19
Expert Evolution Home Study Course	$297
Traffic Secrets Home Study Course	$497

Sales Price if Bundled: $840

Figure 11.3:

When you create huge offers, you can sell them as a bundle in a presentation
funnel or as individual products/services in an unboxing funnel.

I could have used a presentation funnel (such as a webinar or
a product launch funnel) and sold this offer for $840, but instead
I decided to unbox this offer and put it into a book funnel that I
could sell lower on the value ladder. I unboxed this offer by pulling
out each product and putting it into a step of the unboxing funnel.

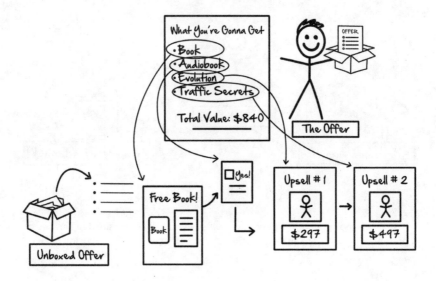

Figure 11.4:

Instead of selling a huge offer for $840, I can unbox the offer, sell each piece separately throughout the funnel, and get more customers to ascend my value ladder.

By "unboxing" this offer, I'm able to get a lot more people to become customers and start moving up the value ladder. If I do it correctly, my average cart value that I make from each sale will be high enough that I can spend a lot of money to acquire customers and I can add a lot more fuel (people) into my business.

There are a few core concepts we will use in all the unboxing funnels. I'll explain them so you'll know how they work in the actual funnels when we get to them.

FREE-PLUS-SHIPPING FUNNELS

Some funnels are referred to as free-plus-shipping funnels because I introduced this concept in the first edition of *DotCom Secrets* using the "100 Visitor Test" inside my "Best Bait" chapter. I ran this test many times in different environments with different target audiences and products, and the results were pretty consistent in almost every test we ran. We ran this test with hundreds of thousands of website visitors, and I broke it down and simplified the findings to show what our core numbers looked like for every hundred visitors we sent through this test funnel.

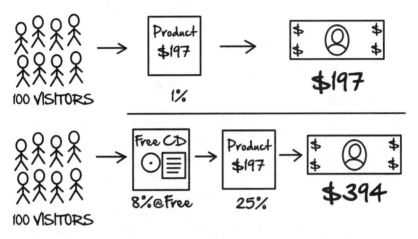

Figure 11.5:

In the 100 Visitor Test, we discovered we could make more money from one buyer if we gave them something free first (and charged a small shipping and handling fee) before offering them the actual product we wanted to sell them.

Here's how it worked: I sent 100 people to a website where they could purchase a product. The product was offered for $197. We paid a talented copywriter and tested different pitches until we got a high-converting page. After all the testing and tweaking, we wound up getting about one percent of cold traffic to convert and buy the product. So for every 100 visitors, we made $197, and we got one new customer on our list. Most marketers would consider that result about average.

Then we started shifting things around and experimented with offering something for free. We wanted to see how this new offer would change the metrics and our income. We splintered off one of the best parts of our product and put it into a form we could ship to our customers for free if they'd help cover the shipping costs. We offered to put this information on a CD, on a DVD, or in a book. After people signed up for the free-plus-shipping offer, we'd immediately upsell them on the same $197 product we were trying to sell before. I figured I would lose money because I was making people pull out their credit cards and buy the free-plus-shipping offer before they even saw the $197 offer. I mean, if only one-tenth of potential customers ever saw the $197 offer, logically I should make less money, right?

Here's what happened, though: we sent people to the website, and on average, a whopping 8 percent of people purchased the free-plus-shipping offer. (Remember, that's up from one percent on the original page. And the free-plus-shipping page needed almost *no* copy to sell, whereas on the original $197 page, we had to include really convincing text to persuade people to buy.)

Now, this is where the magic happens. Because the customer had *already* pulled a credit card out of their wallet and made a commitment toward the concept we were selling, about 25 percent of free-plus-shipping customers bought the upsell offer. That means we made $394 per 100 visitors, and we got eight new buyers on our list. I doubled my money and got seven times more customers by adding in a *free*-plus-shipping offer!

When we first started doing these upsells, people would have to retype in their credit card on each upsell page, and they did. Eventually technology caught up and actually stored their credit card information for a short time frame, so on the upsell pages, if they clicked yes, then it would bill their cards for the agreed-upon prices. By making the buying process even easier, the conversion rates for upsells shot up!

There is something very powerful that happens inside the buyer's mind after you get them to make a commitment by saying the first yes. They've already done the hard work, and because they have already started on the path that this solution offers, it's so much easier to get them to say the second yes. The friction is gone. You get them started by saying yes to a small thing, and they are much more likely to say yes to a larger thing later.

People ask me if they can just sell (or just give away) a digital product instead of the free-plus-shipping offer. The answer is yes, you can (and we do inside lead funnels), but you are missing out on the ability to quickly discover who your buyers are. If I just give it away free digitally, I lose the power of qualifying the buyer when they pay the shipping costs, and I also lose the ability to do a one-click upsell on the next page.

Some people don't feel comfortable giving away their products for free, so we recently tested the strategy of selling the product and giving them "free shipping." We saw almost no dip in conversion rates, and oftentimes we saw an *increase* in conversions.

Regardless of the strategy you use, the key is having low-ticket products that allow you to get more buyers into your funnels and have them commit by saying the first yes, and then you show them the other pieces of your offer.

ORDER FORM BUMP

After people started to learn about free-plus-shipping offers with one-click upsells, they got excited and created what the market called "upsell hell": dozens of upsells in a sales funnel. While this often made more short-term money for the marketer, it usually left them with very upset customers who refused to buy from them again. It would stop people from progressing up the value ladder.

After lots of testing, we found the sweet spot. If we had two upsells in our unboxing funnels, it didn't annoy most customers, and it gave us the ability to make money with our funnels after paying for our ad spend. Any upsells more than two and it hurt the lifetime value of our customers; any upsells less than two made it hard to make any money.

Then one day, we found something new. I don't remember where I first saw it, but I know I found it when I was buying something online one day. It didn't have a name that I knew of, so I started calling it an "order form bump." It was a small checkbox on the order form *after* someone filled in their credit card information but *before* they clicked on the submit button, and that checkbox offered a lower ticket product.

It reminded me of the checkout line at the grocery store, where you can add quick impulse purchases like gum, Tic Tacs, and a *National Enquirer* magazine. The order form bump was the digital version of that.

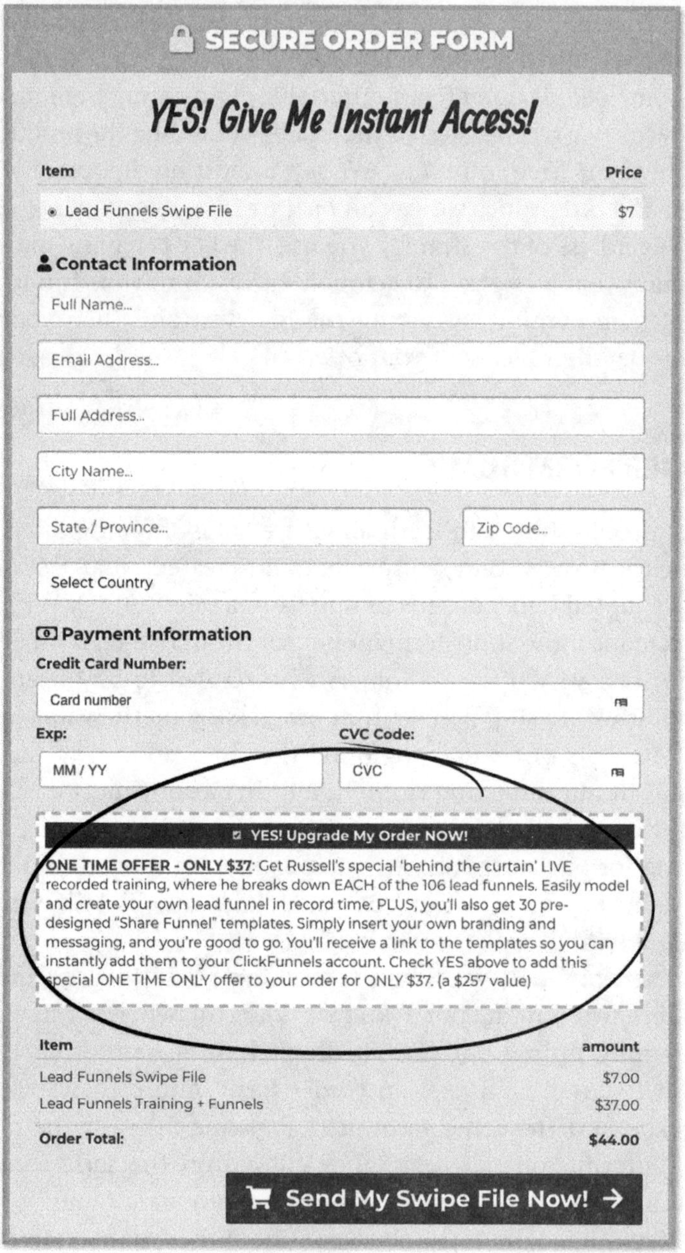

SECURE ORDER FORM

YES! Give Me Instant Access!

Item	Price
Lead Funnels Swipe File	$7

Contact Information

Full Name...

Email Address...

Full Address...

City Name...

State / Province...

Zip Code...

Select Country

Payment Information

Credit Card Number:

Card number

Exp:

MM / YY

CVC Code:

CVC

YES! Upgrade My Order NOW!

ONE TIME OFFER - ONLY $37: Get Russell's special 'behind the curtain' LIVE recorded training, where he breaks down EACH of the 106 lead funnels. Easily model and create your own lead funnel in record time. PLUS, you'll also get 30 pre-designed "Share Funnel" templates. Simply insert your own branding and messaging, and you're good to go. You'll receive a link to the templates so you can instantly add them to your ClickFunnels account. Check YES above to add this special ONE TIME ONLY offer to your order for ONLY $37. (a $257 value)

Item	amount
Lead Funnels Swipe File	$7.00
Lead Funnels Training + Funnels	$37.00
Order Total:	**$44.00**

Send My Swipe File Now! →

Figure 11.6:

As people fill out their credit card information to buy our *Lead Funnels* e-book, they can click the small "order form bump" checkbox to add a special offer to their purchase for just $37: a behind-the-scenes video training on lead funnels plus 30 lead funnel templates.

I started adding these bumps to each of my funnels and found that about 33 percent of the people who bought my first product purchased this stealth upsell, and it had no decrease in lifetime value of the customers. They didn't see it as an additional upsell in the sales funnel.

In most funnels, my profit from the order form bump covers all my ad costs, leaving the other upsells in the funnel as pure profit!

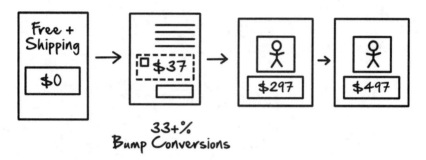

Figure 11.7:

Instead of adding a third upsell that would hurt my lifetime customer value, I added an order form bump that my customers could add to their order during the checkout process.

AVERAGE CART VALUE

There are two core metrics that I look at when I'm driving traffic into my funnels. In Secret #28, I'll show you how to use these metrics to make changes to your funnel if it isn't working, but for now we just need to understand what the metrics are.

The first metric is cost per acquisition, or CPA. How much money does it cost you on average to get a new customer? If I'm running Facebook ads to sell a copy of my book, how much money does it cost to sell that book? If I'm spending $20 in ads to sell a book, my CPA is $20.

The second metric is average cart value, or ACV. This is how much money you make on average inside of the funnel for each customer you acquire. If I get 10 people to buy my book, and I make $1,000 in total sales throughout that entire funnel, then my ACV is $100.

Then I look at these two numbers together. If my CPA (how much it costs me to get one customer) is $20, and my ACV (how much I make for each customer) is $100, then I know my profit for each customer is $80.

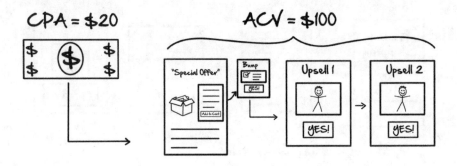

Figure 11.8:

If I spent $20 to acquire a customer and I made on average $100 per customer in the funnel, then I would make a profit of $80 per customer.

If my CPA is less than my ACV, my funnel is working and I can spend as much money as possible to keep getting customers. It's like a slot machine where I put $20 in and I get $100 back. I'll keep putting money in for as long as that lasts. But if my CPA is bigger than my ACV, the funnel isn't working and I need to go back to the drawing board.

Throughout these chapters I'll be showing you things that you can do to increase your average cart value, but I wanted to point these metrics out now so you can understand the math behind funnels. It's not complicated, but it's the real secret to creating funnels that will grow your company.

Just like lead funnels, there are different types of unboxing funnels that you will use for different situations. The two core unboxing funnels include a book funnel (for authors, speakers, coaches, consultants, or anyone using information products at the front of their value ladder) and a cart funnel (for e-commerce and physical products companies). While these two funnels are structured the same, the strategies behind each are a little different.

The last type of unboxing funnel is a challenge funnel. It's one of the most powerful types of funnels that you can bring your dream customers through at the beginning of your value ladder. It will help them get a quick result with you, receive massive value, and become indoctrinated to how you like to work with your tribe.

BOOK FUNNELS

Figure 11.9:

A book funnel has these pages: a sales page (often with an order form bump), an upsell page (often with another upsell page and downsells, as well), and a thank-you page.

It was a little after 7:30 P.M., and I was sitting at Carl's Jr. with my funnel-building chiropractor, Chad Woolner. We watched our kids playing on the playset while we ate food that we knew we'd regret the next morning. We were dreaming about the future, and then he said something to me that changed the course of my life.

"You know the difference between you and Tony Robbins or Brendon Burchard?" he asked.

"No," I responded. "What's the difference?"

"I think that your content is as good as either of theirs, but the biggest difference between you and them . . . is that they have a book. They seem more legit," he said.

Wow, I had never thought about that before. I knew I wanted to write a book someday, but that night it hit me like a ton of bricks. The reason that more people didn't know my name was I didn't have the authority or credibility that a book can bring to someone like me. That night when I got home, I decided to write this book.

After almost a year of work, it was finished. I sent the manuscript to the publisher, and within a few weeks, I got the first copy in my hand. It was one of the coolest moments of my life to hold my own book with my own hands. After looking at it for about an hour, I knew that I didn't want to sell just a few copies of this book on Amazon; I wanted the world to know about it. So I did what any good funnel hacker would do and I looked for ways that people were selling books online. I found dozens of different book funnels, each that had different things that I loved. I took these ideas and sketched out what I wanted my book funnel to look like. Then I logged into ClickFunnels, built the funnel that launched this book, and sold over 100,000 copies before I wrote this second edition!

Since that time, I've had a chance to create book funnels for some of the most respected influencers in the world, including Tony Robbins, Dave Asprey, Grant Cardone, and Robert Kiyosaki, as well as for other book and information products that I personally sell. There is a proven framework that we can plug almost any book into and it will work.

But—and this is a BIG *BUT*—this funnel isn't just for selling books. We call it a book funnel because that's how most people use it, but it works for any free-plus-shipping-style information product. For example, I used it to sell an MP3 player that was preloaded with 257 episodes of my podcast.

Figure 11.10:

Book funnels aren't just for books; you can use them for any information product you give away for free in exchange for a small shipping and handling fee (like this MP3 player).

I've also used this book funnel to sell dozens of other types of information that we ship to someone, including CDs, DVDs, MP3 players, reports, and booklets.

Figure 11.11:

I used a book funnel to sell my "Perfect Webinar" script (one piece of paper) with a DVD teaching how to use the script.

I'm telling you this because if you haven't written a book yet, you can still use this funnel. Writing a book, for me, is one of the hardest things that I do and it takes the most time. Making a CD or a DVD is a lot faster and easier, and it works just as well.

PAGE #1: THE SALES PAGE

There are two types of page layouts that I use for book funnels. The first I use when it's a free-plus-shipping-style product. On the top of the page, I use the "Curiosity-Based Headlines" scripts from Secret #18 to hook them into the page.

On the left side of the page, I tell a story and make the offer for the product. I usually create a video using either the "Who, What, Why, How" script from Secret #19 or the "Star, Story, Solution" script from Secret #20. Both scripts are very effective at telling your story and making the offer.

Figure 11.12:

Both my books are sold with a similar funnel style: curiosity-based headline as my hook, video as my story, and free-plus-shipping offer.

On the right-hand side of the page, we have the order form. The first step on this order form asks visitors, "Where should I ship this?" Once prospects fill out the shipping address form (that's step one), they move on to step two, where they fill in their credit card information for the shipping and handling charge. It's important that you mention on the first page that the buyers will be charged for shipping and handling. Otherwise, it's unethical and you'll upset your customers before they even have a chance to get into your value ladder, which is never a good idea.

The majority of your prospects are emotional buyers and they'll buy from this top block. For the buyers who are more logical, I put a section under the top block with a long list of bullet points showing them logically what they will learn when they invest. Finally, for the buyers who buy because they fear the offer will be taken away, I end the page with urgency and scarcity to push them off the fence and buy.

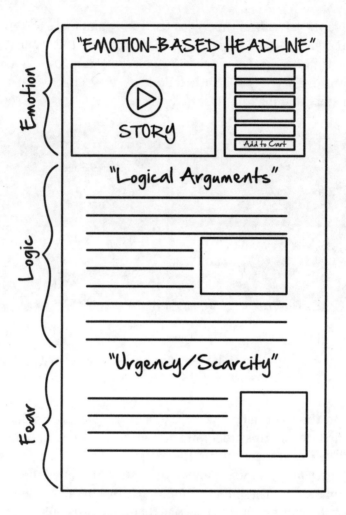

Figure 11.13:

When building your funnel, envision it built out with three blocks (from top to bottom: emotion, logic, and fear) to help lead your prospects to buy.

We use the two-step order form at the top of the page when the offer is a free-plus-shipping style offer. The psychology behind this two-step order form is amazing. People are more likely to fill out the first step because they don't see you asking for credit card information. Then once they do get to the credit card form, they keep filling it out because they have already committed to the process. Interestingly, I often find conversions to be higher on step one of this order form than on a regular email squeeze page, even though I'm asking for an entire shipping address instead of just a short email. This is probably because receiving something physical in the mail has a higher perceived value than receiving digital information via email.

Figure 11.14:

For our free-plus-shipping offers, we use a two-step order form, where the prospect first puts in his/her shipping information (step 1) and then the credit card information (step 2), where they can also add an order form bump.

If I am selling something that I need to spend more time building up the value before I display the price, I don't put the order form at the top. For example, if I am selling a front-end digital information product between $7–$27, I will likely have the order form at the bottom of the page because I don't want the price to push them away before I have a chance to help them see the value of the offer.

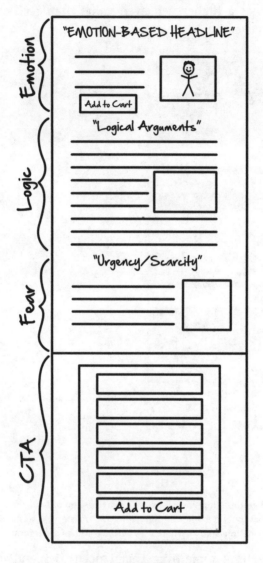

Figure 11.15:

For other offers where I need to build up the value first,
I put the order form at the bottom of the page.

Order form bump: The secret to a good order form bump is it needs to be something that doesn't take any effort to explain. Think again about being at the checkout stand at the grocery store. I only have a few seconds to convince you that you should add this to your order, so it needs to be simple. With books, some of the easiest order form bumps are:

"Would you like to add the audio book for an extra $27?"

"Would you like to add a special behind-the-scenes training where you'll learn _____ for an extra $37?"

"Would you like me to throw in our templates that let you _____ for an additional $47?"

If you have to explain more than that, the order form bumps traditionally won't convert very high. The order form bump is in the sales flow after someone has put in their credit card information but before they click the Submit button.

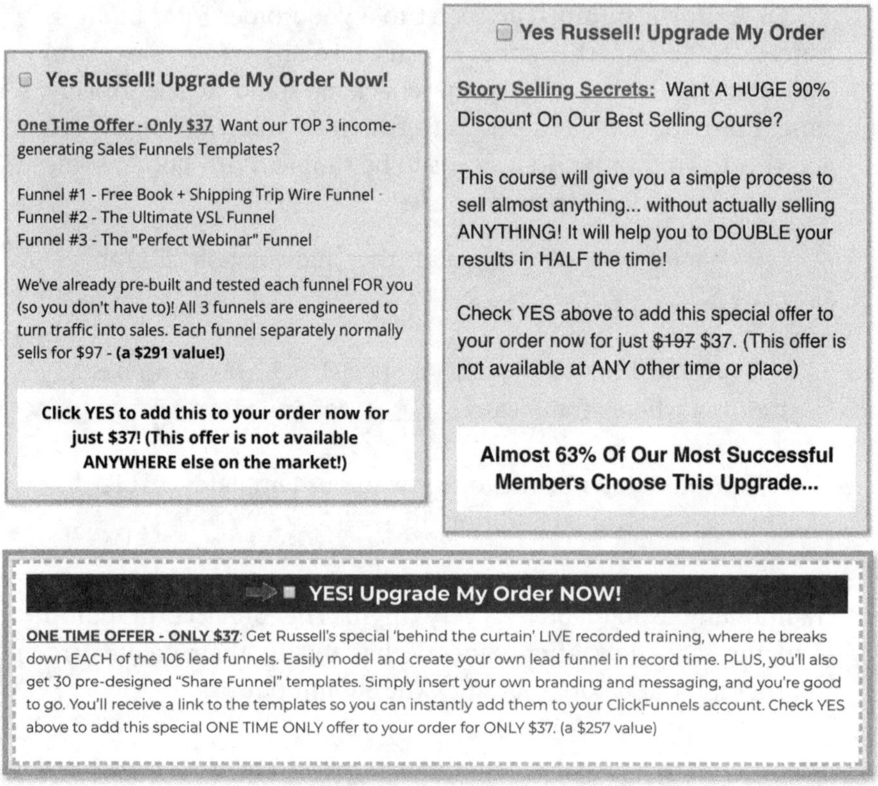

☐ **Yes Russell! Upgrade My Order Now!**

One Time Offer - Only $37 Want our TOP 3 income-generating Sales Funnels Templates?

Funnel #1 - Free Book + Shipping Trip Wire Funnel
Funnel #2 - The Ultimate VSL Funnel
Funnel #3 - The "Perfect Webinar" Funnel

We've already pre-built and tested each funnel FOR you (so you don't have to)! All 3 funnels are engineered to turn traffic into sales. Each funnel separately normally sells for $97 - **(a $291 value!)**

Click YES to add this to your order now for just $37! (This offer is not available ANYWHERE else on the market!)

☐ **Yes Russell! Upgrade My Order**

Story Selling Secrets: Want A HUGE 90% Discount On Our Best Selling Course?

This course will give you a simple process to sell almost anything... without actually selling ANYTHING! It will help you to DOUBLE your results in HALF the time!

Check YES above to add this special offer to your order now for just ~~$197~~ $37. (This offer is not available at ANY other time or place)

Almost 63% Of Our Most Successful Members Choose This Upgrade...

➡ ■ **YES! Upgrade My Order NOW!**

ONE TIME OFFER - ONLY $37: Get Russell's special 'behind the curtain' LIVE recorded training, where he breaks down EACH of the 106 lead funnels. Easily model and create your own lead funnel in record time. PLUS, you'll also get 30 pre-designed "Share Funnel" templates. Simply insert your own branding and messaging, and you're good to go. You'll receive a link to the templates so you can instantly add them to your ClickFunnels account. Check YES above to add this special ONE TIME ONLY offer to your order for ONLY $37. (a $257 value)

Figure 11.16:

Order form bumps must be simple to explain in a few sentences so it's a no-brainer for your prospect to add to their order during the checkout process. The top two order form bumps are from a two-step order form, and the bottom order form bump is from a long-form sales page.

Having the bump earlier usually hurts conversions. You want the purchase to have already happened in your customer's mind; at this point, they're at the checkout stand just grabbing an impulse offer on their way out the door.

PAGE #2: THE UPSELL PAGE(S)

After someone purchases a product from you, you can upsell them with an OTO.

Figure 11.17:

By offering an upsell, you can keep the buying loop open and
increase your conversions on the back end of your funnels.

The first thing that you'll notice on this page is that I need to keep the buying loop open. If I say, "Thank you for your purchase," in the mind of the consumer, they are done buying, and you will see your conversions stop. On the OTO page, we want to keep the buying loop open. Traditionally the language we use on this page includes something like: "WAIT! Your order is not yet finished. Please customize your order now." This keeps the buying loop open and your conversions high. We then move into the OTO script where we confirm their initial decision and get them to upgrade their order.

For an OTO, you'll use the "OTO" script found in Secret #21. When you're creating your offer for your OTO, you need to be aware of the OTO rule for upselling information products. This rule is different than the OTO rule you'll learn later for upselling e-commerce physical products.

The OTO rule for upselling information products is this: don't sell more of the same thing. This is the biggest mistake most entrepreneurs make when it comes to upselling information products. If your customer just bought an e-book about how to get six-pack abs, your upsell should not be another course on how to get abs. In their mind, even though they don't yet have a six-pack, as soon as they have made the purchase, that problem has been solved. That itch has been scratched.

Instead, you need to sell the next thing that they need. Every time you solve a problem for someone, it creates a new problem. For example, as soon as you buy a new car, you'll need to buy gas. As soon as you read this book about funnels, you'll need funnel software, right? Think about what they just purchased from you, and ask yourself, *What is the next logical product or service they need to reach their goals?* That is what you sell them for your OTOs.

Under the Order button, you need to add a No Thanks link where they can say no to this offer. I like to have this close to the Order button and big enough so that they can see it; that way they don't think their order is done and just exit or leave the page. If that happens, they won't progress to the thank-you page, which means they won't be able to download what they purchased and they won't get to see the other offers in your funnel.

On the No Thanks link, don't put a positive action in the wording. For example, don't say: "No Thanks, Take Me to the Member's Area Instead" because that is a positive benefit for clicking. I don't want to increase click-through rates on the No Thanks link, so instead I may say: "No Thanks, I Don't Want to Add This Amazing Bonus at a 95% Discount to My Order Right Now." By seeing this, they have to acknowledge that they don't want something awesome at a huge discount. It will encourage people to look one last time at the offer before saying no.

Downsell (optional): If someone says no to my one-time offer, I can offer them a downsell. Typically, on a downsell, I will either make the price cheaper by taking away elements of the offer or move from a physical product to a digital product. Another downsell option is to offer a payment plan. Downsells aren't essential for every funnel, but they are a very powerful way to increase your average cart value with little extra effort.

Figure 11.18:

If someone says they don't want your one-time offer (left), one of the downsells you could offer them is a digital-only version for a lower price (right).

Upsell page #2 (optional): This page is almost identical to our first upsell page; it's just making another offer to your audience. Remember the OTO rule for upselling information products: don't sell more of the same thing. Ask yourself, *What is the next logical thing they need to be more successful?* What new opportunities have you created for them that you can now help them solve?

PAGE #3: THE THANK-YOU PAGE

On the final page of your funnel, you can thank them for their purchase and give them information on how they can get their digital product (e.g., provide access to the member's area) or how and when their product will be shipped to them. You can also use this page to point them to the next funnel in your value ladder.

Inviting them to attend a webinar (a type of presentation funnel) or fill out an application to work with you directly (a type of back-end phone funnel) is a powerful offer you can add to this step in your funnel.

After someone requests Dean Graziosi's free book, *Millionaire Success Habits*, Dean asks the buyer to reserve their seat in his upcoming web class. Notice that the presentation was already included as part of the book offer they purchased, so he encourages them to register for the web class and continue to move up his value ladder.

Figure 11.19:

On your thank-you page, you can invite your customers to continue moving up your value ladder by offering them the first step in your next funnel (in this case, a webinar).

CART FUNNELS

Figure 12.1:

A cart funnel has these pages: a sales page (often with an order form bump), an upsell page (often with another upsell page and downsells as well), and a thank-you page.

I had just finished working out with my friend BJ Wright, who was not only a fellow wrestler but also obsessed with online marketing like me, and he asked me if I had seen the new ad for Squatty Potty.

I rolled my eyes because for years BJ had been trying to get me to try out a Squatty Potty. "It'll change how you poop forever" was usually how he would start the conversation, and then he would pitch me on this new product that his cousins had invented. Earlier that year, they had been on *Shark Tank* and gotten a deal for $350,000 from Lori Greiner for 10 percent equity in their company, and recently they had launched their new viral video.

"The video has a unicorn that poops ice cream," he said. "It's amazing!"

Confused, I grabbed my phone and searched for the video. Within seconds I was dying laughing watching this new video created by Harmon Brothers to sell Squatty Potty. This video was all I needed to push me off the fence, and I decided to finally order one. Over the next few weeks, I ended up showing this video to hundreds of people and I watched as it got tens of millions of views.

The more I watched their success, the more I wanted to meet the people who made this video. I contacted Harmon Brothers, and within a few days they reached back out to me. They told me that they had just launched a new video for a company called FiberFix, and while the video was going great, the sales when people hit their website were not. They said they had heard that I was the "funnel guy," and wanted to see if I could help them with their funnel. I was excited because I wanted their help with a video for ClickFunnels, so we decided to trade services: I'd create a funnel for FiberFix, and they'd help script a video for ClickFunnels.

I went to the FiberFix website, and it was an e-commerce-style site that looked similar to their Amazon listings. It showed some features of the product and had an Add to Cart button. If you added it to your cart, then it would suggest other products they also sold. In short, it looked like a very traditional e-commerce shopping cart. The problem, as Harmon Brothers told us, was that it wasn't converting.

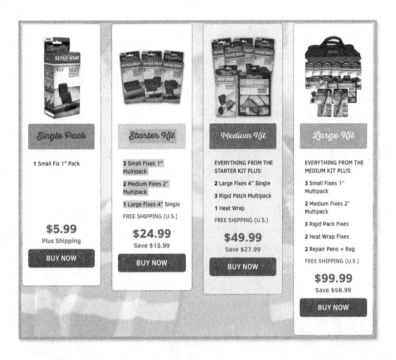

Figure 12.2:

The FiberFix website (top) had a similar feel to their
Amazon listing (bottom): picture, features, and a Buy Now button.

This is pretty normal with most e-commerce sites. Most e-commerce sellers have to focus on free organic traffic because they typically don't have a high enough average cart value to pay for ads. The problem: "A confused mind always says no!" When you show up to a page with dozens of different products on them, it can get confusing, and because of that, even people who are interested don't end up buying.

When creating an offer for an e-commerce company, I typically look at all the SKUs they have inside their normal Shopify or Amazon store, and I try to pick the sexiest, most interesting thing to become the front-end lead offer. When we built a funnel for Marcus Lemonis, the CEO of Camping World, we went to their store and asked about a dozen employees what the best-selling product was. They all told us it was their dissolving toilet paper, so the front-end offer for their cart funnel became a four-pack of their dissolving toilet paper for free.

Figure 12.3:

Choosing which front-end product should go in your cart funnel
could be as simple as using your best-selling product.

As I looked at the FiberFix project, I started to do the exact same things I have been talking about in this book. The video Harmon Brothers created had an amazing hook and story, but the offer was horrible. Instead of saying "buy some FiberFix," we changed the offer to "when you get three wraps of one-inch FiberFix today, we'll throw in two wraps of two-inch FREE and one wrap of four-inch for FREE!" We made a bundle by selling their best-selling product and giving away a few of their lesser-known products for free. This gave me the ability to say the world "FREE" in the headline twice, creating a very sexy offer.

Now that we had shifted their product into an actual offer, we were ready to build out the funnel. As I go through the pages of a cart funnel, I'll show you the funnel we built for FiberFix, but pay more attention to the principles for each page. They are similar to a book funnel with a few key differences.

PAGE #1: THE SALES PAGE

The best way to sell a physical product is with a demo. As a kid, I used to watch Billy Mays pitch dozens of different products on TV from OxiClean to the Quick Chop. He became one of our country's greatest pitchmen, and every commercial he made had a great product demo. The demo typically serves as the hook and the story, and then makes the offer.

On the first page of the FiberFix funnel, we show the product demo video and the headline explains the offer. One interesting thing with most e-commerce products is that the headline is usually less about invoking curiosity and more about telling people exactly what the offer actually is.

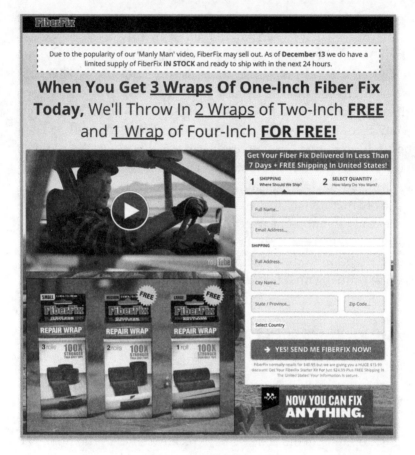

Figure 12.4:

You can create an offer bundle by selling your best-selling product
and giving away lesser-known products for free.

Just like a book funnel, we then use the two-step order form,
with the first step asking them where we should ship the product
and the second step asking for their credit card information.

Product selector and order form bump: On the second step
in the order form, we actually have two levers that we can use
to increase our average cart value. The first is by increasing the
quantity of products that someone purchases above the order
form and the second is by adding an order form bump.

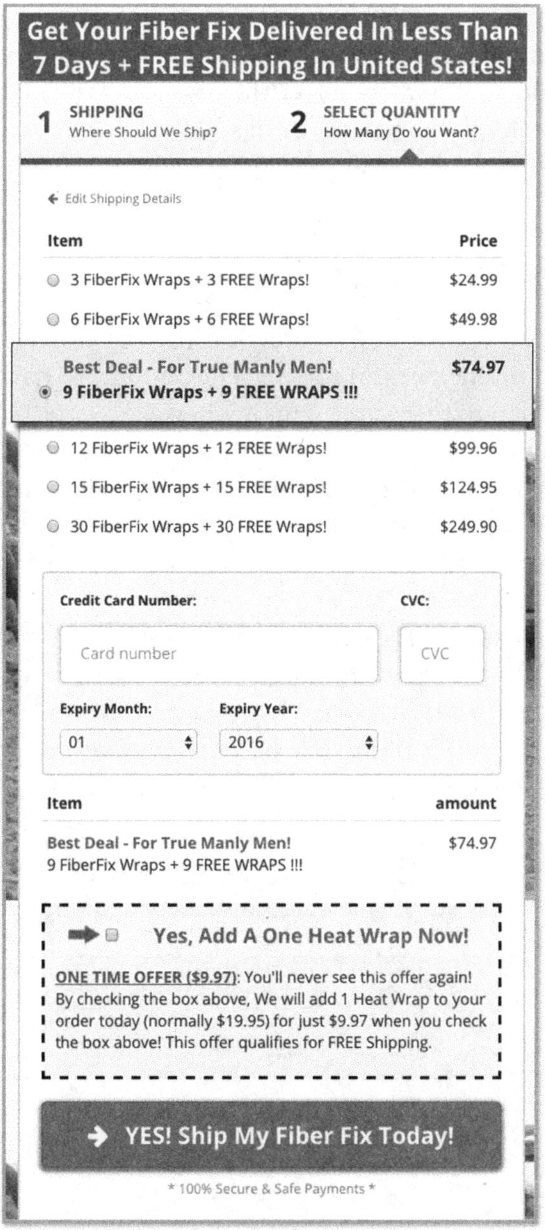

Figure 12.5:

Unlike other funnels, cart funnels have the ability to increase their average cart value on the order form simply by offering different quantity amounts.

Once again, think about the order form bump as if someone were checking out at the grocery store. What could your customer quickly add to their order? With physical products, I've often seen order form bumps be things like rush shipping or other complementary products.

PAGE #2: THE UPSELL PAGE(S)

After they buy our sexiest product on Page #1 and we have their credit card on file, we can use one-click upsells to have them add other products to their order. This is where we see the biggest difference in strategy between the book funnel and the cart funnel. In a book funnel, the OTO rule for information products is to *never* sell more of the same thing; instead, we sell the next logical solution to the problem we just created. With a cart funnel, we *do* sell more of what they just bought, but at a discount.

In the first FiberFix upsell, we sell more repair wrap, but at a discount. We give them the ability to add one or two more starter kits for just $19.99 each (they had just paid $24.97 each for this offer on the earlier page), but because they've become a buyer, they get a discount to get more for themselves or to give away as gifts.

Figure 12.6:

Once someone has already bought a physical product, it's easy to get
them to buy more of the same product when you offer it at a discount.

Notice how simple the first upsell is, because we aren't
re-explaining a new offer; we're giving a discount on more of the
same thing, so we don't need a video to sell it. Just stating the
special, one-time offer is usually enough. We also make sure that
the No Thanks link is close to the Order button and uses text that
shows what they will miss out on if they say no.

Additional upsells (optional): Once you hit the second upsell,
it starts to function more like a traditional shopping cart you've

likely seen online. We start looking at the other SKUs that they offer and figure out which next logical product they can add to their cart. If I were selling hot dogs, I would start selling buns, ketchup, and mustard as they move through the next set of upsells. If I were selling supplements, I would think about what other things my dream customer may be suffering from and what other supplements I could provide them. With FiberFix, we looked at the other SKUs they were selling on Amazon and listed them in the order of what was selling best.

Figure 12.7:

After the first upsell, you can create special one-time
offers around your best-selling products.

We added their heat wrap (their number two best-selling product on Amazon) as the upsell offer, and when people say yes or no to this offer, we take them to the last offer in the funnel, which is the "Manly Man" Kit for just $49.95.

Figure 12.8:

You can also create special one-time offers based on
the next logical product your customer will need.

You'll probably notice that with book funnels I never go over two upsells (either two upsells, or one upsell and one downsell) because it tends to lower the lifetime value of a customer. I haven't noticed that as much with cart funnels, probably because people are used to looking at Amazon or a more traditional e-commerce store and seeing lots of different options and SKUs, so having three to four offers after they buy doesn't seem to hurt the lifetime value of the customer.

PAGE #3: THE THANK-YOU PAGE/OFFER WALL

The thank-you page for a cart funnel usually has two primary functions. The first is to thank them for their purchase and let them know what to expect next. We'll often tell them when their order will come, how to get customer service, etc.

The second function is to direct people into your next funnels. In a cart funnel, we do this by creating what we call an "offer wall," where you show the other offers that you have. This will guide people into other funnels that you have created. On the thank-you page from Trey Lewellen's flashlight cart funnel, Trey shows multiple offers (such as bottle targets, gun cleaning oil, and silhouette targets) that his customers can get for free when they click the Tell Me More buttons.

Figure 12.9:

By creating an offer wall on your thank-you page that leads your customers to your other funnels, you can increase your sales from your hyperactive buyers.

CHALLENGE FUNNELS

Figure 13.1:

A challenge funnel has these pages: a sales page (often with an order form bump), an upsell page (often with another upsell page and downsells as well), and a thank-you page.

For years, I've watched people run "challenges" to get new customers in their businesses. Most notably are gyms that do weight-loss challenges every new year to fill up with people looking to hit their New Year's resolutions. I had tried many times to replicate a challenge online with varying degrees of success. While some versions did okay, none did well enough that we kept it as part of our core marketing strategy.

A few years ago, though, one of my Inner Circle members, Natasha Hazlett, developed a new way to run a paid challenge. I watched from afar and saw the results she was having. I was so excited by her new funnel that I called her up and asked her to walk me through her model. Within minutes, I began jumping around with excitement! I knew this was going to become the future of our value ladder. All book funnels would lead into a challenge where we could:

- Get a result quickly for our dream customers
- Give all our customers a similar vocabulary and foundation so we could work with them quicker and get them bigger results up the value ladder
- Indoctrinate our customers on what we do and how we do it
- Warm up our dream customers and repel the people who aren't a good fit to work with us

There are many other benefits from a challenge, but these were the ones that got me the most excited. We created our own One Funnel Away Challenge (also known as OFA) and did a test to our lists. Over 5,000 people went through the first challenge, and it changed our customers and our business more than anything we had done prior. We started weaving this challenge into the upsell flow of every funnel, our email follow-up funnels, our onboarding calls, and more. It became the value ladder doorway that everyone would have to go through.

I've asked Natasha to write this chapter because I want you to hear it the same way I heard it from the pioneer who helped to bring this funnel type into our company and into the ClickFunnels community.

CHALLENGE FUNNEL SECRETS BY NATASHA HAZLETT

"There *has* to be a better way!"

That was the thought running through my mind once I wrote my first book, *Unstoppable Influence: Be You. Be Fearless. Transform Lives.*, and started brainstorming the best way to get it out into the world.

At the time, the free-plus-shipping book model was the hot strategy . . . but when Rich (my husband and business partner) ran the numbers, it didn't seem to be a very profitable option for us.

Then we had an idea . . .

What if we take the challenge model we used with one of our clients, add in a copy of my book, and then bolt on Russell's "Perfect Webinar" during the challenge?

We could sell the challenge for $47 and get books into people's hands, but we would make way more money on the front end than the free-plus-shipping model.

We didn't know how well it would work, and honestly, I was just hoping that I could sell the 60 books I had sitting in our house.

I wasn't prepared for what happened next . . .

We were sending cold traffic via Facebook ads straight to our sales page with a $47 challenge offer. The sales page started converting like crazy!

Before I knew it, 450 people had joined our first challenge, forcing me to quickly find a warehouse and fulfillment company, rush-order a ton of books and bring on more customer service help . . . all in the first two weeks of launching our challenge funnel.

Talk about building the airplane in the air!

Even *more* exciting was what happened *during* the challenge. Remember how we added in Russell's "Perfect Webinar"?

When we ran traffic to our webinars pre-challenge, we had a disappointing 18 percent show-up rate and a 4 percent conversion rate to our $997 product offer. This was the exact same presentation that previously converted to live audiences at 24 percent or higher! It looked like we were the victims of webinar fatigue in our market.

But our challenge funnel saved the day!

Seventy-five percent of our challengers registered for the webinar, and a whopping 50 percent or more showed up for the webinar *and* stayed through the end. Our sales conversion rate on the webinar skyrocketed from 4 percent to 20-plus percent!

Our first challenge funnel generated over $105,000 in revenue and helped us earn the highly coveted Two Comma Club award 10 months later.

Best of all, our challengers were getting amazing results and a community of friends. Because they got a lot of value, many of the challengers could not wait to join our high-ticket programs! In fact, the average customer lifetime value of a $47 challenger shot over $420 and continues to grow!

If you want to build a tribe of loyal followers ready to ascend your value ladder, a challenge may be the solution you've been looking for! The magic of the challenge funnel that Rich and I designed lies in both the structure of the challenge funnel AND the way we run our challenges, so I'm going to teach you both parts! Sound good?

Designing the Challenge

As the challenge is your actual offer in this funnel, I want to spend a little time showing you how we run our challenges to give you ideas on how you could run yours.

Challenge length: We try to keep challenges between 14–30 days. Less than 14 days is too short to build trust and a tribe, while a challenge lasting longer than 30 days will cause people to lose interest. The Unstoppable Influence challenge is 21 days long while Russell's challenge takes place during a 30-day period.

Challenge location: Russell and I host our challenges inside a closed Facebook group. When the challenge is over, we simply archive the group and create a new challenge group. I love Facebook groups because our audience is already on Facebook daily and they know how to use it, so it's easy to fit into their daily routine.

Training format: The secret sauce of our challenge style is that it allows people to truly get to know us while building a very powerful, loyal, high-vibe tribe. We've found that the best way to get large numbers of people to do that is through the video . . . more specifically, LIVE videos. Why?

Live videos create a sense of urgency to participate at the designated "class time." This encourages people to show up, which means they're more likely to take action, and therefore are more likely to get results. When they get results, they're going to want to work more with you! That's why we focus on incorporating elements that encourage people to participate. Live videos have the added benefit of building community as people watch the training together. Our challengers love interacting with one another!

You can prerecord videos as your challenge content, but you will miss out on the community building potential and the scarcity element to encourage consumption of your training. That said, prerecorded videos are huge time-savers! There are a few software tools such as OneStream and LIVEpigeon that you can use to live stream prerecorded content. This has been a huge help for me personally . . . especially while I have twin babies with unpredictable needs!

You can deliver your challenge training through written posts or emails. However, if that's all you do, you will miss the opportunity to build a deep connection with your challengers. So if you choose to deliver written training, I recommend adding some videos (preferably live ones) to build connection and rapport.

While I deliver my content directly to the Facebook group, Russell houses his challenge content inside a ClickFunnels members area so it can deliver the content each day on autopilot. He also uses the Facebook group to offer support, accountability, and connection.

Moving your challengers up the value ladder: Near the end of the challenge, I host a webinar using Russell's "Perfect Webinar" format where I offer our three-month coaching program for $997. Because the challengers have already achieved the result I promised, nearly 70 percent of them register for the webinar. Our average show-up rate is 50 percent (it was 18 percent when just advertising the webinar directly) and the average sales conversion rate increased from 4 percent to 20 percent. We attribute these huge increases to our challenge!

One of my most successful challenge clients, Cristy "CodeRed" Nickel, offers a custom nutrition program and accountability coaching for $997. Unlike our challenge, Cristy doesn't even do a webinar. Instead, she offers a limited-time discount on her custom program package and nearly 10 percent of her challengers take her up on that offer. The fact that Cristy doesn't even do a webinar to sell her program is a testament to the immense value she provides during her challenge.

As you can see there are different ways you can run your challenge; the key is understanding that challenges are one of the most powerful ways to:

- Build a relationship with the Attractive Character
- Get your dream customers a tangible result
- Have them actually move up your value ladder

With that said, let me walk you through our challenge funnels.

Page #1: The Sales Page

For this type of funnel, the offer is to participate in a challenge to get X result in Y days, and you can get that message across in your headline.

A clear hook: The most important thing to include on your challenge sales page is *a clear hook*. What is the result that you are promising? The result must be *simple and believable*.

The 21-Day Challenge to Becoming The Fearless Influencer You're Meant to Be!

Figure 13.2:

For your challenge to be successful, make sure you have
a clear hook that shows the result you're promising.

We've tested quite a few challenge funnels; many have crushed it and others have flopped. What we've discovered is that the success or failure of a challenge funnel appears to be based on three things:

- The clarity of the promise
- The belief that the challenger could see themselves accomplishing the result
- AND the credibility of the expert

Cristy is in the weight-loss niche, and her hook is: lose 10 pounds in 30 days. The benefit was clear and believable, and the headline of her challenge was the hook that promised the result. Her challenge has transformed tens of thousands of lives, consistently generated 3x–4x return on ad spend, and quickly earned her a Two Comma Club award.

Figure 13.3:

Cristy's "10 Pound Takedown Challenge" result is to lose 10 pounds in 30 days (top). ClickFunnels's "One Funnel Away Challenge" result is to launch your first (or next) funnel (bottom).

Other important elements of your challenge funnel sales page are:

The story: The story needs to be short and compelling. It should help the visitor quickly bond with your Attractive Character and have confidence that they have walked the journey and know how to deliver the promised result.

The path: What are the topics you will cover during the challenge and how will it benefit the visitor? Clearly show the journey your challengers will walk on as they go through the process of transformation.

The prizes: Everyone loves prizes! When choosing your prizes, consider seeding the offer you will make at the end of the challenge that ascends the challenger up your value ladder.

Figure 13.4:

Both Natasha (top) and Cristy (bottom) chose to add prizes to their challenge that let their customers know about (and desire) the products that were higher on their value ladder.

A stack: Ever since Russell taught us the "Stack" back in 2012, we have put a Stack in all of our offers. The Stack is a recap of everything that your buyer will get when they purchase the challenge. It is important to differentiate between *price* and *value*. Price is the actual "price tag" of the item, while value is the transformational effect that the "thing" will give the customer.

For example, our challenge costs $47 to enter, but people have consistently said that knowing what they know now, it is worth thousands of dollars to them. So the value we place on just the 21 days of training is $2,100. Remember to consider the value of the transformational effect when creating your stack!

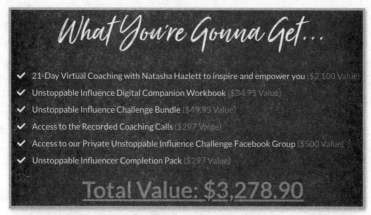

What You're Gonna Get...

- ✓ 21-Day Virtual Coaching with Natasha Hazlett to inspire and empower you ($2,100 Value)
- ✓ Unstoppable Influence Digital Companion Workbook ($34.95 Value)
- ✓ Unstoppable Influence Challenge Bundle ($49.95 Value)
- ✓ Access to the Recorded Coaching Calls ($297 Value)
- ✓ Access to our Private Unstoppable Influence Challenge Facebook Group ($500 Value)
- ✓ Unstoppable Influencer Completion Pack ($297 Value)

Total Value: $3,278.90

Here's A Recap Of

EVERYTHING You'll Get FREE

When You Accept The 'One Funnel Away' Challenge Today!

- • 30 Days of Video Missions From Russell Brunson ($997 Value)
- • 30 Days of Coaching From Stephen Larsen & Julie Stoian ($997 Value)
- • One Funnel Away Challenge Customized Kit (30 Day Plan) ($247 Value)
- • **BONUS:** Physical Copy Of The Challenge Workbook ($97 Value)
- • **BONUS:** MP3 Player ($297 Value)
- • **BONUS:** 30 Days Hardcover Book ($97 Value)
- • **BONUS:** Unlimited Access to 30 Days Interviews ($197 Value)
- • **BONUS:** Behind The Scenes-Two Comma Club Interviews ($197 Value)

Total Value: $3,126

Figure 13.5:

Add more products and services to your challenge so you can build up the value as seen in Natasha's stack (top) and One Funnel Away's stack (bottom).

Testimonials. Once you've run your first challenge, encourage your challengers to write a testimonial on Facebook they're willing to let you share. Having screenshots from social media platforms will increase the credibility of your testimonials.

Order bump. When adding an order form bump, make sure it's not just random additional training. Instead, make sure it's something a challenger believes they *need* to be successful in your challenge. You want them to commit to consuming all your training because when they do, they will get results. When they get results, they want to buy more from you so you can help them become even more successful!

Because we included my book with their challenge purchase, we added the audiobook as our order bump. We position the offer as something that truly committed challengers want so they can take the information everywhere with them. This order bump has consistently converted at well over 30 percent.

Other great order form bumps include templates, workbooks, supplements, and swag. The possibilities are endless; just remember that it needs to be something that enhances their challenge experience.

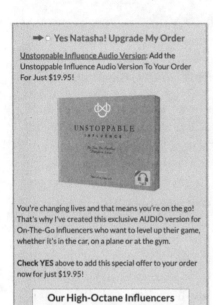

➡ ☐ Yes Natasha! Upgrade My Order

Unstoppable Influence Audio Version: Add the Unstoppable Influence Audio Version To Your Order For Just $19.95!

You're changing lives and that means you're on the go! That's why I've created this exclusive AUDIO version for On-The-Go Influencers who want to level up their game, whether it's in the car, on a plane or at the gym.

Check YES above to add this special offer to your order now for just $19.95!

Our High-Octane Influencers Will Choose This Upgrade

☐ Yes Cristy! Upgrade My Order for $19.95

Code Red Revolution Digital & Audio Version: Want a little bit of an advantage in the 10-Pound Take Down Challenge?

This book will answer TONS of your questions while giving you a really good shot at not only losing MORE than 10 pounds, but winning the BIG prizes (including a Custom Home Study Program with a Code Red Certified Coach valued at $997)! And you can read it and listen to it ANYWHERE!

Check YES above to add this special offer to your order for just $19.95 and get the digital and audio versions of my book now!

OUR MOST SUCCESSFUL CHALLENGERS WILL CHOOSE THIS UPGRADE

➡ ■ Yes Russell! Upgrade My Order Now!

One Time Offer - Only $37: People always wonder: "What happens if I build a funnel, and it FLOPS?" Don't worry (Most people's do the first time...)! At last year's Funnel Hacking Live, I gave a special workshop called Funnel Audibles. It shows you a simple process to take ANY funnel that's broken, and turn it from a 'zero' to a 'HERO'! Click YES to get the training, plus the transcripts and companion workbook that will walk you through how to do a funnel audible on your own funnel now for just $37! (This offer is not available ANYWHERE else on the market!)

Figure 13.6:

Your order form bump should enhance your customer's challenge experience. Natasha offers the audio version of her book (top left), Cristy offers an additional digital book (top right), and One Funnel Away offers a training to fix a broken funnel (bottom).

Page #2: The Upsell Page(s)

We recommend at least one upsell and possibly two. We've found that the best upsells for challenge funnels are ones that the buyer believes will help them complete the challenge. One of our upsells is a private accountability coach. The biggest perceived benefit from an accountability coach is that the coach will help the challenger finish what they start, which is our target market's biggest desire.

Figure 13.7:

After your customer buys your challenge, you can keep the buying loop open by offering an upsell that helps your customers complete the challenge. Natasha offers an accountability coach (left) and Cristy offers a starter kit with physical products to help during the challenge (right).

Another upsell that has worked well for us is a physical journal and workbook. As these two items are required materials for the challenge, we let the challengers know that they can either buy their own journal and print out 100-plus workbook pages, or we can make their lives easier by simply mailing them everything they need for the challenge.

The key to a solid challenge funnel upsell is to ensure that it's not adding a lot of extra information they feel they must consume to get results, but instead simple tools that will help them complete your challenge and get amazing results.

Page #3: The Thank-You Page

On the thank-you page, you'll thank them for their purchase and explain how they can access their challenge materials. If any products are being shipped to them, explain how and when those will be shipped as well.

Presentation Funnels

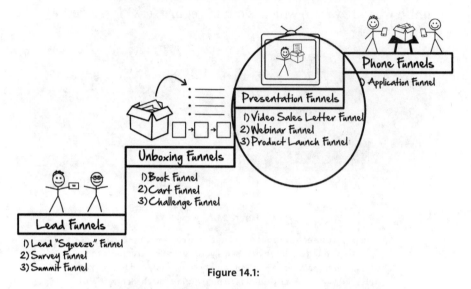

Figure 14.1:

The three best presentation funnels we've used are video sales
letter, webinar, and product launch funnels.

As we keep moving up the value ladder, the price of what we sell also goes up. Typically with lead funnels and unboxing funnels, because the price is lower, you don't usually need to spend as much time to get someone to see the perceived value of what you are selling them. I can do a product demo or use the "Who, What, Why, How" script and within a few minutes they can see that the value of the product is higher than the amount of money I am asking for it.

But as you move up the value ladder, when the price increases, you also have to increase the perceived value of the thing you are trying to sell, and you do that by creating a sales presentation to actually sell the offer you have created.

Inside *Expert Secrets*, I spend the majority of that book focused on how to create your Perfect Webinar. Even though it's called the Perfect Webinar, it can be used for all your presentations. We go slide by slide through the presentation showing the psychology of the sales scripts and how to use it to increase sales for your offers. You can get a simpler version of the Perfect Webinar in the "Funnel Scripts" section of this book, but I recommend going deep in *Expert Secrets* to really master your Perfect Webinar, as you'll be using it in each funnel in this section of the book.

Figure 14.2:

Any presentation that you give, whether on stage or online, uses a variation of the Perfect Webinar found in *Expert Secrets*.

The presentation's goal is to educate the person on the problem they have, break the false beliefs that are keeping them from moving forward with you, and get them to take action now. If structured correctly, it will take your cold traffic and help them to identify their problem, discount all other solutions, make them aware of your product, and get them to give you money.

Figure 14.3:

Your presentation will focus on turning cold traffic into hot traffic using the "Perfect Webinar" script.

Depending on what you're selling and its complexity or price, your presentation can quickly move someone from cold to warm to hot in minutes, hours, days, or weeks, depending on which funnel you use. There are three basic types of presentation funnels that we use based on what we are selling.

The video sales letter funnel (20- to 30-minute presentation): This looks similar to a book or cart funnel, but you can use it when your offer needs a longer presentation to explain the product or you need to break false beliefs before someone sees the order form. You can use this funnel to start selling products that are low ticket, up to about the $100 range. If you go higher than that, I would typically recommend moving to a webinar or product launch funnel. I have also used this funnel when selling access to membership sites and continuity programs.

Webinar funnel (60- to 120-minute presentation): When your price is between $100–$2,000, the best solution is to use a longer-form presentation set up inside of a webinar or automated webinar funnel.

Product launch funnel (presentation dripped out over multiple days/weeks): When you have a new product coming out priced between $100–$2,000 and you want to build anticipation and pressure for its release, a product launch funnel is often the best. It will follow the same "Perfect Webinar" script as the others, but the presentation will be dripped out over several days or weeks.

VIDEO SALES LETTER FUNNELS

Figure 14.4:

A video sales letter funnel has these pages: a sales page
(often with an order form bump), an upsell page (often with
another upsell page and downsells as well), and a thank-you page.

It was the day after Christmas over a decade ago. Most marketers had been emailing their lists like crazy before Christmas to capitalize on the holiday season, but once Christmas came, the emails slowed down as they went home to be with their kids and take some time off. When I opened my email on the morning after Christmas, I wasn't expecting to see many new emails, so that's why it was so strange when my inbox was full of a dozen or so emails talking about a new video that just went live.

I clicked on the link and was taken to something that I had never seen before. Now, you have to understand that a decade ago, the way we sold things online were with long-form sales letters. They were modeled after the old-school direct response sales letters that your parents would have gotten in the mail to sell them products that they might have been interested in.

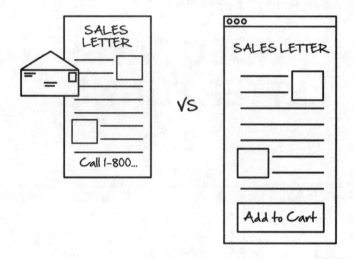

Figure 14.5:

Old-school direct response sales letters have been transformed
into modern-day video sales letter funnels.

When the internet started, we didn't change how we sold things; we just changed the media we used to sell through. So we took the long-form sales letters that we would mail to potential customers and turned them into long web pages that showed the same sales letter. Instead of sending that letter to people, we would buy traffic and send those people to that letter.

That's why it was so strange when I got to the page and all I saw was a headline and a video. I clicked Play, and the video was simple: no images, just the text of the sales letter being delivered on video, one sentence at a time, with a voice-over reading the sentence.

Figure 14.6:

Video sales letters feature a video with text on the screen
and someone reading the sales letter out loud.

They were reading the sales letter to me! I couldn't believe it! At first I thought it was dumb, but then I couldn't stop watching. I didn't have the ability to scroll down and see what they were selling or the price; I had to listen to every word, in the order they had designed for me to read and listen to them! I was sucked in, and for the next 30 minutes I listened and read every word in that video. After about 30 minutes, when he started to ask me to get my credit card out and order, an Add to Cart button appeared under the video. It was like magic!

I knew in that moment that how we sold things online was going to change forever. Bandwidth for videos was still expensive and streaming was difficult, but I felt that this was going to be the future. Over the next few years, more people started creating these types of videos. At first, they looked just like the one I had watched where someone read the text as it showed up in the video, but it soon transformed into complex videos pioneered by Vince Palko and his team at AdToons.com, where they hand drew your video while people listened to the voice-over.

There are now dozens of types of video sales letters you can create, including the Attractive Character just talking direct to camera. I believe that the most important part of your video is the presentation. (I wrote *Expert Secrets* so you could master this most important element.) How you present the message is secondary to the actual words you use.

PAGE #1: THE SALES PAGE

This page will look similar to the sales page of the book or cart funnel, but you'll notice that the order form is not at the top of the page. That is because we need the presentation to increase the perceived value of the product before we introduce the price. Because of that, all the focus at the top of the page is to get someone to actually watch the presentation. If we have a curiosity-based headline (see Secret #18), then the only goal of that headline is to get them to watch the video.

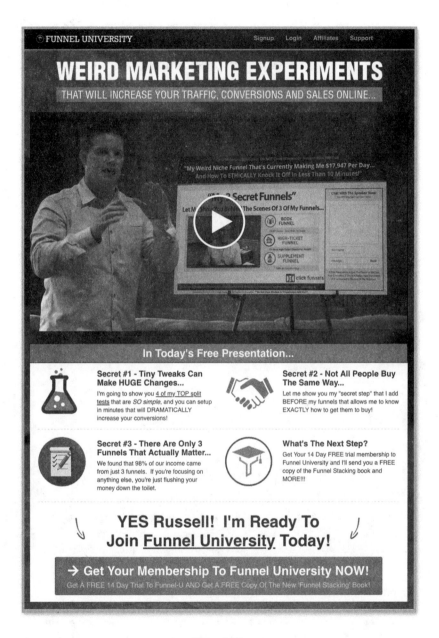

Figure 14.7:

The goal of your sales page is to get your audience to watch your presentation.

Funnel scripts: The video presentation should follow the "Star, Story, Solution" script in Secret #20 or the "Perfect Webinar" script in Secret #22. Either of these scripts will help grab their attention, break the false beliefs they have that would keep them from buying from you, and present your offer in a way that makes it truly irresistible.

Below the video, I like to create a "video spoiler box" that has a goal to push people back into watching the video. It starts with "In Today's Free Presentation" and then shows four things they will learn inside the presentation. These four things sync back to the "Perfect Webinar" script. There will be one block for each of the three secrets, and then one block showing them what's next, hinting to the CTA.

Figure 14.8:

The spoiler box remains up during your entire presentation. Depending on your audience, you might choose to have the CTA (YES Russell! . . .) section viewable during the entire presentation or have it pop up when you discuss the CTA.

Under the video spoiler box, I'll have the CTA section that will point to my Order button. Sometimes I'll hide this section and have it appear when we talk about the CTA in the video. Other times I'll have it there the whole time. We've tested both ways with mixed results. Sometimes hiding the button until the CTA wins, and other times having it open during the entire presentation wins. It's something that is simple to test with ClickFunnels and worth finding out which works best for your specific traffic in your market.

PAGE #2: THE UPSELL PAGE(S)

The upsell pages in this funnel are identical to the book and cart funnels. Whether you're selling information or physical products will depend on which types of offers you should sell here (either more of the same thing for physical products or the next thing for information products). I'd recommend reading those two chapters for more insight on the best practices when structuring your upsell offers.

PAGE #3: THE THANK-YOU PAGE

The thank-you page is also similar to the other funnels. If you're selling physical products, I'd recommend an offer wall, and if you're selling information products, I'd recommend inviting them into the next funnel on your value ladder.

WEBINAR FUNNELS

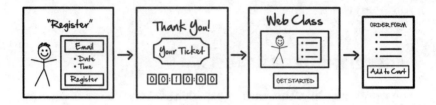

Figure 15.1:

A webinar funnel has five pages: a registration page, a thank-you page,
a webinar room, an order form page, and a replay page (not shown).
(You can also add bumps, upsells, downsells, and a thank-you page.)

It was February 23, 2018, and I was in Las Vegas at the Mandalay Bay Events Center. I was a speaker at Grant Cardone's 10X event, and he had a packed house with over 9,000 people in attendance, all there to learn how to grow their companies online. I was up next.

I had given a version of my presentation hundreds of times online, but as I waited for my name to be announced over the loudspeaker, the butterflies in my stomach were almost too much to handle. I was so excited but also sick to my stomach at the same time. It got louder and louder in that room and then the voice came over the loudspeaker:

> For the past 10 years, this man has built a following of entrepreneurs in the millions. He's sold hundreds of thousands of copies of his books. He popularized the concept of sales funnels. He's cofounded the software company ClickFunnels that has gone to over $100 million in sales and has 55,000 active customers in just three

years. He is the king of funnels, the internet's favorite entrepreneur, a marketing genius; he is an American storyteller . . . Ladies and gentlemen, bring to the stage with a thunderous 10X applause: Mr. Russell Brunson!

As I heard these words, I started to climb up the small stairs that led to the stage. When I got to the top, I stopped, took a deep breath of air, and listened for a second to the loudest noise I had ever heard. I looked out and saw 9,000 people on their feet cheering.

I knew there was no turning back now, so I took my first step out onto the stage. I introduced myself, and then I started my presentation. For the next 90 minutes, I went slide by slide, doing my "Perfect Webinar" script to a T (yes, the same one I give you in Secret #22 of this book and teach in detail in the *Expert Secrets* book). As I finished the presentation, I made an offer for a $2,997 course that came with one year of access to ClickFunnels for free. After I made the offer, I watched people start to stream from their seats over to the order tables outside the arena. It was the biggest "table rush" I had ever seen.

After I ended my presentation and got up to the sales table to take pictures with everyone who bought (also part of my offer), I was shocked to see a line that wrapped around the Mandalay Bay Events Center three times! As I got to the picture line, I saw hundreds of entrepreneurs who had seen the vision of funnels, and how funnels would work for their specific business. I took pictures with each person for the next four and a half hours.

By the time we were done, I could barely stand. Between the nerves from giving the presentation and standing and smiling for the pictures for four and a half hours, my body was destroyed. My wife and I snuck back to our room and I passed out for a few hours.

When I woke up, I was excited to hear the results. How many people had signed up? How much money had we made? How many lives were we going to be able to change through this offer we had just presented? We found the hotel room that our small team was in, processing orders, and I asked them the numbers.

They had been processing orders for hours and had only made a dent in the order forms. For the next few hours, I would get updates from them through text.

$650,000 processed . . .

$1.2 Million processed . . .

$1.8 Million processed . . .

$2.3 Million processed . . .

$2.9 Million processed . . .

$3.2 Million—final number!

Yes, from one presentation, I had sold $3.2 million! I'm not positive, but I'm pretty sure that is a world record for the most sales from stage in the shortest period of time.

I want you to think about that for a minute. Most salespeople would spend their entire lives selling one-on-one to people and never make $3.2 million, yet I was able to do it in 90 minutes because I had crafted a presentation in a way that was proven to get people to buy. I didn't do it to just one person at a time either; I presented it to 9,000 people at one time. So even if my close rate was a lot less than a really good salesperson (and it was), because I was able to give 9,000 sales presentations in 90 minutes (one for each person who heard it), I was able to make more in that 90 minutes than the best salespeople will make their entire life.

But what's even more interesting to this story wasn't the fact that I did $3.2 million in 90 minutes; the more interesting part was that this same presentation that I did live on stage in front of 9,000 people was being seen online through webinar and automated webinar funnels over 30,000 times per month, making consistent revenue like clockwork!

Most people will probably not have a chance to be on stage in front of 9,000 people to deliver their presentation, but everyone has the ability to create a presentation, put it inside a webinar funnel, and get thousands of people to watch it every month! Me speaking on stage like that is not scalable, but doing it through webinar funnels is.

When we launched ClickFunnels, webinars were the funnel type we used to grow the company. My role was to do as many live webinars as possible. I was often doing at least one per day, and often two or three per day during the first year we went live. Only after a year, where we had perfected the presentation, did I switch it into an automated webinar.

I go into much more detail inside *Expert Secrets* on how to perfect your sales script and presentation, so I won't go deeper here, but do know that you want to use a normal live webinar funnel for as long as possible before you transition it into an automated webinar funnel. I will show both models here in this chapter, but I'll focus more on the live webinar as it's the most important to master.

PAGE #1: THE REGISTRATION PAGE

The goal of the registration page is to get someone to register for a webinar. On this page we want to create a curiosity-based headline (Secret #18 will give you dozens of templates you can use) that will get someone to want to register and show up for your presentation. I don't spend time telling my story on this page; instead, I focus hard on a hook that will pull them in and get them to register. Here is an example of the first registration page we used for the original ClickFunnels webinar:

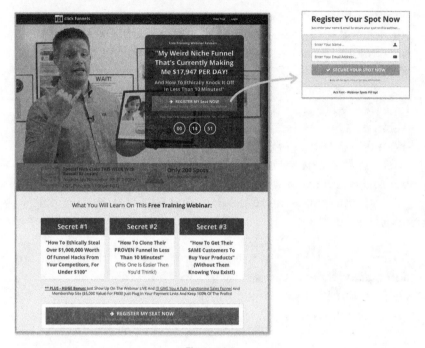

Figure 15.2:

Your registration page creates as much curiosity as possible so your audience will feel compelled to register just to find out more.

Notice that the page causes a lot of curiosity. The picture is kind of strange; the headline ("My Weird Niche Funnel That's Currently Making Me $17,947 Per Day! And How to Ethically Knock It Off in Less Than 10 Minutes!") raises a lot of questions but gives no answers. We specifically tell them when the web class is starting so they can put it on their calendar, and other than that, we push their entire focus to the Register My Seat button.

When they click on that button, a pop-up appears so they can enter their email address to register for the webinar. Then they're added to a Soap Opera Sequence to warm them up before the presentation begins.

ClickFunnels doesn't have its own webinar software, so most people use ClickFunnels to create all the funnel pages and integrate with either GoToWebinar or Zoom to run the actual webinar. It's simple to integrate either of these platforms into your ClickFunnels pages.

PAGE #2: THE THANK-YOU PAGE

While the goal of the registration page is to create enough curiosity to get them to register, the goal of the thank-you page is to build a relationship with them and get them to show up to the webinar.

Funnel scripts: I usually have a video here using the "Who, What, Why, How" script from Secret #19. This is where I explain who I am, what my viewers are going to learn on the webinar, why it's so important, and how to get it on their calendar so they don't miss it.

Figure 15.3:

The most important part of your thank-you page is to build a relationship with your registrants and make sure they show up to the webinar.

One other thing you can do on this thank-you page is to push people into a low-ticket offer (usually a book or a cart funnel) before the webinar. I tell them it will help to prepare them for the webinar, which it does, but it also can help to cover your ad spend. Most of my ad spend to get someone to register for the webinar is recouped immediately from this thank-you page, and then anything I make on the webinar is pure profit.

One thing to note: Make sure that your thank-you page offer doesn't compete with your webinar offer. Doing that will cannibalize your webinar sales. Make sure it's something that complements your offer and will create more of a need for the thing you are about to offer them.

PAGE #3: THE WEBINAR ROOM

This webinar will happen inside your webinar software. Most people use either GoToWebinar or Zoom. We've used both with great success in the past. Those platforms will send out notifications to make sure people log in to their software, and when the time begins, you can open your slides on your computer and deliver the perfect webinar!

Figure 15.4:

Two platforms you can use to deliver your webinar presentation include GoToWebinar (presenter control panel shown at right) and Zoom.

I would highly recommend spending the time to master your presentation. This is the difference between a webinar that flops and one that can make you millions of dollars. You will learn the basic structure of the "Perfect Webinar" script in Secret #22, but make sure you thoroughly read *Expert Secrets* to really understand and master the psychology of the script.

PAGE #4: THE ORDER FORM PAGE

At the end of your presentation, you will make a CTA to push someone to an order form to buy. The mistake people make on this page is they try to resell people on the order form. Every time I've done that in the past, it's hurt my sales. If they have watched your presentation and gone to the order form, your job is just to recap the offer and then let them purchase.

Figure 15.5:

On your order form page, you should recap the offer, not try to resell.

There are a lot of cool things that you've learned in other secrets that you can also plug into your checkout process. You can add order form bumps, upsells and downsells, offer walls, or links to your phone funnels on your thank-you pages. All the best practices can be added here in these funnels as well.

PAGE #5: THE REPLAY PAGE

No matter how hard you try to get people to show up for your live webinar, the vast majority of people (usually 80 percent) still won't show up live. Because of that, we set up a replay page with a recording of the presentation you made earlier. We don't keep this page up forever; usually we'll give it a 48- or 72-hour countdown where they have to watch the video before we pull it offline. Without this urgency and scarcity, it can be really hard to get this 80 percent to actually go and watch the presentation; with the deadline, you will get a huge percentage to go and watch it.

Figure 15.6:

To add urgency and scarcity to your replay, offer a limited viewing time of two to three days before the video is taken offline.

After the live webinar, we'll send out emails pushing people to this replay page, letting them know what they missed in the presentation and how long they have until we pull it offline.

VARIATION: AUTOMATED WEBINAR FUNNEL

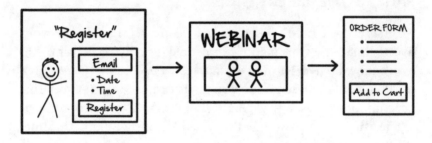

Figure 15.7:

Present your webinar live until you master it, then you can automate it with a prerecorded webinar.

Registration page: The automated webinar is similar to a traditional webinar funnel, except there is no live event or external webinar software. Everything can be done in ClickFunnels. The presentation is prerecorded, and people are registering to watch it either in real time or at a future date. We still use curiosity to drive the registration for an event that is happening in a few minutes.

Figure 15.8:

Just like a live webinar funnel, your automated webinar registration
page should be simple, with a curiosity-based headline, an eye-catching
image, and all focus directed to the Register button.

Presentation page: After they register, they are taken immediately to a presentation page (similar to the replay page in a traditional webinar) where they can watch the actual webinar.

Figure 15.9:

The page where you show your automated webinar
looks similar to a live webinar replay page.

Order form page: From that webinar we push them to the order form where they can purchase the offer we make them on the webinar.

Figure 15.10:

The order form for an automated webinar is the same as the live webinar order form where you should only recap the offer, not try to resell.

Then we have email sequences that push them to watch the presentation before it expires, just like we did with the replay emails in the traditional live webinar.

I want to restate that while I love automated webinars, and they are one of my favorite funnels long-term, if you haven't mastered your presentation, they are not worth doing. So put in the time doing live webinars until you have mastered your presentation; when you have one that has converted the best, use that presentation as the video in your automated webinar.

PRODUCT LAUNCH FUNNELS

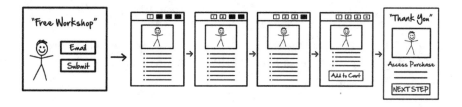

Figure 16.1:

A product launch funnel has these pages: a "free workshop" page, multiple video pages, an offer page (with order form at the bottom or on a separate page), and a thank-you page.

Every month, we get a front row seat to watch Hollywood practice a formula where they launch new movies. They start by showing a trailer that builds buzz and anticipation for the movie. Then they'll start running ads giving a date when people can buy tickets. As the date gets closer, they drop another trailer to get people even more excited.

Then the time to buy tickets comes, and everyone gets their seats for opening night. A few days before the premiere, the actors and actresses show up on the early morning and late-night talk shows, all talking about opening night. This causes more people to buy tickets, and then opening weekend hits.

Millions of people hit the theaters on opening night. If the movie lives up to the hype, the word of mouth continues, and more tickets are sold all weekend long. On Monday, you hear the official stats for how much money the movie grossed during the opening weekend. If sales were good, then people will keep buying tickets for months to come.

Can you imagine getting that type of buzz when you're launching your new business or releasing a new product to the market? What if you could get that same anticipation of people actually counting down and waiting anxiously for the second that they can buy?

Well, you can with the product launch funnel made famous by Jeff Walker. Jeff said to look at the product launch funnel as a "sideways sales letter."[16] The presentation is the same, but instead of someone reading or watching it from top to bottom, you are tipping it on its side and delivering part of it each day to build anticipation and buzz.

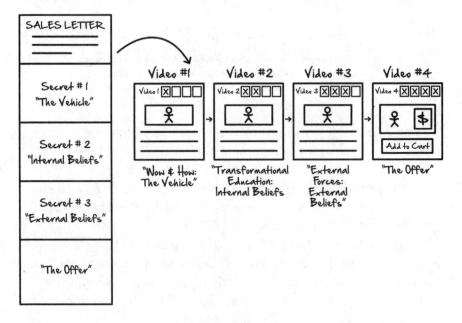

Figure 16.2:

The product launch funnel is like a sales letter flipped on its side.

Product launch funnels are best used with warm or hot traffic. We usually send people to the videos from a link in an email—either to our own list or to an affiliate or joint venture (JV) partner's list. You break down your sales presentations into more digestible chunks, delivered over the course of a few days or weeks to build up excitement. You teach in the first three videos and then sell your product in the fourth video.

The way this funnel works is someone will register for a free online workshop. You'll then give them the first of four videos with the first part of the presentation that hooks them to watch the second video.

A few days later, you release the second video, which is the second part of your presentation. At the end, you get them to comment on the page to increase engagement and then you hook them to get them to watch the next video. A few days later, the third video comes out that finishes the presentation and sets up the special offer they will receive in the fourth video. In this last video, you make the offer and push them to your order form.

The presentation isn't much different than what you would do on a webinar presentation (using my "Perfect Webinar" script); it's just breaking the presentation down over multiple days to build anticipation so you have people lining up and waiting for the moment that the fourth video drops so they can buy whatever it is you're selling!

PAGE #1: THE "FREE WORKSHOP" PAGE

This page looks just like a simple squeeze page that you learned about during the lead funnels section, but the lead magnet is the actual training workshop. They are registering to get access to the live training! At the bottom, I like showing screenshots of the videos to help them understand that they are registering for a series of videos that will help them to get a specific result.

Figure 16.3:

The first page of your product launch funnel gives someone your lead
magnet (a free workshop) when they register for the training.

Funnel scripts: We use the "Curiosity-Based Headline" script
from Secret #18 as well as the "Who, What, Why, How" script
from Secret #19 to get them excited for the training they are about
to register for.

PAGES #2–4: THE VIDEO PAGES

The video pages are simple, but they have a few essential elements
to understand. On each page, you'll see thumbnails of the videos
in the series. The videos that are live are usually in color and have
a Play button on them, so they can go back and watch ones they
have missed. The ones that have not come out yet will often be
black-and-white and/or have an icon of a lock on them.

Figure 16.4:

**As you unlock a new video every few days (with upcoming videos seen at top),
you'll build anticipation for the upcoming videos to be released.**

Funnel scripts: Under the thumbnails, we have the actual video. The script you use (the "Perfect Webinar" or "Product Launch" script) depends on what will be on these videos. You will notice, however, that both scripts are very similar.

Video #1—Wow and how: You will "wow" them with a big idea, and then show them "how" you and others are using this concept.

Video #2—Transformational education: You will let people look over your shoulder as you walk through the process with them.

Video #3—External forces: You will break any external false beliefs they have, address the external roadblocks that may keep them from success, and show them how to navigate those issues.

Under these videos, we'll often have links to lead magnets they can download for free. These will usually provide value and tie into what we're teaching in the video so they will want to continue watching the rest of the series.

We'll usually have a comments section on the page so people can build the buzz; this provides social proof from others and a feeling of community as people interact with the videos.

PAGE #5: THE OFFER PAGE AND ORDER FORM

After the three videos have been released, you'll release the fourth video where you make the offer. You will send them emails when the date is set and you're ready for them to come and buy. The page they will be taken to is very simple; it will only have a video of you making your offer and a link to your order form.

Figure 16.5:

Your order form page should be simple with just a headline,
a video of you explaining the offer, and a link to buy.

After someone watches the video, they'll click on the link to
the order form. Some people put the order form directly under this
video while others link to an order form on a separate page; either
option works great. When someone gets to your order form, don't
forget all the other elements you've learned in other chapters such
as adding order form bumps and one-click upsells. You can easily
add these into your sales process here to increase your average
cart value.

Most people use product launch funnels to launch a new
business or a new product. However, after you've done it once
live, it's very simple in ClickFunnels to go back and create an
automated version of this funnel that will work on autopilot
around the clock. This is a great way to drive consistent traffic to
your product launch funnel even after the original launch is over.

Back-End Phone Funnels

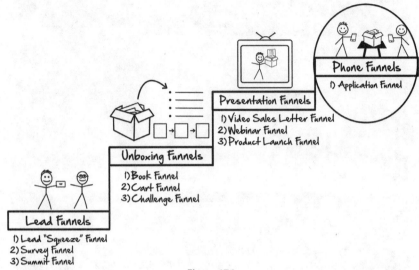

Figure 17.1:

When your product or service is priced above $2,000, you'll have higher conversions if you change the selling environment from online to offline.

As we went through the seven phases of a funnel, you'll remember that the last phase was changing the selling environment. This means we take people offline and into a more intimate setting where you have full control over the selling process.

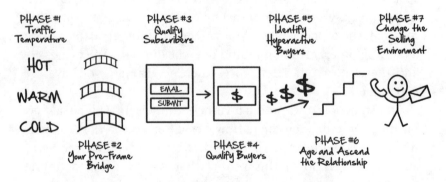

Figure 17.2:

The best back-end, high-ticket funnel we've used is an application funnel.

When someone is behind their keyboard, in their home or office, they have full control over the sales process. They can quickly close your page or scroll past your ad, and the only thing you are able to do is try to throw out better hooks to get their attention, and tell better stories to build more rapport.

In this phase, we have built that rapport, and we are asking them to get away from their computer where they control the environment and move into a different situation where *you* will have more control. A good example of that is taking someone offline and bringing them to a live event. At this event, you have complete control of the selling environment. When they are there, you have their full attention. You can choreograph the event for selling in a way that is impossible online.

Whenever I'm trying to sell an offer that is more than about $2,000 (and even up to a $1 million or more), I try to get them offline as quickly as possible. While there are many ways to do that, the one way that has been the most profitable consistently has been an application funnel. This is where you get someone to fill out an application to work with you, and then you call them on the phone and sell them on your product or services.

For some businesses, all their selling happens on the phone, and that's okay; these application funnels will create higher quality leads and warm up your prospects before they ever get on the call with you or your sales team.

APPLICATION FUNNELS

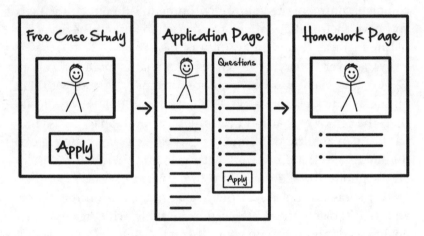

Figure 17.3:

An application funnel has three pages: a landing page, an application page, and a homework page.

I was scheduled to speak in the morning, but I knew that Matt Bacak was speaking the night before, and I wanted to hear his presentation, so I took the earlier flight so I would be at the hotel in time to hear him. As he got on stage and showed his sales funnels and value ladder, I sat in the back taking notes.

"The first thing I do is sell this free CD. They pay $4.95 to cover the shipping and I send it to them right away. Then on this CD, I talk to them about my business model and how it can help them. I don't hold anything back on that CD either; I walk them through exactly how to do it," he explained. "A few days after they have received the CD and hopefully had a chance to listen to it, someone from my team calls them on the phone and offers them my eight-thousand-dollar offer where they come to my office and we help them get it set up for their business. Right now one out of the ten people we call signs up for the eight-thousand-dollar workshop!"

I was stunned. I had sold thousands of items online, but never once had I ever thought about calling my customers on the phone and offering them the next product in my value ladder. I couldn't sleep that night, or the next. As exciting as it was, though, I didn't have the time or know-how to hire salespeople, and I was too introverted to make calls myself, so I didn't do anything.

A few months later on a cold December night two weeks before Christmas, while most people were inside, warm with their families, I was outside on a rickety ladder hanging up lights, wearing a thin coat that couldn't keep out the cold. My fingers were so numb, I couldn't feel them anymore, but the real pain wasn't from the cold. It was the sick feeling of despair I felt in my stomach knowing that the next day, just a few days before Christmas, I was going to have to walk into the office and deliver one of the worst messages that anyone can hear during the holidays. Not only would there be no Christmas bonuses, but after tomorrow, there would be no more jobs for anyone. My closest friends and some of my family members were all going to lose their jobs because of me. Business had slowed down a lot, and the money we were making wasn't enough to cover the costs to keep our doors open.

As I slowly moved the ladder around my house and stapled lights under our frozen rain gutter, my mind was racing, trying to figure out some trick, some strategy, something that would magically save my dying business. And then it happened. I had the epiphany, and it struck me hard and fast. What if I followed Matt's model that I had learned before? I had a customer list, I had products, and I had a coaching program. I just needed to be willing to call some of these people on the phone and make the sales!

The next morning I grabbed our team and I explained the new model. We took one of our best-selling products and burned it on a DVD. Then we set up a quick funnel and sent an email to our small list. Within a few days, we had sold over 800 copies of this new $4.95 DVD! Our small team shipped them out to our customers, then we waited long enough for them to get the DVD and hopefully watch it, and then we all picked up the phones and started calling.

"Did you watch the DVD yet?" we would ask. Most people said no, so we asked them to go watch it right then and we'd call them back in an hour. Call after call we went through our list of 800 hot leads, asking them if they had watched the DVD, and if they had, we invited them to a workshop where we were going to help them implement what they learned on that DVD. Because it was Christmastime, it was hard to get ahold of most people, but we did get on the phone with many of them.

"The workshop is just $5,500 and it will be here at our office in January," we said. The first day in, we had a dozen noes. Finally, on day four, we got our first "YES!"

We were so excited, we all jumped around screaming! Within a few days, we had more yeses, and by Christmas day, 11 people had wired us the $5,500 for their ticket to this private workshop!

This was a huge lesson for me because I learned that creating a lead online and then selling it offline was powerful. Within a few months, I had built a sales team and we started to grow quickly. Within a year, I had over 60 full-time salespeople and we were selling over 6,000 DVDs per week, calling every person who ordered.

While this model worked for a time, it was terribly inefficient. I was spending almost $1 million each month in overhead to keep the operation running. Eventually it got to be too much, and we shut down the call center; for years we never called another customer on the phone.

Over the next few years, we built out all the other tiers of the value ladder and were profitable, but I always knew I was leaving a ton of money on the table. One day we had the idea: What if, instead of us calling everyone who bought from us, we only called people who were interested and applied to work with us? We would only call the cream of the crop.

We did a quick test by launching a new funnel with an application form on it and emailing a few of our best customers. I asked them if they wanted our help, and if so they should apply and tell us why they felt like they were a good fit. Within hours, we had dozens of applications from my dream customers selling me on why I should work with them. Then I had two guys on my team call these applications and find out who would be fun to work with. In the end, we had one of our most profitable, stress-free weeks of our entire lives.

I got so excited by this that we started to test and tweak the application funnel. It went from one page to two pages and eventually to three. We tested hundreds of things until we found the perfect process as well as the perfect phone scripts. I will walk you through each of the pages in this funnel in this chapter, and then give you two sets of scripts that you can use to close high-ticket sales: the "Setter" and "Closer" scripts (for two salespeople; Secret #25) and the "Four-Question Close" script (for the entrepreneur without salespeople; Secret #24).

PAGE #1: THE "SUCCESS STORY" OR "FREE CASE STUDY" LANDING PAGE

This first page is where you are going to show someone the big result that you are capable of getting for them. This is casting a vision for what is possible if you were to work with them. We typically do this in one of two ways.

The first is by showing a success story from someone who has worked with you in the past and achieved what they will likely want to achieve if they were working with you.

Figure 17.4:

You can use a success story to help your dream customers
visualize what they can achieve by working with you.

On this page I call out that I'm looking to work with a few
more of my "Dream Clients" and I show a video from Liz Benny
telling her story of working with me in the Inner Circle. After they
watch the video, they have the ability to apply to work with me to
help get that same result.

You can use this type of success story page for any business, just
as Dr. Chad Woolner used it to generate applications for his clinic.

Figure 17.5:

**You can use a success story video to sell a high-ticket
product or service in any market.**

The other type of page you can use on the front end of this funnel is a "Free Case Study" page. It works the same and has the same goal of showing people what's possible, but instead of someone else telling their story about you, it's you showing the case study of what you did to get yourself or someone else the same result.

FREE CASESTUDY: $89,230 TO A <u>TINY LIST</u> OF PEOPLE, IN LESS THAN 3 DAYS!

THE BLACK BOX...
A Simple 3 Step Funnel To
Sell Almost Anything... *Without*
Actually Selling Anything!

Enter your email for the FREE "Blackbox Funnel" Infographic AND to apply to have me help setup a Blackbox Funnel in your business!

Figure 17.6:

In your case study video, explain the strategy you or someone else
went through but not the tactics of getting the result.

Usually with a case study video, I am showing them exactly *what* I did (the strategy), step by step, but I don't go into *how* I did it (the tactics). That way they see the process, but the desire to really understand the *how* is what compels them to apply to work with you.

The three goals of this first page in the funnel are:

1. Have them watch the success story or case study showing what is possible if they work with you.

2. Let them apply if they want your help to achieve the same results.

3. Get an email address so you can follow up if they don't finish the application.

The next two pages (the application and homework pages) of the funnel will pre-frame and presell your leads on all the reasons they should sign up—instead of worrying about all the reasons they shouldn't sign up.

PAGE #2: THE APPLICATION PAGE

On the first page we only collected email addresses, so that gives us the ability to follow up with them over and over until they complete step two in the process, which is to fill out the longer-form application. The goal of this application is to get them to sell you on why you should work with them. We call this a "takeaway" sale because you're not selling them; they are selling you. As you see how the phone scripts work in Secrets #24 and #25, you'll see how powerful the positioning is that starts on the application.

I also like to include a video on this page that explains in more detail what it looks like to work with me, and then I put in a "testimonial rush" where they see as many video testimonials that I have playing back-to-back. This will give them tons of social proof to listen to while they are filling out the application form.

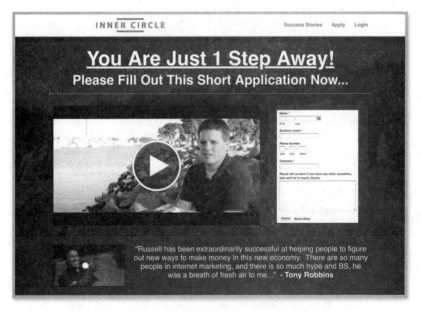

Figure 17.7:

Your application should prequalify your leads and help you get as much information as possible about them before your sales call.

While there are tons of questions that you can ask on the application page, there are a few important questions that will help your dream customer be prepared for the sales call; the answers to those questions will also give the salesperson what they need to be successful on the phone.

- **Revenue qualifier:** This question will be different depending on the type of business you're in, but I want to make sure that the person who is applying isn't just *willing* to buy my higher-ticket programs, but also *able* to buy. I don't just come out and ask them if they can afford it. Instead, I like to disguise this question in something that will give me the answer. Questions like these will give me the answers I need.

  - What type of business do you own?
  - How much money do you spend on ads each month?
  - How often do you go out to eat?
  - How much money do you set aside each month for investments?
  - How much money have you spent in the past trying to solve this problem?

- **What does success look like for you?** I want to make sure that the person I am going to be working with has an accurate picture of what success will look like. If they tell me they want to make $10 million in the next 12 months and they don't have a product yet, I will not work with that person. Their vision of success and what I can achieve are so far misaligned that there is no way I will make them happy. The question I like to use to figure out what success will look like for them comes from the book *The Dan Sullivan Question* by Dan Sullivan.[17] He says:

  If we were having this discussion three years from today, and you were looking back over those three years, what has to have happened in your life, both personally and professionally, for you to feel happy with your progress?

- **Why would you be a good fit for the group?** My coaching is always in a group, so I want to make sure that they will be a good fit for our group. I need them to sell me on why we should bring them into the cool kids' club. I do this to get them to sell themselves to me, but also to make sure I can protect the integrity of our program for the others who are in it.

- **How can you contribute to the group?** I've found that givers are always more successful than takers, so I try to attract the givers and repel the takers. This question helps us to know where they will fall.

PAGE #3: THE HOMEWORK PAGE

After they've finished the full application, I take them to a homework page.

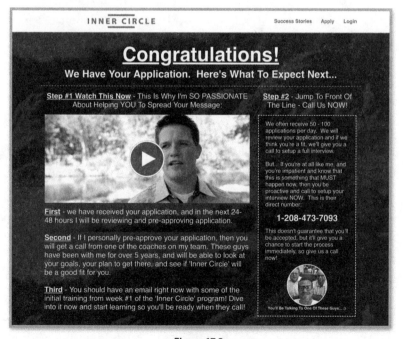

Figure 17.8:

On your homework page, you'll try to build connection with the Attractive Character, tell them what to expect, give them homework, and encourage them to initiate a phone call.

There are a few goals for the homework page.

1. **Build connection with the Attractive Character:**
   Up to this point, they have heard from your success story about you, or heard you tell a case study about a result. They are applying to achieve a similar result, but now they have to decide if it's you they want to go on that journey with. On my homework page, I have a video where I tell my story, and it builds connection with those who are applying. I've had people who call my salespeople in tears after watching the video, telling them that they trust me and want to work with me because my story matches theirs.

2. **Tell them what to expect and give them homework:** Let them know what is going to happen next and have them watch videos or read something to help them prepare for the call that will be happening soon. Anything you can do to preindoctrinate them before the call will help to increase conversions when you do get a chance to talk to them.

3. **Get them to initiate a phone call:** We found that when we call an applicant, we make one quarter as much money than when they call us first. So we will call every application that comes through, but if I can get them to pick up the phone and call me instead, they will be worth four times more to us. So I try to get them to call us after they have applied. This doesn't guarantee that they will get into the program, but it lets us know who is serious, and we look at their applications first.

This high-ticket funnel is simple to create, and it can qualify and warm up leads faster than anything else I've ever seen. We went from having 60 full-time salespeople each making hundreds of calls a week to just two salespeople, calling the applications of people who are selling us on why we should let them into our programs. We make as much gross revenue and almost 10 times as much net revenue with this simple funnel and two people as we did cold-calling warm leads with 60 people.

SECTION THREE

FUNNEL SCRIPTS

"How would you like to get the best salesperson on planet Earth to close sales for your products 24 hours a day, seven days a week (without them ever complaining, asking for a raise, or taking a break)?" That was the question I asked a group of business owners who sold their products face-to-face for a living.

"All a funnel really does is take your proven sales presentation, put it into a process where you can create the pitch once, and it makes the sale for you over and over on autopilot forever. You already know how to sell your product; we just need to create a video of you doing your pitch, put it into a funnel, and then we've taken your time out of the selling equation. Now you can sell every day like clockwork. Even if your overall conversions go down because it's not as effective as selling face-to-face, your actual revenue will dramatically go up because it is a much more efficient way to sell."

When I started creating my own funnels, I quickly realized that the structure of the funnel and the process I took them through was just a small piece of getting someone to buy. The biggest piece was the pitch: the script, the words on the pages that convinced someone to buy my product. In the marketing world, they called this "sales copy," and I started an intense study for over a decade to understand how it worked and how I could use it in my funnels.

For each funnel I created, I would funnel hack a few dozen other people with similar funnels, and if they had sales videos, I would get them transcribed. I would read them over and over again, looking for the patterns. The more funnels I hacked and the more copy I read, the clearer these patterns became. I started to doodle out each sales video, noticing that most of them took the viewer on a very similar journey. I did the same for upsell videos, webinars, and phone scripts. When I would create my sales videos inside of my funnels, I would break out the script, follow the process, plug in my stories and my offer, and almost every funnel we launched became a success because we knew how to sell the products on the pages.

I created these little "funnel scripts" for myself that I could use over and over again, just plugging in whatever product I was selling at the time. Every time I needed to make a video for a landing page, I would pull out the "Who, What, Why, How" script, and I knew exactly what to say. When I did a webinar, I'd pull out my "Perfect Webinar" script and I had a process I knew would get people to buy.

When I wrote the first version of this book, I included the scripts I had with each page of the funnel. After I published the book, my friend and now business partner Jim Edwards told me how much he loved the scripts, and he asked if he could make software where people could fill in the blanks and it would generate the scripts for them. I agreed, and he created the most amazing software you can find at FunnelScripts.com that can help you to quickly implement these scripts. Since then, he has added 50-plus more scripts to cover almost every selling situation you can dream of, from Amazon listings to email campaigns to Facebook ads, and more.

In this second edition of the book, I decided to put all the scripts into their own section so you could find them easier and reference them faster when you need them. This is by no means every possible script you could use, but they are the core ones we use in the funnels you learned about in Section Two. Some scripts (like the "Perfect Webinar" script) have been used so much by people inside our community that more than half of *Expert Secrets* focuses on mastering that one script to use in your ads, video sales letters, webinars, and email campaigns.

I also want to note that these scripts should serve as a framework, not a word-for-word script. You should be weaving your stories, your Attractive Character, and your message into the framework. That is the secret to having success inside your funnels. Your personality is what will keep people coming back for more and ascending your value ladder.

Front-End Lead
Funnel Scripts

"CURIOSITY-BASED HEADLINE" SCRIPTS

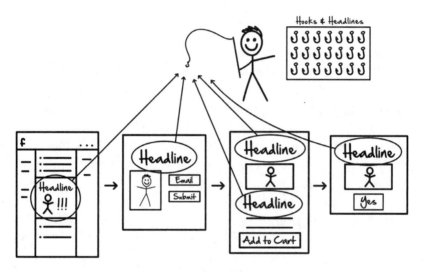

Figure 18.1:

Mastering the art of headline writing is crucial for your success
because you'll be writing headlines everywhere: your ads,
landing pages, sales pages, upsell pages, and more.

I wanted to start this Funnel Scripts section with arguably the most important yet most underrated of all the funnel scripts. I didn't put any headline scripts in the original *DotCom Secrets*, but my partner, Jim, built them into the Funnel Scripts software because they are the most-used script in all of marketing. Think about it: you use headlines on your ads and on your landing pages. After someone joins your list, every email you send them has a headline (subject line). When they see the sales page, it will usually have multiple headlines and subheadlines. The same is true on upsell pages, downsale pages, thank-you pages, blog posts, and articles.

Because there was such a need, I asked Jim to contribute this chapter to the second edition along with all his favorite headline scripts that you can start using immediately.

HEADLINE SECRETS BY JIM EDWARDS

How important is a headline? Why bother? Who reads headlines anyway? If your product or service is awesome, that's what really matters, right?

Let me tell you a quick story about a time I was teaching a class 3,000 miles away from home to a group of Realtors in California.

A title insurance company hired me to teach direct response advertising to their number one client in Orange County. The top sales rep told me the group I was speaking to was the smartest but toughest group in the whole company. Nothing impressed them, and they didn't take kindly to out-of-towners coming in and telling them how to do business. To say I was intimidated would be a stretch, but it did make me think I needed a good hook to grab their attention.

The morning that I was speaking to the group, I stopped in the hotel gift shop and grabbed a copy of the *LA Times*. On the way to the office, I sat in the back of the taxi, looking at the headlines. (Yeah, a taxi! Uber was about 15 years in the making at that point.) That's when it hit me! I knew how to grab their attention *and* teach an important lesson.

When I arrived at the office, I went straight to the office manager and asked if she had some duct tape or masking tape. She pulled out a huge roll of duct tape from her desk and handed it to me. (I didn't ask why she had the duct tape; I just assumed it was fate.) I went in the conference room and got ready for my "tough" audience. In the 10 minutes before class, I'd covered all the headlines on the front page with duct tape. I'd also found a full-page ad by the company I was speaking to, but I didn't cover anything up.

As the attendees filed in, I definitely got the vibe the title rep warned me about. This group was not going to be an easy one to impress. Instead of going through a big, long introduction about myself and what we'd cover in the class, I held up the paper and asked, "What's missing here?"

Instantly everyone said, "The headlines!"

"Why does it matter that I covered up the headlines?" I asked.

They said, "Because we don't know what the articles are about."

"Why does that matter?"

"Because without the headlines, we don't know if we're interested in the article or not!"

"Oh, that makes sense. Without a headline, nobody knows if they're interested in the content or not. So without a headline, the content is useless, right?"

"YES!" they all cried.

Then I turned to their ad on the back page of the same paper and asked, "So what's missing from this ad?"

One of the agents yelled out, "How do we know? You didn't cover anything up!"

And that's when I dropped the hammer with a one-word answer: "Exactly."

You could have heard a pin drop as I let it sink in for about 10 seconds until the silence became uncomfortable even for me. Then I said, "I didn't cover up anything on this ad because there is no headline. And since there's no headline, how could you expect anyone to know if it interests them or not?"

And with that, we got started with the session. At the end of the day, the group manager told me it was the most impactful training they'd ever had, and he'd never seen his agents so open to learning about ad writing and direct-response sales techniques. They understood how important headlines were, and their lives and businesses were permanently changed for the better as a result.

When it comes to writing sales copy, most people leave the headline until the end, as an afterthought. That's a huge mistake, and here's why: you can have the greatest product in the world with the greatest sales copy, but if your headline is junk, you won't sell much, if anything at all.

On the flip side, if you have an amazing headline that stops your ideal prospect dead in their tracks, pre-frames them perfectly, and sets the stage for your product like a message sent from heaven above, your sales copy can basically suck and you'll still make a *ton* more sales than you will with a bad headline.

Why? The reason is really simple: a better headline gets more people to stop and read your sales message. It's like a batter in baseball. The more times you get up to bat, the more hits you can make. Your batting average might stink, but if you swing the bat enough, you'll connect sooner or later.

You can be the best batter in the world, but if you don't get up to the batter's box (i.e., you have a crappy headline), you'll never get to take a swing at the ball. With a great headline, you can be a hack and still outperform every player who never gets off the bench. A bad headline means you *never* get off the bench. A good headline means you always get off the bench, even if you're the worst player on the team!

A lot of people have the wrong idea about headlines. They think headlines sell. They don't. The number one purpose of a headline is to hook the right people to stop what they're doing, pre-frame them for your story or sales message, and get them to the next step in your sales copy.

- **In an ad**, that means a good headline gets them to stop, read the ad, and click over to your funnel landing page.

- **On the actual funnel page**, a good headline stops people in their tracks, arouses their curiosity and desire to learn more, and gets them to move on to the next step in your sales copy (like watching your sales video or reading the first few paragraphs of your sales letter).

- **In an email**, a good headline is the subject line that gets them to open the email.

- **In a video,** a good headline is the first sentence out of your mouth that gets people excited and curious enough to stick around to hear the next sentence.

No matter where you use a headline, its job is *not* to sell! The job of the headline is to hook the right target audience members to *stop* what they're doing, arouse curiosity, and then seamlessly move them to the next step. Curiosity is the key!

Question headlines: A fast way to create curiosity is to ask a question about something your target audience really desires to have or really wants to avoid. Here are some simple question headlines for using curiosity to grab their attention.

- What If You Could (Desire) Without (Pain)?
- Worried About (Pain)?
- Isn't It Time You Stopped Struggling with (Pain)?
- Sick and Tired of Not Having Any (Desire)?
- Are You Getting Enough (Desire)?
- Do You Want to Be a Successful (Target Audience)?
- Isn't It Time You Got the (Desire) You Really Want?

Now let's talk about why headlines matter so much in ads, especially in a competitive marketplace. If you can get twice as many people to click on an ad with one headline as opposed to another, that means you will, at a minimum, double your revenue. How is that possible? Basic math, my friend! Two times the number of readers clicking over to your funnel from the ad equals two times the number of sales.

Also, if you can get twice as many people from an ad to click over and read the sales copy on your funnel, you have just cut your traffic expenses in *half*! If you spend $1,000 to get 500 people to read your sales copy, you're paying $2 a person. Double the number of people who click over to read (2 x 500 = 1,000 viewers for the same $1,000. Your traffic cost just dropped to $1 per person).

But here's where it really kicks in. Let's say you're selling a product for $1,000. For every sale you make, let's say you're spending $900 in ads. That means for every $900 you spend, you *net* $100 in profit ($1,000 revenue - $900 ads = $100 profit).

If you double the number of people who click on your ad, that means you doubled revenue to $2,000 (2X the people = 2X the revenue), *but* your ad spend didn't go up. That means instead of $100 profit you made $1,100 profit ($2,000 revenue - $900 in ads = $1,100 in profit). By doubling the clicks on your ad, you did *not* double your profit—you increased profit by more than 10 times!

That is the power of the right headline. That is the power of testing headlines. The key is you don't know what the right headline is until you've tested a bunch to find the winner. In order to come up with a bunch of good headlines fast, you need to use scripts. Creating headlines on your own is like stumbling around in a gold mine with no flashlight. You know there's gold there, but you can't see it, and you could spend your entire lifetime wandering around in the dark just inches from gold and never find it.

Headline scripts are the flashlight in the gold mine. They are the key to cashing in with your funnels as fast as possible.

Headlines come in many shapes, sizes, and flavors. Everyone has an opinion about how long they should be, how they should be phrased, whether they should be in "quotes" or not, even what color they should be! The best advice I can give you besides modeling proven templates and scripts is to know the audience you're targeting with your headlines.

Russell talked earlier about traffic temperature by giving credit for the original idea to Eugene Schwartz. Hot traffic knows who you are and about your products. Warm traffic knows there's a solution out there somewhere, but they don't know about you yet. Cold traffic just knows they have a problem.

Figure 18.2:

You should create separate landing pages to match the temperature of your traffic.

As a general rule, you should *never* send all these types of traffic to the same landing page in your funnel. They each need their own headline at the proper temperature, at a minimum, to start the sales conversation off on the right foot.

Hot traffic headlines: Typically, this means you can mention your name and your product name in a hot headline. For example:

- Finally! Discover How (Product/Service Name) Gives You the Secret to (Big Result) . . . Without (Pain) . . . Today!

- (Product/Service Name) Is the Secret to Automatically (Big Result)! . . . Guaranteed!

- Watch This Free Video to Learn How (Product/Service Name) Gives You an Unfair Advantage with (Main Topic) . . . Guaranteed!

- It's True! You Too Can (Big Result) in (Specific Timeframe) with (Product/Service Name) . . . Guaranteed!

- (Big Result) with (Product/Service Name) . . . Guaranteed!

Warm traffic headlines: In a warm headline, you talk about the payoff or benefit they're seeking:

- See How Easily You Can (Big Result) Without (Pain)!
- For (Target Audience) Who Want to (Big Result) but Can't Get Started!
- The Secret to Automatically (Big Result) Without (Pain)!
- Here's a Quick Way to (Big Result) . . . Guaranteed!
- How (Target Audience) Just Like You (Big Result) in Just (Specific Time Frame)!
- The TRUTH About How to (Big Result) and Avoid (Pain)

Cold traffic headlines: In a cold headline, you would typically use their problem to hook them:

- Don't Let (Pain) Stop You!
- You Can Laugh at (Main Topic) Problems If You Follow This Plan
- How (Target Audience) Can STOP (Pain)
- When Pro (Target Audience) Have (Main Topic) Problems, Here's What They Do
- How to Eliminate (Pain) from Your Life . . . Guaranteed!

"Hot, warm, and cold" is a good starting point, but do *not* think of this temperature system as a hard-and-fast rule you should apply like the Ten Commandments (which don't have any exceptions to the rules as far as I know). Remember, the purpose of a headline is to grab the attention of the right people (your hook), get them to stop what they're doing, create curiosity to find out more, and pre-frame them for what's coming next (the rest of your sales copy/story). In the end, people buy to satisfy a desire or solve a problem (preferably with a high emotional punch behind it), and 99 times out of 100, the headline is what starts the buying conversation.

Curiosity headlines: Sometimes a good old-fashioned curiosity-generating headline like these can form the basis of an amazing headline that paves the way for that one funnel to change your life and business forever. Sometimes their biggest problem is they don't have what they desire . . . and if your headline hooks them with a promise of a big payoff, you've got a winner.

- You Can Laugh at (Main Topic) Worries—If You Follow This Simple Plan

- Imagine (Desire) in Just 30 Minutes

- You May Be Sabotaging Your (Main Topic) Success . . . and You Don't Even Know It

- Don't Even Think about (Desire) Without Reading This!

- Here's What (Enemy) Doesn't Want You to Know about (Main Topic)

In fact, here are three great areas to focus on when it comes to headlines—no matter what the traffic temperature—if you want to amp up the emotional punch behind them.

1. A clear desire they want to satisfy

2. A pressing problem they really want to solve

3. A nagging or intense pain they want to avoid or eliminate

A final word of *caution*: In the end, the only opinion about your headline that matters is the opinion of the person with a credit card in their hand who decides whether to spend money with you based on your sales copy. Let me share a story with you that perfectly illustrates this point.

Back in the early 2000s, I published a CD called *Five Steps to Getting Anything You Want*. It was a two-CD set that explained a practical system I figured out for manifesting anything you could imagine, whether it was physical, spiritual, or financial. We poured our heart into the product (long before the days of MP3 players), including a significant amount of studio time and recording fees. I had a lot tied up in this product financially and emotionally. I felt like I was sharing a part of my soul with people.

Soon the launch day came and I thought I was ready. I'd written my sales copy, gotten my testimonials lined up, and made a great case for why people should buy. I had a lot riding on this launch. This was where I'd prove I had my act together and belonged in the "big leagues" of online marketing. (No pressure, right?)

I sent my carefully crafted email to entice my subscribers to the sales page. I was almost dizzy with anticipation of the lives I'd change with this amazing product. I saw the traffic start to show up to the landing page and kept hitting Refresh on my shopping cart page, ready to see the mountains of cash that were surely just minutes away.

One hundred visitors came . . . no sales.

Two hundred visitors . . . no sales . . . What the heck?! (I double-checked the cart and everything was working.)

Three hundred visitors . . . no sales . . . My list wasn't that big. The traffic was going to run out. I thought, *My online career is over! This stuff doesn't work! I'm gonna have to go get a job!*

I took a deep breath . . .

I asked myself a question: "What would a great marketer or copywriter do?" Great question, apparently, because I instantly got an answer that saved me that day and taught me a principle that has made me more money than anything else I've ever done. The answer I got was simple: "A great marketer or copywriter would test a different headline . . . *now!*"

My original headline was "How I Went from Trailer Trash to Piles of Cash," which I thought was an amazing headline. (Turns out I was the only one who liked it! By the way, there's a lesson here. In my experience, every headline I fall in love with rarely works. The headlines I use that do the best *always* speak *to* the target audience on an emotional level about something *they* care about . . . which is *not* me.)

So I tried another headline really fast. I can't remember exactly what it was, but what I do remember is that within about three to four minutes, I got a sale. (Woo-hoo!) At that point, a lot of people would just stop. They'd say, "You know what? I got a sale. Problem solved. Let me move on with my day. I guess this just isn't a great offer and this is the best it's ever going to do."

Not me. I thought, *Hey, maybe I can do even better.* So I modeled a headline I knew worked from another site. I knew that headline worked because I'd recently spent money on the site. (Great lesson, by the way. If sales copy gets you to spend money, it's good copy and worth paying attention to and studying.) This particular headline was "How to Gain a Positively Unfair Advantage in the Search Engine Wars." I modeled that headline and turned it into "How to Gain a Positively Unfair Advantage in Business and in Life!"

I changed nothing else in the funnel except the headline. Within five minutes of making that change, I made five sales. A 500 percent increase over the second headline and an infinite increase over the first headline that made *no* sales.

Why the big change in sales because of this headline? Two big reasons:

- The two new headlines were about *them* (the reader), not about me.

- The last headline created curiosity in a unique way for each person who saw it (each person has their own idea of what an "unfair advantage" would be for them in their lives).

The big lesson here: make the headline about them and use proven templates or "scripts" to shortcut the process when creating headlines (or any other pieces of sales copy).

I could have stumbled around in the dark for weeks or months trying to come up with that headline on my own. But when I used a proven script, I came up with a viable headline in less than a minute.

"WHO, WHAT, WHY, HOW" SCRIPT

Figure 19.1:

For more information on where to use this script, see Secret #8:
Lead "Squeeze" Funnels, Secret #11: Book Funnels, Secret #12: Cart Funnels,
Secret #15: Webinar Funnels, and Secret #16: Product Launch Funnels.

The "Who, What, Why, How" script is simple and easy to remember because of its name, and it's one that you will use all the time. I still use this almost daily for my ads (both video and text) to get people to click into my funnels, on landing pages to get people to join my list or register for my webinars, and on my book and cart funnels to sell low-ticket products. Let me walk you through how to use this script.

SCRIPT STRUCTURE

This script answers four basic questions and then moves into a fast CTA.

Question #1: Who are you? This script is usually used at the front of your value ladder with colder traffic. For the majority of people who watch this video or read this text, this will likely be the first time they have ever seen you, so you want to quickly introduce yourself.

> *Hi, I'm Russell Brunson, and I'm one of the cofounders of ClickFunnels.*

Question #2: What do you have? Here is where you will quickly hook them and introduce them to your offer.

> *In the past five years, over 100,000 entrepreneurs have ditched their websites for a funnel, and I want to give you a free two-week trial to ClickFunnels today so you can create your first funnel for FREE!*

Question #3: Why do they need it? This is where you help them to understand why they need to get your offer. There is an old copywriting formula called PAS: Problem, Agitate, Solve that I often use inside this question. I raise the problem using the same words they would use to describe it and agitate it by twisting the knife, and then our offer becomes the solution.

> **Problem:** *I know that your website isn't generating the number of leads you want, and it's not really making any sales either.*

> **Agitate:** *Most people spend thousands of dollars to get a website that ends up being nothing more than a glorified brochure that doesn't actually do anything.*

> **Solve:** *That's why I want you to get your free two-week trial to ClickFunnels so you can build a funnel that will generate*

leads for your business and actually sell your products . . . and you won't have to spend thousands of dollars. In fact, I'll let you try it out for FREE so you can get your funnel live and generating leads for you before you pay your first penny!

Question #4: How can they get this offer? Tell them exactly what they need to do to get access to the offer you just made them.

Just click on the link below, or go to ClickFunnels.com to start your free trial today!

That is the core part of the "Who, What, Why, How" script. I showed you how we use it for a free trial, but the same process works if you're offering a free teeth cleaning, a free report, or a free webinar you want them to register for.

To amplify this script, I will often add these other four elements to help increase conversions.

The catch: Tell them why you're presenting this offer for such a great deal. People always think there's a catch. So instead of avoiding the topic, let them know what the catch is, if there is one, or that there is no catch.

You may be wondering why I would give you a free trial. The reason is because I know that after your first funnel is live and generating leads for you at a fraction of the cost you've ever experienced before, you're never going to want to leave, and I'll have you as a customer for life.

Urgency and scarcity: What are the real elements of urgency and scarcity that you can weave into this offer?

This week we are also going to be giving anyone who gets a trial, 10 of our favorite lead funnel templates. These templates are proven to convert visitors into leads, and you'll get them for free if you sign up before Friday at midnight. After that, you can still get your trial account, but you won't get the free funnel templates.

Guarantee: Reverse any risk in ordering the product.

If for some reason you decide that you don't love ClickFunnels as much as the other 100,000 entrepreneurs who use it daily, just let us know and we'll cancel your account with no hassle. In fact, you can just log in to your account and click a button to cancel and never talk to anyone ever! You only stay a member if you love it!

Recap: Remind them what they are getting and why.

So don't forget, go to ClickFunnels.com or click on the link below to get your free 14-day trial to ClickFunnels. And if you create your account before Friday at midnight, you will also get 10 lead funnel templates for FREE!

Unboxing Funnel Scripts

"STAR, STORY, SOLUTION" SCRIPT

Figure 20.1:

**For more information on where to use this script,
see Secret #14: Video Sales Letter Funnels.**

I didn't invent the concept of the "Star, Story, Solution" script. I first heard it when I was interviewing Vince James, a guy who had made $100 million in 23 months selling supplements.[18] He documented his journey in one of my favorite books, *The 12-Month Millionaire*.

During his interview, he told me that there was a script he had learned and used to sell all his products. The script formula was so simple! First, you need a star (I call this person the Attractive Character), then you need a story that agitates a problem, and finally you need to provide a solution (your offer).

I thought it was a powerful format, but it took me almost 10 years to figure out how to frame each section of the script. After I figured out how to lead a prospect through each section, I was able to build out a framework that my companies (as well as hundreds of our clients) use again and again. It works great for both text and video sales letters. In video format, this script is usually about 20–30 minutes long and is typically used to sell products that are low ticket but need a longer presentation to explain the product or to break a false belief pattern before they see the offer. We use it to sell low-ticket products up to about the $100 price range.

As with all the scripts I'll share with you, it is a framework and shouldn't be used word for word. Weave in your Attractive Character, your stories, and your offers to make this script come to life. Let's go through the scripts for all three sections: star, story, and solution.

SECTION 1: STAR

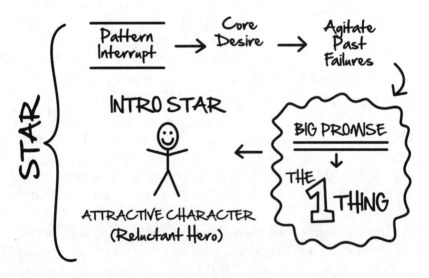

Figure 20.2:

The first part of this script will introduce the Attractive Character as the star.

Pattern interrupt or hook: This is usually the first thing prospects see. It's important to grab their attention, get them out of their current environment or activity, and pull them into your sales copy/story. Often, my hook here is modeled after my curiosity-based headline that I created for the presentation. I will lead with that hook as the pattern interrupt making a big promise for what they will learn during the presentation. I open the loop and then I move on.

> *During this presentation, I'm going to show you my weird niche funnel that is currently making me $17,947 per day and how you can ethically knock it off in less than 10 minutes. But first, I have a few questions for you . . .*

Core-desire questions: Now that I have their attention, I want to ask them questions about their core desires. These questions move the brain to the topic you want to discuss, which is the outcome or results they wish they could achieve. Here's an example of core-desire questions I might ask if I were selling something teaching people how they could work from home:

> *Have you ever wanted to work from home? Own your own business?*

> *Come on, you know you want that lifestyle . . . the one that everyone talks about . . .*

> *Where you can work from home in your underwear or on a beach with your laptop . . .*

Do you see how those questions get them saying yes in their head as they think about the core desires they have that relate back to your product or service?

Agitate past failures: If prospects are taking the time to read your sales letter, chances are pretty good that this isn't the first time they've tried to solve this problem. We want to raise the problem, then twist the knife to agitate it even more.

> *So, why hasn't it happened for you yet? Come on, admit it.*

This isn't the first time you've been looking for a proven way to make money, is it?

When is it your turn?

or

This isn't the first time you've been looking for a proven way to lose weight, is it?

Why didn't it work last time?

Every person that buys your product or service is doing it because they are trying to meet one of their core desires. When you know what these desires are, it's easy to plug them into this script.

Big promise/the One Thing: Here's where you introduce your big promise, the One Thing that if you were to solve for them, they would pay you anything to help them solve this problem. What is your big promise that you can deliver on?

Well, by the time you finish this video, that will change forever. I'm going to reveal to you [your big promise here]!

Introduce the star: Right after you introduce your big promise, you get to introduce the star of the story, the Attractive Character. After you introduce the Attractive Character, you transition to the second section of the script, where you tell that person's story.

SECTION 2: STORY

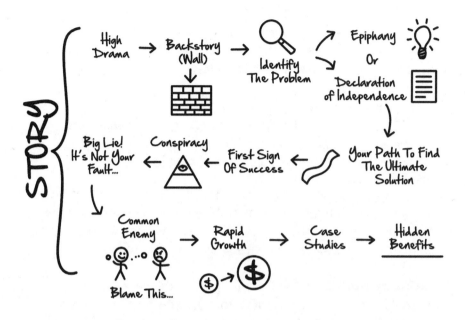

Figure 20.3:

The second part of this script will tell a story that agitates the prospect's problem.

Now it's time to move on to the second section of the sales letter, your Attractive Character's story. If you've already written your Soap Opera Sequence, this section will seem very familiar.

High drama: Whenever you're telling a story, you want to start at the point of high drama. Frequently, the beginning of the story is the most boring part, so instead, figure out the peak of high drama and start the story there. After you get their interest in the story, then you can go back and fill in the details of how you got there with the backstory.

> *I crawled out from under my desk, almost hitting my head as I grabbed the phone.*
> *"Hello," I muttered.*

"WHAT THE #@%$ ARE YOU DOING!?" responded the stranger on the other line.

Confused, I asked him what he was talking about.

"In the past six hours, we have received over thirty spam complaints from YOUR IP address. Russell, you're a SPAMMER, and we're shutting off your internet access."

"What?!"

I was so confused.

I got a lump in my stomach as I hung up the phone and realized that I now had to explain to my new wife of just six weeks that I'm the reason our internet is shut off.

Do you see how that story pulls you in? Now you're interested in who I was talking to and why they were calling me a spammer. And since I have your attention, I can go back and spend much more time on the backstory without losing your interest.

Backstory (wall): Next you want to fill in the backstory that led up to the point of high drama. How did you, or your Attractive Character, get there? It's important that the featured character eventually hit a wall, a point where he was completely stuck. This, by the way, is where your prospects probably are right now. They have likely tried to make money online or lose weight or get whatever result you're promising, but they can't seem to get the result they want. It feels hopeless.

You see, just six hours earlier, I had "officially" started my new business as an email marketer.

Or so I thought . . .

I had been trying to learn online marketing for almost a year, and I kept hearing people talk about how the MOST IMPORTANT thing you can have is:

Your own email list.

It made total sense to me.

I did the math. If I had one million people on my email list, and I was selling a $50 product, then I ONLY had to get one percent of them to buy in order to make $500,000.

(1% of 1,000,000 was 10,000 people x $50 = $500,000)
It made total sense . . . right?
And I saw others doing it. All I needed was an email list.
I just had no idea how to get one . . .

This backstory starts to explain why I was getting yelled at on the call. I would keep telling the story all the way up to where I hit the point of high drama, and then I would move to the next step in the script where I finally was able to identify the problem.

Identify the problem: Now reveal the problem you faced. Let them know why your Attractive Character was stuck (which is also probably the reason they are currently stuck). In fact, the more closely you can relate your Attractive Character's problem to the readers' problems, the better.

After going through that experience, I realized the problem I had wasn't _____, but it was actually _____.

Epiphany, or Declaration of Independence: Once the Attractive Character pinpoints the problem, it's usually not long before they have an epiphany or decide to make a major change in their behavior or mindset. For example, your Attractive Character might have an epiphany that to make money online, he has to build a list. Or in order to lose weight, he has to change his eating behavior once and for all.

Epiphany example: *As I was sitting there trying to figure out what to do, I had an idea . . .*

Declaration of Independence example: *I knew the answer, but I didn't want to do it. But right then, I decided that I HAD to make a change, so this is what I did . . .*

Your path to finding the ultimate solution: Take the reader along your journey. Describe some of the different things you, or your Attractive Character, tried before you found success. These will likely be similar things that they have tried, or are currently trying, to get the same results that you're promising in this story.

The first thing I tried was _____, but the problem I found was _____. So then I tried _____, but nothing seemed to really work, until . . .

First sign of success: This is where they get the first glimpse of success in your journey as well as a glimpse at what you ultimately discovered.

And that's when I finally tried _____. And guess what? This time it worked!

Conspiracy: Show them how you finally realized that the cards were stacked against you from the start. Your prospects are probably convinced that the cards are currently stacked against them. Because they believe it, you need to address this fear through the Attractive Character's story.

And that's when I realized it wasn't my fault! All these years of failure, and it was actually because of _____. No wonder I was struggling!

The big lie: Explain why it's not their fault that they haven't succeeded before now.

For years, they had been telling me _____, and when I figured out that it wasn't true, I was finally able to break out of their chains and get the results I deserved.

Common enemy: This is who or what is really to blame for the big lie that was holding the star back and blocking their success.

The real problem is _____. They were the ones keeping me and you from _____.

Rapid growth: Now show them how fast the Attractive Character progressed once they realized the truth.

Once I realized _____, that's when we started to _____ really FAST!

Case studies: Highlight the stories of others who've had success similar to your or the Attractive Character's story.

> *But it wasn't just me. Take a look at what _____ has done for others.*

Hidden benefits: Explain the benefits you didn't expect that have resulted from the product/discovery you are describing to the reader.

> *I didn't realize when I started that not only does it _____, but it also _____ and _____.*

SECTION 3: SOLUTION

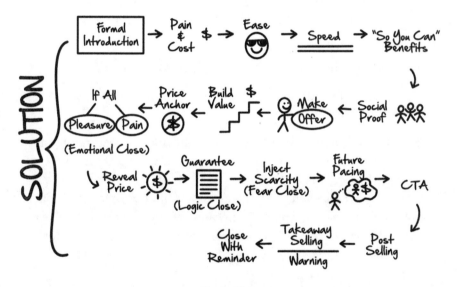

Figure 20.4:

The third part of this script will introduce your product
as the solution to the prospect's problem.

Now it's time to bring it all together and wrap up your pitch in a nice, neat package (that the readers can buy).

Formal introduction: Introduce the offer.

And that's why I created _____.

Pain and cost: Tell them what you had to go through to create the product.

This took _____ [time] to create, and cost me _____. But it was totally worth it because now you can use it without going through the same pain I did or spending what I did for this solution!

Ease: Share the contrast between the pain and cost you had to go through, and then the ease that they'll be able to go through to get the same results because you blazed this trail for them.

Because I went through all the pain to create this offer, you don't have to go through any of that pain! It will be so much easier for you!

Speed: How much time does the product save you?

What used to take me _____ [time], I can get done in _____ [time].

"So you can" benefits: Here you will talk about a feature of your product, followed by the phrase "so you can," and then you will explain the benefits of that feature. So many people sell the features of their product, but the reality is that people don't buy based on the feature, they buy because of the benefit of that feature. Adding the phrase "so you can" after each feature will force you to realize and explain the benefits they get from that feature.

Burns fat while you sleep **so you can** *lose weight without exercising.*

Builds your email list on autopilot **so you can** *concentrate on running your business.*

Social proof: This is where you show them that it isn't just you who has had success with this offer, but that you've been able to successfully use it with other people as well.

But don't just take my word for it. Here's what other people who are just like you are saying after they tried it.

Make the offer and build value: Explain everything that they will get inside of this offer. I would recommend using the Stack Slide from the "Perfect Webinar" script in Secret #22. This is the best way to present the offer.

Secret 20.5:

For more information on this Stack and Close section, read Secret #22.

Price anchor: Explain the total value of the offer. It should be at least 10 times higher than the actual price. If it's not, then you need to add more things to your offer.

The total value of everything you get inside of this offer is $_____.

Emotional close (If all): I want to make sure that people believe that the offer is actually worth the value I just shared with them, and we do that by using "If all" statements. I ask them: "If all this did was _____, would it be worth the full asking price? I get them to say yes, and they've subconsciously agreed that the offer is worth the full asking price.

If all this did was give you the house of your dreams, would it be worth it?

If all this did was let you fire your boss, would it be worth it?

Reveal the real price: Here is where we do the price drop and give them a reason why you are dropping the price.

I'm not going to charge you the $_____ that this is worth.

I'm not even going to charge you the $_____ that you were probably thinking.

Because you are here today, I'm going to give you a very special price of just $_____.

Guarantee (logic): Now that they know the price, we want to take away any risk they may have if they purchase. We make them a guarantee that speaks to their logical mind.

I want to make sure that this offer will actually work for you, so I'm going to put my money where my mouth is. I'm going to give you a full 30-day money back guarantee. If for any reason you aren't happy with the results, just let me know and I'll give you 100 percent of your money back.

Inject urgency and scarcity (fear close): Give the buyers a legitimate reason to buy *now*.

But you must act now because _____.

Future pacing: Help them see how awesome their lives are about to become—after they buy your product.

Just imagine what life will be like after you start getting these results . . .

Call to action: Tell them what to do to make a purchase. Also, tell them what's going to happen next.

So click on the button below right now and you'll be taken to a secure order form. After you put in your credit card information, you'll be taken to a secure members' area where you can download _____, even if it's 2:00 A.M.!

Post-selling: Make the readers feel like they might be left behind if they don't hurry.

For those who are already signing up, this is what's going to happen next . . . As soon as you submit your order, you'll be taken to a page where you can create your account. When you get to the member's area, the first thing you should do is . . .

Takeaway selling (warning): Explain that they need to make a decision, and it doesn't matter to you whether they order or not.

You see, it doesn't matter to us if you sign up right now or not.

We'll still be going about our daily business and hitting our financial goals with absolute certainty—whether you join our team or not.

However, without our help, you'll ALWAYS be working harder than you really need to.

I know it sounds kind of harsh, but I think you'll agree that it's true.

Close with reminder: This is a summary for the skimmers, but it can remind all readers of the offer.

Remember, when you get started today, you will get _____ [restack the offer].

"OTO" SCRIPT

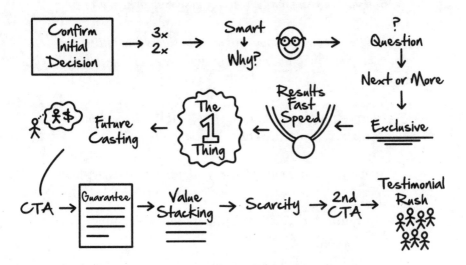

Figure 21.1:

You can use this script on any one-time offer. For more information on how to use this script, see Secret #11: Book Funnels.

In the past, I made a huge mistake with my "One Time Offer" (OTO) sales videos and I always had really low conversion rates. I assumed that I needed to go through a full "Star, Story, Solution" script again to get someone to buy my upsell, so each of my upsell videos was 20–30 minutes long, telling a new story and trying to get them to buy my next offer.

One day, one of my friends, Tim Erway, bought one of my products. He went through the funnel and messaged me on Facebook.

"How's your funnel converting?" he asked. A few seconds later, he said, "The upsell's not converting, is it?"

"How did you know?" I asked.

"Ha ha, I knew it! It's because you made the cardinal upsell mistake. You tried to resell the prospect on why they needed to buy from you. They're already sold on you; they already said the first yes. You just need to convince them to say yes again. It's a much simpler script."

He then showed me a few of his upsells, and I saw my mistake. I immediately went back to over a dozen funnels and reworked all the upsell videos with this new OTO script and my conversions went from almost nonexistent to double digits over night!

This script focuses on confirming the initial purchase decision and quickly convincing them to say the second yes for the next offer that will help them to better achieve the result they were looking for. This offer will be different depending on what type of product you sold on the front end. If you sold them an information product on the front end, then this upsell is likely your next product that helps solve the next problem they will encounter now that they have your first product.

For instance, if I sell you a book on how to create funnels, now that you know you need funnels in your business, the next logical offer could be funnel software, or a training course on how to get traffic into your new funnels. If you're selling physical products, then it's probably more of the same product at a discount as explained in the Cart Funnels chapter.

Usually this OTO video is only three to five minutes long, yet it will close people on price points from $27–$997 or more.

SCRIPT STRUCTURE

Confirm initial decision: It's important to put any possible buyer's remorse to rest by reinforcing the decision to purchase the initial offer. It's also important to make sure you keep an "open loop" at this stage. We used to say things like, "Congratulations, your order is complete," before we made the upsell offer, but this language closed the sales loop. The prospect's brain was thinking, *I'm finished*, and it was hard to get that second conversion.

But once we changed that language to, "Wait! Your order is not yet complete," the sales loop remained open, and our conversions went up. Why? Because subconsciously the reader was still open to being sold on something else.

> *Congratulations on purchasing _____! Don't close your browser yet because your order is not quite finished.*

Smart → why: Tell the buyer they've made a great decision by making the first purchase and why.

> *You've made a smart choice, and here's why . . .*

or

> *You ordered this because you wanted _____, and that's exactly what it's going to do for you.*

Question (Next or more): Based on the type of product, ask them a question about the next offer, or ask them if they want more at a discount.

> **Information products:** *Let me ask you a question. Now that you have _____, many people ask me about _____.*

or

> **Physical products:** *Let me ask you a question. How would you like to get more _____ at a huge discount?*

Exclusive: Explain why this OTO is not for everyone.

> *This offer is NOT for everyone. We're only making it available to you because you proved you're an action-taker when you took advantage of _____ [initial offer]. So I'm going to make you a special one-time offer that's only available right here, right now.*

Results, fast, speed: Explain that this OTO will complement the original purchase by delivering better results, faster.

> *What I'm going to share with you right now will help you to _____ [the results the customer is wanting] in a fraction of the time.*

The One Thing: Here you need to find the One Thing in your product that is the key to the buyer's success. This part is often tricky because it is tempting to explain everything about the offer. But if you do that, you will kill the sale. You need to figure out the One Thing that is the *most* valuable and will yield the best results. For example, in my OTO selling my "Perfect Webinar" system, I have over 24 hours of videos. But instead of telling the buyers everything they will learn, I focus on one thing: a special video where I teach the Stack. I explain what it is, how much money it has made me, my results, and what type of results the buyer can expect from this One Thing.

> *I have another product called _____. I don't have time to go over everything inside of the product because we could be here for hours, but one of the strategies inside that will give you the results you're looking for FAST is _____. Let me explain to you what it is and how it can help you. [Explanation.] And that is just ONE of the things that you'll learn with this product. I wish I had time to explain everything else!*

Future pacing: Help the buyer imagine achieving goals faster and with greater ease.

> *Can you imagine what your life will be like when you have _____ [the One Thing]?*

Call to action (CTA): Tell the buyer how to order the special offer.

> *So click the button below right now to add _____ to your order.*

Guarantee: Offer a guarantee to help reverse the risk and make them feel more comfortable adding this to their order.

Value stacking: I like to try to use the word FREE as many times as possible in my upsell videos and on the page. I start looking at all the other things inside the offer and I quickly tell them about each cool thing they are getting, and how they get it for free when they act now.

If you act now, you'll also receive _____ (worth $_____) for FREE.

And _____ (worth $_____) for FREE . . .

And _____ (worth $_____) for FREE . . .

Scarcity: Give them a reason to order right now! Make this a truly one-time offer.

This _____ [product name] is available on my website for _____ [higher price]. But right now, you have this ONE CHANCE to get it for only _____. This one-time offer is only available right here, right now. When you leave this page, it's gone forever.

Second CTA: Repeat your call to action.

Now is the time to get started, so click on the button down below to add this to your order now.

Testimonial rush: Add in testimonials about your product—more is better.

If you're still here trying to decide if this is right for you or not, I'll show you a few videos from others who were just like you, trying to decide if they should take this offer, and they took the leap of faith, got started, and saw success. I want you to hear what they said in their own words.

Presentation
Funnel Scripts

"PERFECT WEBINAR" SCRIPT

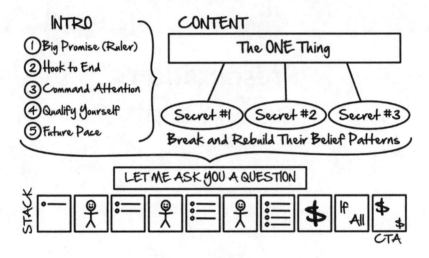

Figure 22.1:

For more information on where to use this script, see the Presentation Funnels introduction chapter as well as Secret #14: Video Sales Letter Funnels, Secret #15: Webinar Funnels, and Secret #16: Product Launch Funnels.

Whenever you are doing a webinar or an automated webinar, the script you should use is what we call the "Perfect Webinar" script. *Expert Secrets* goes deep into the psychology of this script as it's the one that I use most often. I use it when I sell from stage, and I use it in webinars, video sales letters, product launch video sequences, email sequences and more. In fact, recently one of my Inner Circle members, Jaime Cross, adapted this script for her physical product brands and created the "Five-Minute Perfect Webinar" script for short-form sales videos and video ads (this version of the script is in the FunnelScripts.com software as well as the new edition of *Expert Secrets*). This script, of all the scripts, is my favorite.

If you break this script into a 90-minute presentation, you'll typically spend the following amount of time on each section:

- 15 minutes: Introduction
- 45 minutes: Content
- 30 minutes: The Stack and Close

You can compress the time to 60 minutes, five minutes, etc., but the ratios of time will stay about the same.

Over the past 10 years, I've had the opportunity to speak and sell on stages all around the world, and I've learned from some of the best stage closers in the world. This script incorporates strategies I learned from at least a dozen different people.

There are a lot of pieces to this script, but try not to get overwhelmed. Think of it as just three sections (introduction, the content, and the Stack and Close), then fill these three sections in with the scripts provided.

INTRODUCTION

When people first log in to the webinar or start watching your presentation, you need to hook them fast and get their attention. This first section of the script is designed to do just that.

INTRO

1. Big Promise (Ruler)
2. Hook to End
3. Command Attention
4. Qualify Yourself
5. Future Pace

Figure 22.2:

The first part of this script hooks your viewers and sets the stage of what's to come.

1) Big promise: Share your big promise. This is the One Thing that got the participants to sign up in the first place. It's also the ruler they will use to judge your webinar's quality. If you don't set this ruler, then they will measure the value of your webinar based on something outside of your control. What is the big domino you need to knock over for them in the next 60 minutes?

> *Hi, I'm Russell Brunson, founder of ClickFunnels, and in the next 60 minutes, you are going to learn my exact strategy on "how to _____ without _____."*

2) Hook to end: Give the participants a reason to stick around all the way to the end of the webinar. Free giveaways are popular. You could also promise to do something funny or show them something cool.

> *Don't forget! At the end of the webinar, I'm going to give you a secret link where you can download a transcript of everything I'm going to show you today. You have to be watching live in order to get this, so stick around. I promise it will be worth your time.*

3) Command attention: Tell them to close out of Facebook, turn off their cell phones, and give you their undivided attention. Also, you might ask the participants to grab a pen and paper for taking notes.

I know there are distractions all around us, but this strategy I'm about to share can change your life. I don't want you to miss a single crucial step. So please, make a commitment to stay focused. Can you do that for yourself? Close out of Facebook. Stop checking your email. Turn off your cell phone. Give me your complete attention.

4) Qualify yourself: Let the participants know why you are qualified to speak on the subject.

You're probably wondering why I'm qualified to teach on this topic. Here's my story: _____.

5) Future pace: Lead the viewers through some imagination exercises where they can picture what life could be like once they learn the secrets you're about to reveal. Be descriptive and appeal to all five senses, if possible.

Imagine what your life will be like after you know how to _____. Can you see _____? Would that make things better for you?

CONTENT

This is the majority of the webinar. It should run about 45 minutes and deliver on the big promise that you made to them earlier. Your goal isn't to teach them everything; it's to help them break their false beliefs around the topic that you're teaching so they will be willing to let you help them to solve this problem in their lives.

Generally, this part will teach them the "what" but not the "how," so the content of the presentation is focused around the "what": your unique system, process, or framework. In *Expert*

Secrets, we call this the "vehicle." For my business, my vehicle is funnels. Through funnels, people can achieve success in their business. Later, during the Stack and Close, you'll introduce your product or service, which gives them the "how" to do it (the step-by-step tactics to implement it into their lives).

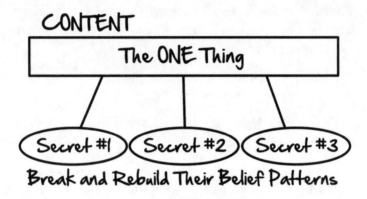

Figure 22.3:

The second part of this script delivers on the big promise you made in the introduction.

The One Thing: My whole presentation revolves around the *One Thing* that I want them to understand. For my webinar teaching people about funnels, the One Thing I need them to believe is:

Funnels are the number one way to growing their company.

If I can get them to believe that, the big domino will fall, and they'll have to give me money. So during the first part of my presentation I'm telling my *own personal origin story* that will show why I believe that my system, process, or framework is the secret to change their lives.

Recently I did a presentation to sell my High-Ticket Secrets course and this was the headline for the presentation; it was also the One Thing that I needed them to believe, and it was the big domino for the presentation.

How to add high-ticket sales to your sales funnel instantly— without you personally talking to anyone on the phone . . . ever!

For this offer, I looked at what the other "gurus" were teaching about making high-ticket sales. They were all teaching how to close people on the phone. Well, I *hate* talking on the phone, and I think most of my audience does too. So I decided to show people how they can still take advantage of high-ticket sales *without* talking on the phone. I need them to believe that it is possible, and if they do, they will buy my program showing them how to do it.

During this first section of my presentation, I presented this idea, and I told my origin story about how I discovered it was true for me. At this point in your presentation, after you tell your own personal origin story, there will be many people who are ready to buy.

Three Secrets: After I tell my origin story and why I believe this vehicle is the right one for them to achieve their goals, I need to look at what would hold them back from actually buying. They usually have false beliefs about one (or more) of the three things below:

- **The vehicle:** False beliefs about the vehicle you are presenting them
- **Internal beliefs:** False beliefs about themselves
- **External beliefs:** False beliefs about things outside of their control

After I explain this big idea (the One Thing), I share three secrets that will break the three false beliefs I listed above.

For my High-Ticket Secrets webinar, there were three belief patterns that I had to break in order to get people to buy. Below are the common false beliefs and the secrets I created to destroy that line of thinking.

- **Secret #1: False belief about the vehicle**

  Break false belief:

  The best model for making money online is to sell information products or e-commerce products.

  Rebuild new belief:

  You can make more money in one day selling high-ticket products than you can in a MONTH by selling normal products.

- **Secret #2: False internal belief**

  Break false belief:

  To sell high-ticket products, I have to sell on the phone.

  Rebuild new belief:

  You don't personally have to sell anything! (Big plus because I hate phones!) Let me show you how to build a two-person mini call center to close all the sales for you.

- **Secret #3: False external belief**

  Break false belief:

  It probably costs a fortune to drive enough traffic to make this work.

  Rebuild new belief:

  You only need a little bit of traffic to make this work (about 100 clicks a day).

For each of these secrets, I'm using stories to break and rebuild their false belief patterns. I tell them the story about how I used to believe what they believe, but because of some experience, I now know there is a different, better way. When you tell them that story, they will have the same epiphany that you had, and their beliefs will change as well.

THE STACK AND CLOSE

After you have finished the content section of the presentation, we move on to the Stack. This is where you present the offer in a way that makes it completely irresistible.

Figure 22.4:

The third part of this script introduces your solution and makes an offer your viewers can't refuse.

It starts with the transition from teaching to selling.

Let me ask you a question: The hardest part of selling on a webinar, for most people, is transitioning into the close. They start to get nervous, and the hesitation shows in the voice and confidence level. The best way I've found to transition is simply to say, "*Let me ask you a question . . .*" and then ask:

> *Is it okay with you if I spend 10 minutes going over a very special offer I created to help you implement _____?*

You can feel confident transitioning to your close at this point because it's your moral obligation to show them you have something that can help them achieve their desired result. After that, you move straight into how your product will help the participants with whatever your One Thing is. Once you transition to your sales pitch, you're going to move into the Stack.

The Stack: I consider the Stack my secret weapon. I learned it from one of my mentors, Armand Morin. I saw him speak onstage and close nearly half the room with almost no effort. I pulled him aside to find out what he was doing, and he explained the Stack to me. I started using it immediately, and I went from closing on average 5–10 percent of a room to consistently closing 30–50 percent or more. Then I started using it on my sales webinars and saw a dramatic increase in how much I made from each presentation. It's worked so well and so consistently that I will never give a sales presentation again without it.

Armand taught me that the only thing your prospect remembers when you sell is the last thing you showed them. He explained that most sales presentations focus on the core offer, then a list of bonuses; when the speaker shows each element of the offer individually, the prospect doesn't remember everything they can get. They can only consciously remember the last item you showed them. So then they look at the value of the last bonus versus the price you ask for the entire offer, and if they don't feel it's worth that price, they won't buy.

So Armand builds a presentation slide called a Stack slide. This slide has everything included in the offer, presented in a long, bulleted list. He introduces the first bullet point, talks about it, moves to the second bullet point, and so on. But when he shows the slide with the second bullet, he restacks the offer.

> *So what that means is that you're first going to get _____ and also _____.*

He then talks about the next component of the offer and reveals the next Stack slide, but this time, there are three products listed in the offer, stacked from the first mentioned to the last.

> *So what that means is that you're first going to get _____ and also _____ AND also this _____.*

He keeps doing this throughout the entire close. When he gets to that last part of the offer, he shows the final Stack slide with *everything* listed and recaps each item on that slide.

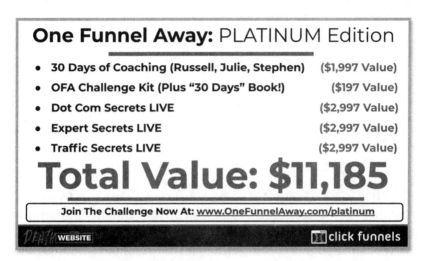

Figure 22.5:

A Stack slide shows the entire offer with the total value attached
so buyers can see all they're getting when they buy.

Then he finally introduces the price. Now prospects associate the price with the full offer—not just the last thing he mentions.

After you reveal your full Stack slide, you want to show the total value of everything the buyers are going to receive. Even though the price you name first isn't what buyers will actually pay, you need to anchor that price in their minds before you move on. We do that by introducing "If all" statements similar to the ones we used in the "Star, Story, Solution" script.

If all: At this point in the presentation, I've built up the value of the offer, and I want to get them to tell me that it's actually worth what I'm asking for it, so I use the words "If all" to anchor the offer and help the buyer justify the price I have given. These statements also help the buyer remember they're trying to move toward pleasure and away from pain, and my product will help them achieve that.

> *I'm not going to charge you the $11,185 that this offer is worth, but I have a question for you. Let's say we did charge you the full $11,185. Would it be worth it?*

Toward pleasure:

> *If all this did was give you the house of your dreams, would it be worth it?*

Away from pain:

> *If all this did was let you fire your boss, would it be worth it?*

I like to try to get them to say yes three to five times by asking multiple "If all" questions before I then move into the price drop.

Reveal the real price: Now tell them the actual price. This price should be much lower than the price you gave after the Stack.

> *I'm not going to charge you the $11,185 that this is worth . . .*

> *I'm not going to charge you the $4,997 that we sell this for retail . . .*

> *I'm not even going to charge you the $1,997 that most of you were probably assuming I was going to charge.*

> *Because you are here today, I'm going to give you a very special price of just _____.*

From there I would then give them a CTA, telling them how to purchase. It may be to click on a link, call a phone number, or run to the back of the room.

There are many other closes and things you can do in this script to elicit emotion and break false belief patterns to get people to buy. I wish I could spend another 100 pages going deeper into this script so you could master it, but that's why I wrote *Expert Secrets*. If you are creating a "Perfect Webinar" presentation such as a video sales letter, webinar, or product launch, then be sure to dive deep into that book as I go slide by slide through what to say and how to say it.

"PRODUCT LAUNCH" SCRIPT

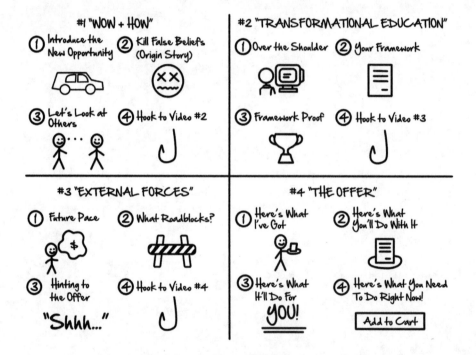

Figure 23.1:

For more information on where to use this script,
see Secret #16: Product Launch Funnels.

The psychology behind the "Product Launch" script and the "Perfect Webinar" script are very similar. As I mentioned when discussing the product launch funnel, it's what Jeff Walker calls a "sideways sales letter." I always look at it as a webinar that is broken down into four videos.

This original script came from some of my friends who focus most of their time doing four "product launch–style" videos, and while there are some things that are different than the perfect webinar, the framework is very similar. If you compare this script to the "Perfect Webinar" script, you'll notice the following similarities:

- Video #1 → Introduction & Secret #1
- Video #2 → Secret #2
- Video #3 → Secret #3
- Video #4 → Stack and Close

With that said, let's dive deep into the core framework that we try to cover inside each video. Remember these are a framework for you to plug in your own stories, offers, and personality.

VIDEO #1: "WOW AND HOW"

This is the first video they will see after they register for the online workshop. Your goal of this video is to hook them and get them excited about what is possible. If you do that, they will eagerly wait for every video in the series; if you don't, this may be the only video they see.

Figure 23.2:

The first video should hook your viewers so they're excited to watch the future videos.

Introduce the new opportunity: In *Expert Secrets*, we spend a full chapter talking about how the best offers aren't "improvement offers" (doing something better than what's currently available) but instead "new opportunities" (offering something completely different).

This whole video series should be about a new opportunity (or a new vehicle) that someone can use to get the result they desire most. They may have tried a dozen other ways to lose weight or to make money or to do whatever your product or service will provide for them. Your goal through this series is to present them with the new opportunity that you've created for them. I may call this the new vehicle at times inside this chapter as well.

Share this new opportunity with them at the beginning of the video series and each video will keep strengthening the position of this as the new process they need to use if they want to get the result that you are promising them.

Kill false beliefs (origin story): It's likely that before you really started to believe in this new vehicle, you had some false beliefs that kept you from doing it earlier. Chances are they will have the same false beliefs after you introduce it to them the first time. The most powerful thing you can do here is to tell your origin story about why you believe that this is the best vehicle to get the result that they want. Telling your story here will build rapport and help them to start to believe that this new opportunity may be right for them also.

Let's look at others: Now that you've told your origin story about this new vehicle and how it is working for you, you can share how it's working for other people. You need to show that not only were you able to have success with this new vehicle, but you have been successfully able to help other people get similar results. Introduce them to your case studies and tell their stories.

In all the content sections here (as well as in the "Perfect Webinar" script), you are focusing on teaching the "what" you did (the strategy and frameworks), and your product will usually be showing them the "how" or the step-by-step tactics on how to accomplish the "what" that they learned about in the video workshop.

Hook to video #2: You've seen this a million times on every TV show, and the reason is that it works. Here you need to hook them and get them excited about what they will learn in video #2. Have them post questions and comments on the page and let them know that you'll be answering some of the questions on the next video.

VIDEO #2: "TRANSFORMATIONAL EDUCATION"

The goal of this second video is for them to be able to visualize themselves doing it. They've seen you do it in video #1, and they've also seen the other people who you have helped; now we need to paint a vivid vision to help them see how they could do it as well.

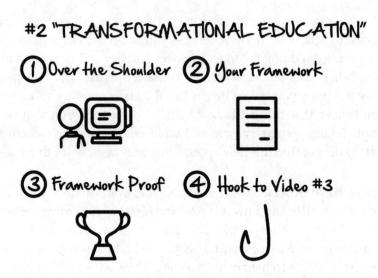

Figure 23.3:

The second video should paint the picture of what it would
look like to have success with your framework.

Over the shoulder: I call this "over the shoulder" coaching, because someone can actually look over your shoulder and watch you do the thing you're trying to get them to do. For me, when I demo ClickFunnels and show them how simple it is and they can see themselves doing it, then their false belief that "this vehicle may work for other people, but it won't work for me" will fade away. Either show them a demonstration of you using whatever it is that you're teaching them about, or show proof of the results that they can get from your new vehicle.

Your framework: Now that they've watched over your shoulder as you've done the thing that you're trying to get them to do, walk them through your framework or system. This is you teaching the "what" for each step in your system. Remember, you are teaching the "what," not the "how."

Here's exactly what I do every time:

Step 1:

Step 2:

Step 3:

Framework proof: Now it's time for more social proof. In video #1 you showed results of others who used your system; here you can pick one of those people and show their story or journey going through your framework. Show how they did step #1, step #2, and so on.

Hook to video #3: Once again, here we need to hook them and get them excited for video #3 in the workshop series. Have them comment and ask questions on the page and get prepared for the day when the next video goes live.

VIDEO #3: "EXTERNAL FORCES"

If you've created the first two videos correctly, then they should believe that this vehicle that you've introduced is the right process for them to get the result they want (video #1). They should also believe that they could actually do it because they've done the process with you (video #2). Now it's time for you to break any external false beliefs they may have. During this video, we will address the external roadblocks that may keep them from success and show them how to navigate those issues.

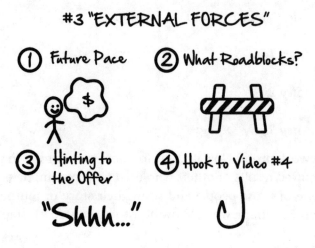

Figure 23.4:

The third video should knock down false beliefs about external
roadblocks and create momentum for the upcoming offer.

Future pace: At the beginning of this video, I want to help them
visualize what it will be like after they are using the new opportunity. I may say things like:

*I want you to take a moment to imagine what would be
different in your life if _____.*

*What possibilities would open up for you if _____? How
would you be different if _____?*

What roadblocks? Now that they believe in your new opportunity
and that they could accomplish it, what are the external roadblocks
or false beliefs that could stop them from finding success? We
need to identify these and then figure out ways to break those false
beliefs or give them tools to navigate the roadblocks.

Maybe they're afraid to try your weight-loss program because
they know that even if they did use your new diet plan, their
spouse would be eating the good food they wanted and they
know they would mess up. Or maybe they do believe that a funnel
would work for their business, but they have no idea how to get
traffic into that funnel.

I need to identify those things and then tell stories about other people who had those issues and what we've found to help navigate or destroy those problems.

Hinting to the offer: Here I start talking a little bit about the offer that is coming and how it will fill in the blanks on how they can accomplish what we are showing them. They have been learning "what" to do, and the product or service you offer will be giving them the missing "how" to implement the framework you've already given them.

Hook to offer video: Just like in the other videos, you want to set a strong hook for people to come back to the last video. Let them know they'll soon learn how to get their hands on the offer you've created for them so they can get the result they've been desiring the most.

VIDEO #4: "THE OFFER"

This last video is where we make our irresistible offer and put them into our new opportunity!

Figure 23.5:

The fourth video should pitch an irresistible offer they can't refuse so they can get started right away with your new opportunity and start seeing results.

Here's what I've got: During the first part of the script, I show them the new opportunity again, quickly recap the "what," and introduce them to my offer. Here is where I show them how to get the "how."

During my offer videos, I structure it very similar to how I do the Stack in the "Perfect Webinar" script. I go through each element, talk about it, and then show a Stack slide with the total value of everything they get at each step. During this part of the video, we're speaking to their emotional side, so the more amazing we can create the offer, the better.

Here's what you'll do with it: Now that they've seen the full offer, I want to paint a picture of the ownership experience. What will it look like after they get access? Oftentimes, I'll even show the buying process.

> *Here is the order form. After you put in your information, you will be taken to this page. After you get access, here is the first thing that I would do . . .*

Here's what it'll do for you: Here is where we re-explain the benefits of getting the product as well as all the hidden benefits that we can think of. I'm trying to appeal to their logical side now, so I will try to think of as many different logical things that this offer will help them to solve.

Here's what you need to do right now: During this last step we make the CTA. Tell them exactly what to do and how to do it. I also plug in urgency and scarcity here. Talk about how long this offer will be available and what happens when this special is over. Does the price go up? Do you stop selling the product for a time? This is your last shot to push people over the edge, so be bold telling them what to do and what will happen if they don't.

Back-End Phone
Funnel Scripts

"FOUR-QUESTION CLOSE" SCRIPT

Figure 24.1:

For more information on where to use this script, see Secret #17:
Application Funnels. You can get printable and editable copies of
the "Four-Question Close" script at DotComSecrets.com/resources.

Congratulations! Your phone funnel has generated an application with someone who is selling you on why you should work with them, so the next question is: What do you say to that person when you get them on the phone? We have two scripts we use depending on who is calling. This first script is usually used when you, the expert, are making the call. The second script (in Secret #25) is used when your sales team is making the call. That script requires two salespeople (a setter and a closer) but also works like magic.

The "Four-Question Close" script works well when you're selling a high-ticket product or service priced between $2,000–$8,000 and beyond. It ties directly back to the questions that you ask them on the application form.

I learned various parts of this strategy from a few different people. This script is based on Dan Sullivan's book *The Dan Sullivan Question*. Perry Belcher coached a few of my friends through the script, and Greg Cassar coached my Inner Circle members and myself through the process. Even though this is called the "Four-Question Close" script, it's more like a four-phase script. There are four primary questions, but you will be asking follow-up questions to dig deeper and get more complete answers.

Before prospects get on the phone with you, they fill out an application form in your phone funnel so you can prequalify them. Then you should have an assistant contact them to set up a 30-minute call.

Once you're on the call, most people will want to open with small talk. That invites them to ramble and waste time. You don't want that. You want to set yourself up as the one running the call right from the start, so you're going to say:

> *Hey, this is Russell, and I'm excited to be on the call with you. So here's how these calls work. I'm going to ask you four questions. Depending on how you answer them and how well we get along, we'll decide whether to move forward. Sound fair enough?*

They should answer yes, or the call can end right there. You're getting a micro-commitment here, or a little yes right at the start. You're also setting the ground rules so you can steer the conversation where you want it to go. Once they agree, it's time to start asking the questions.

QUESTION #1

> *Imagine you and I were to start working together today. I teach you everything I know and do everything I can to help you get*

results. Now imagine we're sitting in a coffee shop a year from now. What would have happened in your life, both personally and professionally, for you to feel happy with your progress? What would make you believe that this was the best decision you ever made?

You're trying to get them to describe their external and internal goals here. You want to hear their true desires. If they can't answer this question, you don't want to work with them because you'll never be able to satisfy them. No matter how much you accomplish—and no matter how much they pay you—if they can't articulate their desires, you won't be able to make them a reality.

Most likely, they'll start by describing external desires. They want to make $10,000 a month or they want a boat or a fancy new house in a better school district. They want to lose weight or have a better relationship with their spouse. This is a great start, but you want to dig deeper and get to the internal desires as well. So ask follow-up questions based on their answers.

Why do you want to make $10,000 a month? Why do you want that fancy new house? What's so important about the school district you're in?

Then they'll start revealing the values and beliefs that are truly important to them. Maybe they want $10,000 a month to prove to their family that they're a good provider. Or maybe they have a favorite charity they want to support in a big way. Maybe they want to be in a good school district because their kids aren't being challenged where they are. Or maybe they are childless and their spouse has given up hope of ever having a family. They are hoping that moving to a good school district will demonstrate that there's still hope.

Do you see how very different these inner desires can be for different people, even though they want the same things? You need to know those inner reasons *why* they want what they want. So keep digging until they reveal these deep emotional connections.

At the end of the day, we all want the same things: respect, inclusion, and purpose. When you dig and dig and eventually they say something that reveals one of these three things, you can stop and move to the next question. They might say, "I just want my parents or spouse to respect me" or "I want my life to have a purpose" or "I want to create a legacy that will live on after I die" or "I want to be part of something bigger than myself." Train yourself to listen carefully for these cues. Then move on to the next question.

QUESTION #2

Clearly, you know what you want. You've painted a really great picture for me. So let me ask you this—why don't you have it yet? What's been standing in your way or holding you back?

Here you're looking for their obstacles and objections. If they don't have what they want yet, there must be a reason. And you need to know whether you can help them with those obstacles or not. If they start blaming other people, you can't help them. Listen for them to say things like "My spouse doesn't support me" or "I tried XYZ program and it didn't work. That guy was useless." If they're blaming other people or outside circumstances for their failures, you really don't want them as a client.

You want people who will take responsibility for their own actions. So listen for some version of "I don't know how." Maybe they say, "I tried XYZ program, but I just didn't understand the finer details. I need to take the time to master the process." The key here is the word *I*. If they talk about themselves a lot, then chances are you can help them. If they don't know how to do something and you can help them, you're going to have a successful relationship.

Next it's time to get them thinking about possibilities.

QUESTION #3

What resources, talents, connections or skills do you have that you're currently not using to the fullest potential that we could use to overcome your obstacles and achieve your goals?

Give them some time to think about it. They might come up with some great answers, or they might come up with something off-the-wall. The point is to get them thinking about the possibilities.

Whatever they come up with is good. Encourage them to keep thinking. Keep asking, "What else? What else?" until they run out of ideas. When they do, you say this:

Okay, so let's review for a minute.

- *It looks like you know exactly what you want. You told me you want _____ because _____.*

- *You haven't been able to achieve that before primarily because of _____ and _____, right?*

- *And last, it looks like you have all these resources you could leverage that you're not leveraging yet, right?*

Then I ask them:

How much more money do you think you'd make (or how much weight would you lose or how much better would your marriage be) if you were able to eliminate the obstacles and leverage those resources?

I let them explain to me what will happen. They might say, "Oh man, if I could do that, I'm pretty sure I could make a million dollars (or lose a ton of weight, be so much happier in my marriage, etc.) . . ."

Then I transition to the final question.

QUESTION #4

So I only have one more question. Do you want me to help you to achieve your goals?

Then I stop talking. I don't say another word until they answer. Most of the time, they will say yes. Then all I have to do is say:

Great! Here's how it works. My fee is $ _____. For that money, you get _____. I'm here to help you. I can transfer you over to my assistant to take care of the financial details right now. Would you like to do that?

If they say yes, you're done. Usually the only reason they won't agree at this point is because they don't have the money. If that's the case, you can help them to find the money or offer them a payment plan.

If you've done a good job with the questions, and they can afford your fee, then you should close most of the people you talk to. Just send them off to your assistant to handle the credit card details, and you're all set.

"SETTER" AND "CLOSER" SCRIPTS

THE SETTER SCRIPT

1. Intro
2. Questions
3. Blast
4. Posture
5. Probe
6. Finding Credit
7. Goals
8. Commitments

THE CLOSER SCRIPT

1. Time
2. Decision-Making
3. Resources
4. Knowledge
5. What's Included
6. Close

Figure 25.1:

For more information on where to use these scripts, see
Secret #17: Application Funnels. You can get printable and editable
copies of the "Setter" and "Closer" scripts at DotComSecrets.com/resources.

If you as the expert won't be making the sales calls, you'll use this script. It really leverages takeaway selling to an even higher level and it's the script we use when we start to grow and scale sales teams. With this script, you will have two salespeople (a setter and a closer) to close the prospect using these "Setter" and "Closer" scripts.

During their call, the setter and the closer will be interviewing the prospect to see if they'd be a good fit for the program. This works for two reasons:

- **It's much easier to sell a $2,000–$100,000 program on the phone.** That extra step helps people feel more comfortable paying the higher dollar amounts.

- **At the higher-level programs, you are typically going to be working more closely with people.** You can screen them to make sure you'll enjoy working with them. If they aren't a good fit, don't accept them into your programs.

Using two salespeople provides consistency in your sales. When you find the right salespeople and they follow the script, it works, day in and day out. In this process, two salespeople work together to close a new client. The setter gathers basic information on the prospect, draws out their emotions, and identifies the prospect's pain and goals. Once that is done, the setter gets off the phone and has the closer call the applicant back. The closer magnifies the pain, gets the prospect to sell themselves on why they are a good fit for the program, and then provides the solution.

THE SETTER SCRIPT

Introduction: For setters, the goal here is to introduce themselves in a low-key way and have a natural conversation with the prospect. The setter is getting to know the prospect and pulling out any emotions related to the topic you're discussing. They must find out where the prospect is right now and *how he or she feels* about where they are.

Questions: Then the setter should focus on finding out where the prospect wants to be. What are their hopes and dreams? What's the real reason, deep down, that they want those things? They may want to make $100,000 per year—that's great. But why? What would that money allow them to do? Quit their current job? Stay home with their kids? Buy a boat and sail around the world? Buy their aging parents a home? Finally show their ex that they're worth something after all? The setter has to find out the *"why."*

That's where the setter will find the emotions. Remember, people buy based on emotion first, then they rationalize the decision with logic.

You've probably heard sales advice saying you need to get to a buyer's emotions, but I find many people just don't know how to do that. Your setter can hook the emotions by asking questions. Always ask additional questions. Does the prospect have kids? Great! How old are they? What are their names? If you know the prospect wants to homeschool their kids, ask why. How would it feel to know they had the freedom to teach their kids any way they wanted? Follow-up questions help you hook into emotions. What would it mean to the prospect if they could buy that new house for their parents? How would they feel standing on a boat in the Caribbean, totally free of debt and worry? Help the prospect paint a picture of the *feelings* behind their dreams.

The setter can get all this information with a few questions; within five minutes, the setter knows exactly why the prospect is going to buy this program. They also know the hot buttons to focus on. The setter should ask the prospect:

> *What's holding you back? Why haven't you achieved your dreams already?*

The setter will probably hear some variation of *I don't know how*. The prospect doesn't know how to build a business online. Or they may say they don't have time—which is really saying they don't know how to build a business in five hours a week. They may say it is because they don't have money—which is really saying they don't know how to build a business using other people's money. Once the prospect realizes it's simply a lack of knowledge blocking their success—and that you can provide them with that knowledge—the setter should ask them this question:

> *If you knew how to build a business in just five hours a week, would you do it?*

Of course they are going to say yes! They have just started to sell themselves on purchasing your product or your knowledge.

The setter cannot move forward with the script until they understand the prospect's emotional hot buttons. The prospect must also admit they don't know what they are doing (in some form or another) when it comes to building a business. They must realize they need help.

Blast—give a taste of what you offer: The setter shouldn't go into great detail about the program they're offering, but the setter should give them an idea of what the prospect could discover or get done.

Now, obviously, it's impossible to work with everyone who applies/buys our information, so I'm here to weed out those who aren't ready and find the right people to work with one on one. I understand you don't know how to build a business in five hours a week. And I don't know, but maybe we can help. Let me explain what we do here . . .

Next, the setter should ask a critical question to get the prospect to sell themselves. It's a pivotal question that will bring home all the reasons they need to pull out their credit card at the end of the conversation.

Let me ask you this: If you could work one on one with Russell Brunson or someone like him, do you think you'd be successful?

Absolutely!

How come?

Here's why this is so important: I can talk for hours about how great our program is and all the reasons the prospect should buy but it might be a lie. If *the prospect* tells the setter all the reasons they'd be successful with our program, then it's the truth because they believe it. When the setter gets the prospect to explain all the reasons they'd be successful, sales become easy. Then the setter should ask:

How come? Why would working with Russell Brunson help you be successful?

Then the setter must shut up! Don't talk. Let the prospect talk.

Once the prospect gives the reasons, the setter should repeat them and confirm the prospect's beliefs.

So if I gave you the chance to work with Russell Brunson, you believe you'd be successful?

Yes!

If you had the opportunity to work with Russell Brunson, you could get _____ [what they want]?

If you had the opportunity to work with Russell Brunson, you'd know how to get there?

Next, the setter should get the prospect to sell themselves and tell the setter why they should work with them.

Why do you think you'd be a good candidate for this program?

Posture: To set up the closer as the expert, the setter should say the following:

Now, I'm not personally an expert at building businesses online in five hours a week. My job is simply to find the people who are qualified to be part of this program. If I feel good about you, I'll turn you over to our program director [the closer]. He is the one to decide who will be the right fit for our program. Before I do that, I need to find out a little more about you and fill out a short profile. I need to understand where you are right now professionally and financially. Then I need to find out more specifics about where you want to be in the future. All this information will help us determine if you're going to be a good candidate.

Is it all right if I ask you a few questions?

The setter has just asked for (and gotten) permission to ask just about anything.

Probe—collect financial information: Your setter is going to start asking some pretty personal questions next and is going to fill out a form with the information. You want people to answer quickly without getting too emotional, so the setter should start by asking about age, marital status, highest level of education, and things like that.

Then the setter must be sure to ask:

Is there anyone else involved in your business: a spouse or financial partner?

If so, get the other party on the phone too, right then and there. It's a waste of time to keep going through the presentation if you don't have all the decision makers present.

The goal of this next set of questions is to find out the prospect's financial status and whether you really can help.

Finding Credit: Your setter is going to find out details about the prospect's credit situation.

How would you rate your credit right now? Why?

If Russell Brunson were to write a check and pay off all your debt, how much would that be?

Of that debt, how much is major credit card debt?

What's the total amount of combined credit that's been extended to you?

Subtract the total debt from combined credit extended, and your setter will find out how much they have available. The setter should be looking for more available credit than the program costs. It's also helpful to get them to talk about their credit balances to show that you're really trying to help pay those off—not add to them. The prospect might need to take one step back to take 10 steps forward, but ultimately we know a program like this can help them pay off all the debt and achieve financial freedom.

The setter should also ask if the prospect has any savings accounts or investments. Do they own their own home or rent? What about retirement accounts?

Goals—talking about a prospect's short-term goals: Your setter is still asking questions and getting the prospect to sell themselves on the program.

> *What would be an optimal situation in six months? Where would you want your business in six months?*

> *How long have you been trying to do _____? How successful have you been?*

> *In 12 months, where do you want to be? What would make you feel good? So in working one-on-one with Russell Brunson, do you think you could achieve these goals? Can you see yourself achieving them? How come?*

Commitments—get four commitments: Now the setter is getting the prospect to declare themselves a good candidate. The prospect is publicly stating they are the kind of person who takes action and finishes what they start. Once they do this, their brain will have a really hard time reversing that declaration and talking themselves out of the purchase.

> *You look like a potential candidate for me to recommend to my director. Before I can make the recommendation and turn you over to them, there are four commitments that must be agreeable to you.*

> 1. *You must have a minimum time commitment of _____ per week. Can you do that?*

> 2. *We need people who are coachable and willing to learn and follow the advice of our experts. Can you do that? Why are you coachable?*

3. *We're looking for people who can start today. We want quick decision makers. When do you think is the best time to start working on _____ [their goals]?*

You want to hear some version of "right now."

Great. If it looks like this is a fit for both of us, is there anything that would hold you back from getting started today?

4. *We want to teach you the concept of using OPM (other people's money) to invest in _____. Are you familiar with this idea? Would you like to learn more about it?*

Explain how to use the bank's money (credit cards) as a short-term leveraging tool to invest in growing their business or reaching their goals.

We have two levels in this program: _____ [lower price] and _____ [higher price].

How much are you comfortable investing to get your business started today? Why would you choose that amount?

This is where the setter's job is mostly done. They have asked all the questions and gotten the information that they must give to the closer (oftentimes the closer will have a title like the Director of Coaching). At this time, the setter lets the prospect know that their information will be taken to the director and the director will call them back to see if they are a good candidate for the program.

Let me have you write down my director's name; it's _____. I'm so happy they're available to talk with you personally, because they are an expert at _____. Most importantly, their job is to make sure we have the right kind of people on our team. So I want you to understand this is not for everybody. Please don't be offended if they don't offer you a spot. Okay?

Before they call you, they wanted me to give you a little exercise to go through while you are waiting. I know we've talked about your goals, but they'd like you to write them down for yourself. Write down a six-month AND a 12-month financial goal. Next, write down three things you want besides money.

Okay? Great! My director will call you shortly.

THE CLOSER SCRIPT

After the candidate has spoken to the setter, the setter will have a lot of information about this person. They will then talk to the closer about them, so they have all the important details before the second call.

This script for the closer will reinforce the candidate's decisions in their mind. The closer will go through the same questions as in the introduction, but perhaps worded a little differently. Get the candidate to picture exactly what life will be like after they have success with your program.

Why are you serious about _____ right now?

How long have you been thinking about _____?

What's the biggest thing that's held you back from _____?

What are you looking to do in six months? What would that do for you?

What are you hoping for in 12 months? What would that do for you?

How about in five years? What would your lifestyle be like?

Then you want the prospect to connect you with their dreams.

If you have the chance to work with someone like Russell Brunson, how would that make a difference in your life?

Anything else?

Next, the closer goes through the four commitments again.

It's my job to find only the very best people for this program. It's not for everybody, and I only want people on board if I know they have what it takes to be successful. So I'm going to ask you a series of questions, and these are things you're either committed to or you're not. So they are simple yes or no answers. Is that something you're willing to do?

Don't move on if you're not getting the answers you're looking for. Either backtrack to find out why the prospect isn't committed or get off the phone because they are not a likely close.

Time: Explain the time commitment.

Are you able to commit to _____ hours per week?

(Yes or no.)

Decision-making: Explain the decision-making commitment.

Opportunities don't wait around. Making decisions is very important. Do you see anything that would hold you back from making a decision to work with Russell Brunson today?

(Yes or no.)

Resources: Explain the investment commitment.

Write this number down: _____.

Now, as long as you see the value, and the program meets all your goals, is there any reason you can think of that would keep you from investing $_____ today?

(Yes or no.)

If the setter and the closer have done all the previous steps correctly and the prospect says you or your product/service is the next best thing to sliced bread, then suddenly the price tag isn't such a big deal anymore. It's all about setting things up in the beginning to keep them from objecting to the money at this step.

Knowledge (teachability): Explain the knowledge commitment.

> *My main concern with taking on students is that they are teachable. They must be willing to learn and then implement what they've learned so they are successful. Do you feel like you're that kind of person?*

> **(Yes or no.)**

> *How come?*

> *So if someone could show you how to do _____, you would be successful?*

> **(Yes or no.)**

What's included: Explain what the prospect gets when they sign up today.

> *We're going to give you everything you need to be successful and avoid mistakes. Your coach will help you work at your own speed.*

Then the closer should simply list out exactly what buyers get with the product or program.

Close: Take it to the finish line and finalize the sale.

> *This is probably the most important question:*

> *Why do you feel like you are a good candidate for this program?*

The prospect is selling themselves *again* on how they will be successful if they are accepted. Then all that's left to do is take their credit card information. Instead of you asking for the sale, they are asking you to *let them* buy. Do you see the subtle distinction there? Sales becomes easier when you use this type of takeaway selling, and it gives you the ability to find people who will actually be a good fit to work with you.

SECTION FOUR

BUILDING YOUR FUNNELS

It was our first ever Unlock the Secrets event, and I decided to not just invite our high-end coaching clients, but I allowed them to bring their kids as well. I did this for a few reasons, but the biggest one was that I wanted my kids to be in the room during that event to start learning funnel building.

I invited a few youth speakers who were having success with funnels to speak on stage telling their stories. One of the people I asked to speak was an 11-year-old kid, nicknamed by his friends "RJ" which stands for "Russell Junior." His real name is Noah Lenz, and he had been mastering funnels for a few years and successfully building them for other business owners.

"How much do you charge people to build them a funnel?" I asked him in front of 800-plus people (including over 350 kids!).

"Well, I used to charge anywhere from $10K to $25K to build a funnel, but I got too busy, so now I only build funnels for equity in their business!"

What was I hearing?! An 11-year-old kid who had mastered the strategies that you've learned so far in this book was in such high demand that he would no longer accept $25K to build a funnel; instead he actually took equity in their companies, and business owners were happily handing it over!

That is the power and the value of what you have been learning so far. If you were to have hired me as a consultant, everything you've learned thus far in the book would be what I would consult you on. We'd focus on your hook, story, and offer. We'd spend time developing your Attractive Character, and then build out a value ladder of where you would take your dream customers.

From there we would figure out which funnels we'd need to create at each step in the value ladder, and then we'd pick one funnel to execute.

That brings us to where we are now. You understand funnel psychology, and now we need to get our hands dirty and actually build the funnels. In this last section, I will be showing you the basic strategy behind ClickFunnels and how we use this tool to quickly build sales funnels that convert. From there I will introduce you to a concept I call funnel stacking, which will show you how we orchestrate funnels in a way that moves people up your value ladder. Finally, I'll teach you about funnel audibles. What do you do if you launch a funnel and it flops? Was it all a waste, or are there things we can do to fix the funnel? This last chapter will show you the things I do to turn an underperforming funnel into a success.

In this last section, we are moving from being a strategist to a technician who can make all these ideas become a reality in your own or other people's businesses. Being able to master the strategy and execute those ideas is one of the most profitable things you can master. Noah understood the strategies, but he gets equity in people's businesses because he can also do the actual work. My goal in this last section is to help give you the tools you need so you can actually build funnels that are successful.

CLICKFUNNELS

I had tried to build ClickFunnels before . . . twice. The first time it was called "ClickDotCom.com" and the second time we called it "ClickFusion.com." Both these attempts cost me millions of dollars, wasted years in failed development, and completely failed. That's why when my friend Todd Dickerson told me he wanted to build software that would make this funnel building process simple, I chuckled and told him that I'd been down that road too many times and it wouldn't work.

Todd had been helping me to custom code all our funnels for the past few years, and despite the fact that we were really good at building them, it still took Todd and a small team of designers and developers about three months to create and launch each new funnel.

Every page had to be hand-coded; every order form and upsell page's code was rewritten and tested over and over. The other problem was I had no tech or design skills, so I would have an idea, explain it to a designer, and we'd go back and forth for weeks trying to get the design right. Then we had to write the copy, so I'd write that and then have the designers plug it in.

Everything was so slow, that for me, a high-energy entrepreneur with a million ideas, by the time I got a funnel done, I was already bored with the idea and on to building our next one. This was our pattern for years: hand-coding over 150 unique funnels for just my own company. We had some big wins, but tons of wasted time and funnels that never went anywhere.

That's why we had tried to build something like ClickFunnels before, because we knew how much pain we were in trying to execute this strategy that we had pioneered. The other problem was when I would try to coach other would-be entrepreneurs on how to get a funnel up and live, well, almost none of them got a single funnel page live.

But Todd wasn't going to take no for an answer. He's from Atlanta, and he had just flown to Boise, Idaho, where I live, for a week of brainstorming on our next funnel. Within a few hours of him getting to the office, he started asking me, "If I were to build something like this, what would you want? What about this feature? What if I made it do this?"

He didn't have to try hard, and within minutes I was in. "Let's do this," I said. "But we need a name . . . SalesFunnels. com? No, that's not available. What about FunnelFusion.com? FunnelDotCom.com?" Every idea was either stupid, or the .com domain was taken. After about an hour of mushing words together, someone said, "ClickFunnels.com!" The domain was taken, but it was for sale! I bought the domain, and Todd and I spent the rest of the week in front of a whiteboard, dreaming about what would be possible with our new tech company, ClickFunnels.

Figure 26.1:

Todd Dickerson, Dylan Jones, and I spent months brainstorming
and creating the software that has now become ClickFunnels.

When the week of whiteboarding was done, Todd flew back home to Atlanta and started coding the first version of the software. Within a few months, he had the early prototypes, and it was amazing. Later we brought in another cofounder, Dylan Jones, who built the original Page Editor.

Each night I would get an email from them asking me to use ClickFunnels, with no explanation on how it worked.

"If we have to show you how to do it, then we failed," they would say.

So I would log in and make a video of me trying to build a funnel. When I'd get stuck, I'd send them the video and they'd go back to the drawing board to try and figure out ways to make it simpler.

By that summer, we had a working app. On September 23, 2014, we went live with our first tech startup, and the rest is history. At the time of this second printing, we have over 100,000 active, paying members with thousands of new people joining each day. I always joke with entrepreneurs that ClickFunnels has become the tool that people use to build funnels, and it's not a matter of "if" you're going to become a member, but "when."

Figure 26.2:

In 2014, ClickFunnels was founded without any VC funding. Its cofounders Russell Brunson and Todd Dickerson grew the company to over 100,000-plus users in just five short years.

This section is not meant to be a full tutorial on how to use ClickFunnels, as you can find step-by-step tutorials inside the software to help you build your funnels. Rather, I'd like to give you an overview of the process you go through from choosing a funnel to launching it to the world.

CHOOSE YOUR FUNNEL

The first step to go through when creating any funnel is to decide which type of funnel you're going to create. You probably have an idea after reading the first few sections of this book as to which funnel you would like to create, but here are some quick ways to identify the right funnel to build if you are stuck.

First, think about the price of the product or service you're going to sell. Then find the step of the value ladder your price fits into:

- $0: Front-end lead funnels

- $1–$100: Unboxing funnels

- $100–$2,000: Presentation funnels

- $2,000+: Back-end phone funnels

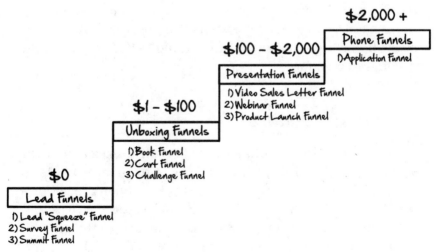

Figure 26.3:

One of the easiest ways to decide which funnel to build is to find which step of the value ladder your offer is priced at, and then choose one of the funnels in that step based on your audience and the offer.

Next, find the step of the value ladder you just selected. Then choose which funnel will be best to sell your product or service. For instance, if you are selling a product or service priced between $100–$2,000, you could use a presentation-type funnel to sell it, so you could choose between a video sales letter funnel, a webinar funnel, or a product launch funnel.

Also, don't forget that just because your offer sells for $1,000 doesn't mean that you have to sell it through a presentation-style funnel. You could unbox the offer and sell it through an unboxing funnel as well. (For more on this, see the "Unboxing Funnels" section.) Likewise, if your product or service is priced at $100, you could sell it with an unboxing funnel. However, you could also sell it with a front-end lead funnel by placing your offer on the thank-you page or special offer page inside each funnel. (For more on this, see the "Front-End Lead Funnels" section.)

At the end of the day, we never know which funnel will work the best, so you make your strongest guess, create the funnel using all the strategies you've learned here inside this book, launch it (and if it fails, read the Funnel Audibles chapter at the end of this book), and keep tweaking it until it's a winner. If for some reason you can't get this funnel to work, this would have been a waste of three to six months of time or more in the past, but because it's so simple to create these funnels fast, you may lose a week or two. Try a new funnel type, follow the process, and keep doing that until you find your winner.

SKETCH YOUR FUNNEL

Once you've picked your funnel, you'll want to sketch out each step of your funnel. You can model any of the frameworks from the funnels you have learned in this book, but don't forget that based on your offer, you may have more or less pages or steps, and ClickFunnels makes it simple to add or change those things.

Here are the first set of questions you should ask yourself:

- What are the pages I will need in my funnel?

- Will I use an order form bump?

- How many upsells will I have?

- Do I want to add a downsale?

■ What is the hook for each page?

■ What is the story?

■ What is the offer?

■ What is the price I will set for each offer?

Sketch out each page and step for the funnel so you know visually what you are going to create first.

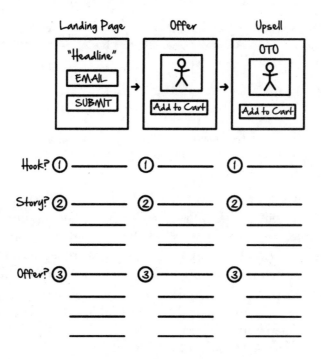

Figure 26.4:

Figure out the hook, story, offer, and price points for each page in your funnel first before you start building them inside ClickFunnels.

BUILD YOUR FUNNEL IN CLICKFUNNELS

After I have a visual representation of what I want to build, then I can go to ClickFunnels.com and let the magic begin. (You can get a free 14-day trial to test-drive the software and see how simple it is to use at ClickFunnels.com.) We've made ClickFunnels easy enough that an entrepreneur or CEO could use it, but also powerful enough that your web and tech guys will love it. Please note that with any software, there will be changes to the user interface (UI) over time, so if images don't look exactly the same as in this book, don't worry, the process will still be the same.

The first step is to log in to your ClickFunnels account and click on the **Add New** button to create your first funnel.

Figure 26.5:

It's easy to build your first (or next) funnel in ClickFunnels: just click the Add New button to start the process.

This will trigger the Funnel Wizard, which will help you to start building your funnel. You can choose to **Collect Emails**, **Sell Your Product**, or **Host [a] Webinar**. If you want to build your email list, click **Collect Emails** to build a lead "squeeze" funnel. If you have a product or service to sell, click **Sell Your Product** to build a variety of unboxing funnels. If you want to sell your product or service with a webinar, click **Host [a] Webinar** to build a live or automated webinar funnel. If you'd like to create a different funnel, you can click **Create a Custom Funnel**.

Figure 26.6:

**Based on your goal, you can choose one of three easy paths
to build your funnel, or you can create a custom funnel.**

After you choose a path, the Funnel Wizard will create a funnel for you to customize. On the left-hand side, you'll see the pages currently in your funnel. Notice how the funnel you sketched out matches the funnel steps. The wizard creates basic funnels, but you can easily add or delete steps to make the funnel match what you sketched on your whiteboard.

Figure 26.7:

**A lead " squeeze" funnel has just two pages:
a landing (opt-in) page and a thank-you page.**

On the right-hand side, you'll see several templates you can choose from to immediately create each page in your funnel. You can choose from our extensive template library and build out a complete funnel, even if you have never designed a website before. Or, if you have more of an eye for design, you can modify our templates however you want or even start a page from scratch. Browse through the available templates and choose one template for each page of your funnel. If you don't find one you like, find one that is close, because it's simple to customize it to fit your brand.

Lastly, if you want to build a funnel just like one of the 10 core funnels in this book, we've created 10 "share funnel" templates that match the funnels in this book to a T. Go to DotComSecrets. com/resources to add one (or all) of these 10 core funnel templates immediately to your ClickFunnels account. That way, you'll have a funnel built out and ready for your custom graphics and text in a matter of seconds.

Figure 26.8:

Choose from hundreds of ready-to-go templates to build your funnel in a matter of minutes or hours, not weeks or months.

After choosing a template, click the **Edit Page** button to open the Page Editor.

Figure 26.9:

You can customize each template by clicking the Edit Page button.

CUSTOMIZE YOUR FUNNEL WITH THE PAGE EDITOR

One of my absolute favorite parts of ClickFunnels is the Page Editor. It's amazing! It allows me, a complete nontechie, to build out my own pages within hours, instead of weeks or months.

Before you start using the Page Editor, though, you should have a basic understanding of how it works and how the pages are structured. When you understand these basics, it's simple to design the pages to look however you'd like.

Pages are made up of sections, rows, and elements. Inside of the Page Editor, we've color-coded each part so it's easy to see what you're working on.

- Sections are green

- Rows are blue

- Elements are orange

Sections: The first step is to create the sections you want to show up on your page, or edit the sections that are on the template you have chosen. Sections are the basic containers for your header, body areas, and footer of your pages. You can arrange them however you want, and each section can even have its own background image or color.

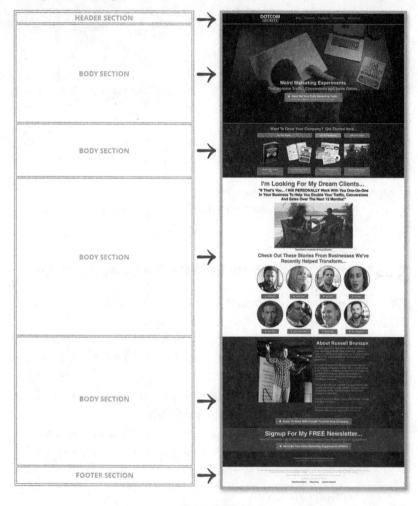

Figure 26.10:

The green sections (shown with double lines on left) are for your header, body, and footer content. Notice how the foundation of the page on the right was created using sections.

Rows: After you create your sections, your next step is to create rows on your page. Rows are the blue boxes on the page and they can be made up of multiple columns. This gives you a ton of flexibility when you are designing your pages, as well as providing a structure that is responsive and mobile friendly.

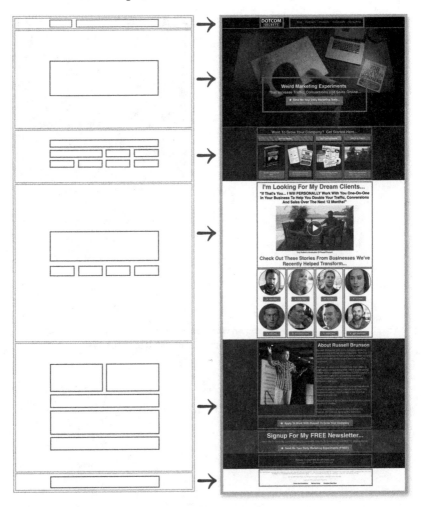

Figure 26.11:

The blue rows (shown with single lines on left) help your pages become mobile friendly and each row can have multiple columns.

Elements: Your last step is to put the elements for your page inside your rows. The page elements are the basic building blocks on the page. You can add various page elements such as headlines, text, images, videos, order forms, buttons, countdown timers, progress bars, opt-in forms, fully customizable surveys, and more.

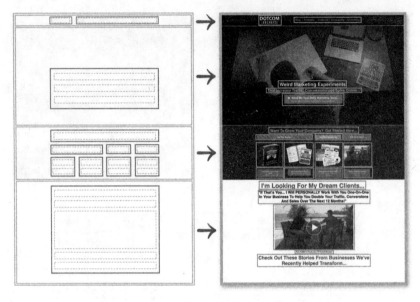

Figure 26.12:

The orange elements (shown with dashed lines on left) are the actual pieces of content (such as images and text) for your pages.

You can quickly add any elements, like videos to a page, with just a few simple clicks of a button.

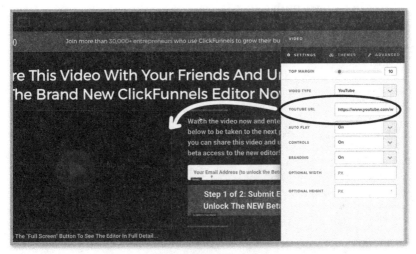

Figure 26.13:

You can add a video to the page simply by copying and pasting a YouTube, Vimeo, or Wistia link.

Besides video, there are over 40 different elements that you can add to your pages to help create your brand and increase conversions.

Figure 26.14:

The Page Editor has over 40 different elements that you can add to any of your types of funnels.

After you've built out the page structure and added in the sections, rows, and elements, then you can go into each element and edit it. It's simple to change headlines, drag and drop elements around the page, and more.

Figure 26.15:

You can edit the text just by clicking on it and typing in any text you want.

One of the coolest things about the Page Editor is that you can rearrange, add, or remove anything to completely customize your pages. You can change sizes, colors, backgrounds—all with the click of a button. All pages are mobile responsive, but you can preview and optimize them even more right inside the Page Editor.

Once you start building, you'll have your pages and funnels completed in no time.

PLUG IN YOUR HOOKS, STORIES, AND OFFERS

As cool as ClickFunnels and the Page Editor are at building the scaffolding of your funnels, the real power is not in the pages; it's in the hooks that you place on the page to get someone's attention and the stories that build connection and increase the value of what you are offering on each page.

As I edit each page in the funnel, I am trying to put in good design and branding, but the most important thing, the thing that will make you the most amount of money and give you the ability to serve the most people, is your hook, story, and offer. As you'll see in Secret #28, when a page or a funnel doesn't convert, the things we tweak are the hook, story, and offer. Don't forget about their importance as you are having fun building cool-looking funnels.

BUILD YOUR FOLLOW-UP FUNNELS

In Secret #7, you started creating your follow-up funnels that you will send to your dream customers after they join your list, either as a subscriber or a buyer. Building out your follow-up funnel is simple inside of ClickFunnels as well.

First, I want to map out my follow-up sequence. Who is my Attractive Character? How do I want to flesh out that character in my emails? What will I say in each email in my Soap Opera Sequence? What types of messages do I want to send out in my Seinfeld emails?

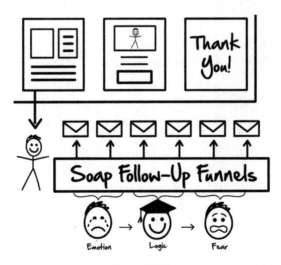

Figure 26.16:

When you're sketching out your funnel, don't forget to plan out your follow-up funnels as well.

The first step is to create a follow-up funnel by clicking on the **New Follow-Up Funnel** button.

Figure 26.17:

After your prospects join your email list, you can continue the conversation with them with a follow-up funnel.

Once you've started a new follow-up funnel, you can create emails for each day of your Soap Opera Sequence. If your sequence has five days, you would create five emails.

Figure 26.18:

Inside your follow-up funnels, you can set up your emails to be sent out on autopilot and they will automatically start tracking the number of sent emails, opens, and clicks.

Then you go into each of these days and write the message that will be sent to your prospects on that specific day. You can use the ClickFunnels Email Editor to design beautiful emails.

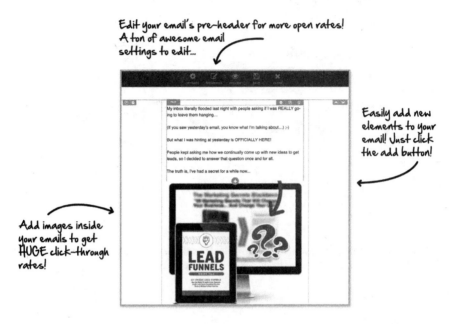

Figure 26.19:

The Email Editor is easy to use; just like the Page Editor, it uses sections, rows, and elements.

After the Soap Opera Sequence has been built out, then you can go back to your funnel and integrate it with the follow-up funnel. That way when someone gives you their email address, they will automatically start getting these emails.

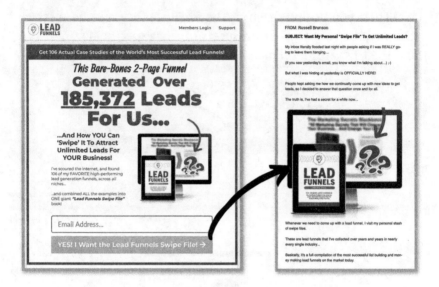

Figure 26.20:

Connecting your follow-up funnel to your funnel pages (so you can collect email addresses) is as easy as clicking a button.

LAUNCH YOUR FUNNEL

After you've built your funnel in ClickFunnels, you'll see that the sales funnel you sketched out on the whiteboard has now come to life. After you've finished building the funnel, you can start driving traffic, tracking your stats, and getting results in record time! Isn't that exciting?! While this once took our team of experts two to three months to create, we can now create everything in ClickFunnels in about an hour.

If you don't have your ClickFunnels account yet, you can get a free two-week trial at ClickFunnels.com so you can get started right away.

FUNNEL STACKING

When I was a wrestler in high school, every summer we would go to wrestling camp and learn "wrestling camp moves." They were the fun moves—the throws and the tricks that are fun to show off to your friends, and that make you feel like you learned a lot but aren't very practical to use in real matches. In fact, when you look at the top-level matches at state, national, and world tournaments, almost every match consists of just two or three moves: single legs, double legs . . . the matches at the highest levels are won with the fundamentals.

Unfortunately, the fundamentals are rarely as exciting, yet the fundamentals are what actually win matches. The same is true with your online sales funnels. The more you focus on the fundamentals and ignore the flash, the more money you'll make.

I review tons of funnels, and I see people who have thousands of variations based on every scenario they can think of: upsells, downsells, cross sales, crazy email sequences, and more, yet most of them are making no money.

While I've shared with you my top 10 core funnels in this book, I don't want you to build out 10 new funnels for your business. Instead, you should choose just one funnel for each step of your value ladder. After all, about 95 percent of my revenue comes from just three basic funnels: my book funnels, webinar funnels, and high-ticket funnels.

As you build out a funnel for each step of your value ladder, you'll be able to ascend your dream customers up your value ladder with a process we call "funnel stacking." For instance, you might send someone from your lead "squeeze" funnel to your book funnel to your webinar funnel and finally to your application funnel. You don't have to choose these specific types of funnels for each step of your value ladder, and you don't have to move your customers through every step in that order. Rather, funnel stacking is moving your customer from one funnel into another funnel higher on your value ladder. This process is done on the pages of your funnels as well as through your follow-up funnels.

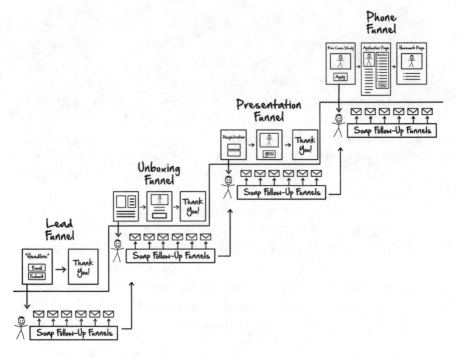

Figure 27.1:

When your customer finishes a step in your value ladder, you can help them ascend by sending them to the funnel on the next step.

If executed correctly, funnel stacking will give you a business that will allow you to outspend your competitors, provide more value to your clients than ever before, and predictably scale your company.

ASCENDING FROM ONE STEP TO THE NEXT

One way that you can ascend your customers from one step of your value ladder to the next is by placing the first step of your next funnel on the last page of your previous funnel.

Figure 27.2:

One example of stacking a funnel on top of each other is to have your Next Step button of your lead "squeeze" funnel push people to the first page of your challenge funnel. Once people finish your challenge, you can invite them to a graduation webinar to pitch your current offer.

Let me show you a few examples of how you can add on another funnel to the end of each funnel type.

Front-end lead funnels: Once you create your lead funnel, you can encourage your leads to become customers right away. Each lead funnel includes an opportunity for you to move people to the next funnel in your value ladder.

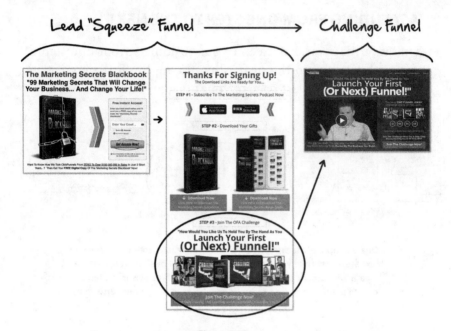

Figure 27.3:

After someone opts in to get our free *Marketing Secrets Blackbook*
and lands on the thank-you page, we introduce them to the next offer in
our value ladder, One Funnel Away Challenge, using a challenge funnel. You
can see this funnel stacking in action at MarketingSecrets.com/blackbook.

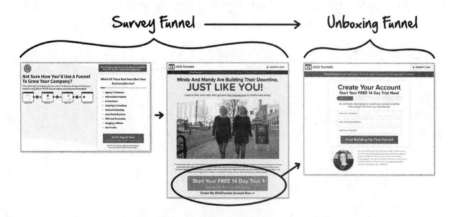

Figure 27.4:

After someone fills out our survey on the ClickFunnels home page and
lands on the results page, we introduce them to the next offer in our value
ladder, a 14-day trial of ClickFunnels, using an unboxing funnel. You can see
this funnel stacking in action at ClickFunnels.com.

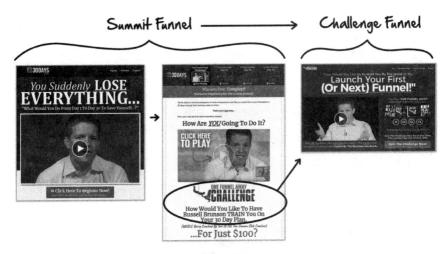

Figure 27.5:

After someone registers for our 30 Days Summit and lands on our special offer page, we introduce them to the next offer in our value ladder, One Funnel Away Challenge, using a challenge funnel. You can see this funnel stacking in action at 30Days.com.

Unboxing funnels: Once your customer has purchased a product or service from you, they're much more likely to buy again from you if you give them an opportunity.

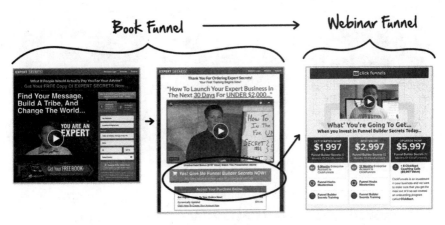

Figure 27.6:

After someone requests our free-plus-shipping *Expert Secrets* book and lands on our thank-you page, we introduce them to the next offer in our value ladder, Funnel Builder Secrets, using a webinar funnel. You can see this funnel stacking in action at ExpertSecrets.com.

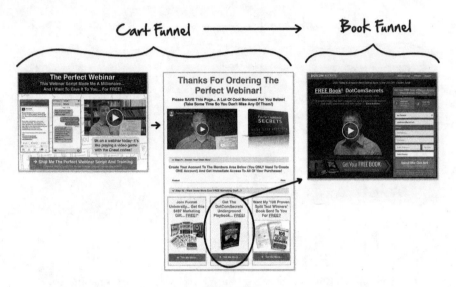

Figure 27.7:

After someone requests our free-plus-shipping Perfect Webinar Secrets
and lands on our thank-you/offer wall page, we introduce them to the next
offer in our value ladder, this *DotCom Secrets* book, using a book funnel.
You can see this funnel stacking in action at PerfectWebinarSecrets.com.

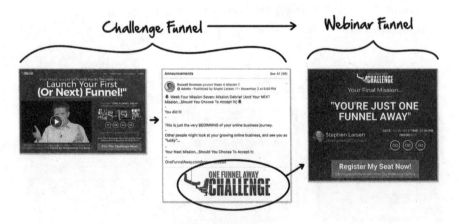

Figure 27.8:

After someone purchases our One Funnel Away Challenge and completes
their training, we post in the Facebook challenge group and invite them to
register for a "top secret next mission" that sells our current offer using a webinar
funnel. You can see this funnel stacking in action at OneFunnelAway.com.

Presentation Funnels: After someone goes through your presentation funnel, the thank-you pages are a great place to push people into either another presentation funnel or into an application funnel.

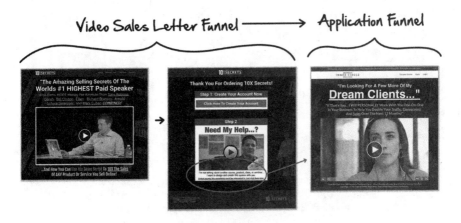

Figure 27.9:

After someone purchased our 10X Secrets course and landed on our thank-you page, we introduced them to the next offer in our value ladder, Inner Circle, using an application funnel.

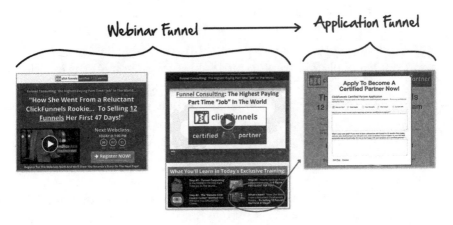

Figure 27.10:

After someone registered for our webinar and landed on our thank-you page, we introduced them to the next offer in our value ladder, CF Certified, using an application funnel.

Figure 27.11:

After someone registered for our Funnel Hacking workshop and landed on our offer page, we introduced them to the next offer in our value ladder, Inner Circle, using an application funnel.

WHY WE FUNNEL STACK

Are you starting to see how funnel stacking works? Just like each page in the funnel builds a relationship with your dream customer and ascends the relationship with them, each funnel will deepen that relationship and send someone up your value ladder.

Some people will want to move slower with you. At the end of the funnel, they will be done, and that is okay. This is where the Attractive Character and follow-up funnels start to progress the relationship until they are ready to reengage with you in the next funnel in your value ladder. For others, they will want to move faster, and so funnel stacking will allow them to move up your value ladder fast.

I've had some people who will buy a book from me and nothing else for three to four years, and then one day they feel comfortable enough to reengage and buy the next thing. Others have bought a book from me and within a week have paid me over $25,000. Everyone moves at their own speed, and I use funnel stacking because if I don't offer the fast movers something now, they will go and look for solutions to their problems somewhere else.

By stacking your funnels together this way, you will notice that you will also start making more money from each person who comes into your funnel because they are seeing more offers. This will give you the ability to make more money from each customer and allow you to outspend all your competitors.

My only fear with teaching this concept (as well as the value ladder) is that you should NOT wait to launch your funnel until you have multiple funnels. Create your first funnel and launch it, and focus on its success and growing it. After you build your second funnel, go back into the original funnel and put in the process to push people from funnel one into funnel two. But don't wait until your stack is complete to launch. I always tell my Inner Circle members that they have to have made at least $1 million (hit the Two Comma Club) in a funnel before they create their second one. That means after your webinar has hit the Two Comma Club, *then* create your high-ticket coaching program, promote it to all your past webinar subscribers, and add it to the thank-you page. Or launch your book funnel, sell 1,000 or 5,000 copies of your book, and *then* create your webinar funnel, promote it to your existing book buyers, and stack it at the end of your book funnel.

There is money to be made now, and customers who are ready for what you have to offer now. Don't wait until all your funnels are done before you start serving them; start serving them now with your first offer and your first funnel.

FUNNEL AUDIBLES

I only had one goal in high school. I wanted to be a state champion in wrestling. The summer before my junior year, that goal was so real in my mind that I would wake up every morning and run, lift weights, and wrestle anyone I could find who was better than me. My dad would drive me all around the state trying to find coaches who could help give me the edge and other athletes who could beat me, so we could find my flaws.

After months of practice, the official season started on November 3, and our first dual meet was a few weeks later. I knew that my first match that season would be against the returning state runner-up. As the big night came, I was ready to beat him—and to prove to my friends, family, and teammates that I was good enough to be a state champion.

Although I had put in countless hours of preparation, as I stepped out onto the mat that night, I quickly found out that I wasn't ready yet. The match was very lopsided, with him easily beating me. I was so embarrassed. I went home that night and cried myself to sleep.

Luckily for me, that night while I was feeling sorry for myself, my dad was upstairs plugging in his camcorder to the TV so he could watch and rewatch my match. He stayed up all night looking at what I had done wrong in the match, taking notes on the adjustments I needed to make if I was going to beat that opponent in the state tournament later that year.

When I woke up in the morning, I was still feeling a little depressed, but my dad was up early with a smile on his face. "I know why you lost!" he said. "And I know what we need to do so you'll beat him next time."

My teenage self was slightly annoyed at my dad and his positive attitude, even more so when he pulled me into the front room and spent the next 30 minutes before school on the carpet showing me the adjustments I needed to make. Then that day, after school and wrestling practice, he showed up and we drilled these things again. He did this every day for the next four months, drilling the positions and the moves that I needed over and over.

Four months later, we were at the state tournament. Because of a good season, I was now ranked second in the state, and the guy I had lost to previously (the returning state runner-up) ranked first. When they posted the brackets, I saw that we were on opposite sides, so if we both won all our matches, then we would be in the finals against each other. As the tournament went on and we had battles with the others in our weight class, eventually we were the last two standing. We were going to be competing against each other in the state finals.

Before the big match, my dad and I drilled the positions again one last time. Then I stepped onto the mat, shook my opponent's hand, and started to wrestle. But this time was much different than before. I had wrestled him hundreds of times in my head. I knew his favorite moves and how to counter them. I also knew where the holes were in his match, and I exploited them perfectly. When the six minutes were up, we both stood up, but with this match it was my hand that was raised, and I became a state champion!

I share this story because soon you will be launching your first funnel. Chances are it is going to flop. Most people's funnels don't work the first time, and that's okay. If you know that going into it, it won't shock or depress you. In my Inner Circle, I used to have people call me the day before they launched any funnels. They would always tell me about how hard they had worked and how excited they were to launch their funnel. I would usually respond with bad news.

"It's probably going to fail."

"What?" they would say.

"Yeah, most funnels fail the first time. Mine all do. The launch is just about getting the initial numbers and data we need so we can make the changes required for this funnel to work, and we have no idea what they are until we send some traffic into it. The sooner we see where the funnel is failing, the faster we can get it fixed."

Then I would tell them my wrestling story and that if the first time I had wrestled that guy was in the finals, there is a really good chance I would have lost to him. But because I had wrestled him four months earlier, I knew exactly where my holes were. I just needed to make adjustments and then it was easy to come back and win.

The launch is just the first match, or the first test. I may spend some money on ads and then just wait. I need to see what happens on each page of the funnel. How many people click on the ad? How much money did I have to spend per click? How many people joined my list? What percentage of them bought my product? Did any of them buy the upsell? After I see all this data, then I can figure out what changes I need to make to create a perfect funnel.

ONE "PROPERLY EXPLOITED" FUNNEL

The late Gary Halbert once said, "Properly exploited, one good idea that occurs to you while walking on a beach is worth more than ten lifetimes of hard work."[19] I may take that statement one step further and say that "one good funnel, properly exploited, is worth more than ten lifetimes of hard work." It's worth putting in the time and energy to take your funnel from a loser, to an okay funnel, to a winner, because when you get one of these funnels to take off, it can transform your life forever. I always tell our funnel hackers that "you're just one funnel away," and it's true. One funnel can change everything for you.

Recently I was on a call with one of my newer Inner Circle members. They had spent months getting their funnel ready and they wanted to show it to me. They then showed me a funnel map that consisted of 50-plus pages with dozens of "if/then" arrows showing countless different paths that someone could take inside the funnel. On top of that, there were countless different follow-up funnel sequences that could be triggered based on actions at any step inside the funnel. While this complex funnel strategy and map looked very impressive, it was really confusing to me. I asked them how the funnel was converting, and they told me that it wasn't doing very well. They wanted my advice, but honestly, there were literally thousands of things that could have been broken inside this maze, and I had no idea where to even start.

You need to understand that complexity is not your friend in the funnel game. Having 8,000 variations of different possibilities could help increase conversions by a fraction of a percentage . . . maybe. But if something is broken, or underconverting, it will be almost impossible to diagnose and fix it (not to mention the countless months of work that go into building out this hypothetical customer journey). While it may seem powerful, it's typically just a consultant trying to make themselves seem valuable.

My funnels are all very, very simple. You'll notice from all the examples inside this book that most are three to five pages with one good Soap Opera Sequence. I do this for a few reasons.

First, we can build it quickly and get our idea to market fast. The reason why most entrepreneurs fail isn't because their ideas aren't good. It's because they either run out of time or money before their ideas get to market. Simple funnels allow you to spend a few hours, or maybe a weekend, and you have a finished funnel that you can start sending traffic to immediately. There is so much power in that. One of my early mentors, Joe Vitale, once told me that "money follows speed," and that rule has been true my entire career.

The second reason is that after I send traffic into the funnel, I want to be able to quickly see what is wrong. With a complex funnel, it could be one of a hundred things that isn't working. With my simple funnels, there are only a couple things I can tweak. The fewer levers I have to move, the less testing I have to do to get to profitability.

Most funnels will start off converting badly, and that's okay. Our job is to take all the best practices you've learned here, try to create the best funnel you can, and then put it out there fast. I then need to send some traffic to that funnel to see what happens. (Inside *Traffic Secrets*, I teach you many ways to get free and paid traffic to fill your funnels with your dream customers, so to master this step, be sure to read the third book in this trilogy.)

After my funnel is live, I like to invest the amount of money in traffic that I would make if one person were to buy my product. So if I have a webinar that sells a $1,000 course, I'll test with $1,000 of traffic. If I have a book funnel with two upsells, I will total up the prices of all the products in the funnel ($0 book + $37 bump + $97 OTO + $197 OTO = $331) and spend that much on ads for my first test. My goal from this test is to break even. I'm going to spend $1,000 in ads for my webinar funnel and try to get one sale so that I make my money back. If I do, then I have what we call a "break-even funnel" because we broke even on our ad spend. Many times on my first test I don't break even, but that's okay; I take the loss of money and write it off as market research and then make the changes that I learned from the test and try again.

I spend the advertising money on Facebook or Google ads (or whatever ad source makes the most sense) and then I sit back and wait for the traffic I purchased to come to my funnel, join my lists, go through my Soap Opera Sequence, and see all the pages in the funnel. This will usually take a few days to a week after I spend the money.

Then I let the market tell me if my funnel works. People always ask me to look at their funnels and tell them whether it will work or not, and my answer is always no. I could potentially destroy your funnel because I am not your market. The *only* opinions you should care about are the ones belonging to your customers. The question we are trying to answer from this initial test is, "Will my dream customers pull out their wallets and vote with their credit cards for this offer I created?" My customer's opinion is the only one I care about. I don't even trust my own opinion. I've done enough split-testing to know that I'm wrong most of the time. You shouldn't trust your own opinion either. Create the most awesome funnel that you can based on the funnel-hacking skills you have learned, and then invest the amount of money you would make if you got one customer to buy everything in the funnel.

From here we just wait and let the market tell us if our hooks were right, our stories built up enough value for them, and we actually created an irresistible offer. The market never lies. They vote with their credit cards, and that's the only vote that matters.

After the test is done, we need to start looking at the numbers. They will tell you exactly what you need to change. After you've made those changes, I invest the profit I would make from one sale again and do a second test. Then I wait for a few more days to let the market tell me if the changes I made worked. Then I will look at these new numbers, make more tweaks based on the data, and do another test. Usually we'll go through this process three or four times before we start getting a winner.

MARKETING MATH (NAIL IT SO YOU CAN SCALE IT)

Let's talk about funnel marketing math. The good news is that I'm not that good at math, so this is not complex, but understanding these simple numbers is how you know what funnel audibles you will need to make. There are two numbers that drive everything inside your funnel and will tell you exactly what you need to adjust in your funnel.

Cost Per Acquisition (CPA): Your CPA is how much money it costs you to get a customer. If you watch *Shark Tank*, you'll notice that one of the first questions the sharks ask the entrepreneurs is, "How much does it cost you to acquire a customer?"

Let me show you how this works. If I spend $1,000 on Facebook ads to drive traffic into one of my free book funnels, and I sell 100 books from these ads, then my CPA is $10. From these ads, I acquired 100 new customers, and I spent $1,000, so each customer cost me $10. If I spent that same $1,000 but only got 10 customers, then my CPA would be $100. That is the first number you have to understand. For every ad you run, you will want to look at it afterward and see what the CPA was.

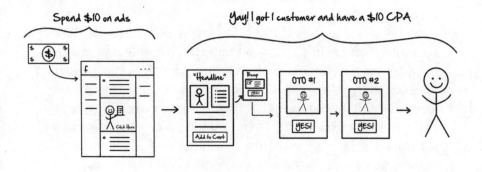

Figure 28.1:

You can find your CPA by taking the cost of your ads divided by the number of sales from your funnel (e.g., $10 ad spend/1 sale = $10 CPA).

Average Cart Value (ACV): Your ACV is the average amount of money that someone will spend with you once they are in your funnel. So if I use the example above and I sell 100 copies of my book, a percentage of these people will buy my order form bumps and upsells. Then I take how much total money I made from all these upsells and divide it by the total number of customers who bought. If we had $2,500 in total funnel sales from these 100 customers, that means we averaged $25 in sales from each customer, so our ACV is $25.

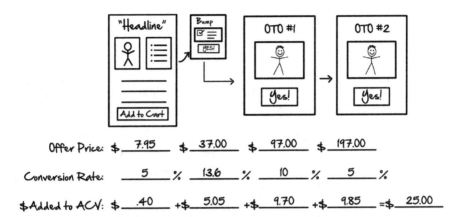

Figure 28.2:

You can find your ACV by taking your funnel's total sales divided by the
number of customers (e.g., $2,500 total sales/100 customers = $25 ACV).

Now that I have these two numbers, my goal is to make sure
that my CPA (how much it costs me to get a customer) is less than
my ACV (how much I make from each customer). If my CPA is less
than my ACV, then my funnel is working and I want to spend as
much money as possible, because for each dollar I put into ads,
I'm making *more* than a dollar back! Now, on the other hand, if
you're spending more money to acquire a customer than you are
making from each of them, this is where we need to start calling
some funnel audibles.

That's all you really have to understand. It's not calculus;
it's simple arbitrage. You have to look at the numbers and make
sure that you're making more money than you're spending. Just
remember this:

- If CPA > ACV, your funnel is broken.

- If CPA < ACV, your funnel is working.

Every ad you run will have a different CPA. The ads where the
CPA is too high, I will turn off. The ones where the CPA is low, I
will keep running for as long as they remain profitable.

This doodle shows a basic mockup of how we evaluate a funnel.

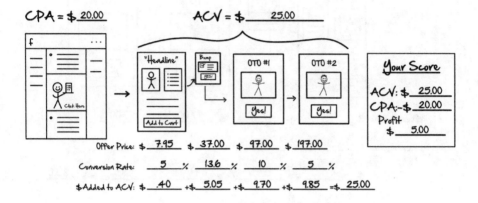

CPA = $ 20.00   ACV = $ 25.00

Offer Price: $ 7.95 $ 37.00 $ 97.00 $ 197.00

Conversion Rate: 5 % 13.6 % 10 % 5 %

$ Added to ACV: $ .40 +$ 5.05 +$ 9.70 +$ 9.85 =$ 25.00

Your Score
ACV: $ 25.00
CPA: -$ 20.00
Profit
$ 5.00

Figure 28.3:

If your ACV is higher than your CPA, your funnel works and you should spend as much money as you can while it remains profitable.

As you can see, this sketch is very simple. After we spend our test budget, we fill in the blanks on this sheet to see where the chips fell. On the left-hand side, we will write down what our actual CPA was during this test. How much money did you spend, and from that ad spend, how many customers did you acquire?

Next you will go to each page of the funnel. I write down how much the actual offer price was for each page in the funnel, followed by what the conversion rate was on each page. ClickFunnels will show you these stats inside your funnel dashboard. Then I take the order price and divide it by what percentage of the people took that offer, and on the bottom line I write in how much money it contributed toward my ACV. After I do this for each page in the funnel, I can then add up the numbers and it will give me my total ACV. (NOTE: ClickFunnels will also do this math for you and display your ACV at the top of your reporting stats so you can find it quickly.) Then I go to the Your Score box, write down my ACV, and subtract it from my CPA to find out if my funnel was profitable.

FUNNEL AUDIBLES

Now that your first test is done and you have your numbers back, the market has told you what it thinks about your funnel! If you lost money, it's telling you that it's not ready yet, and we need to look at the numbers to see which part of the funnel is underperforming. If you broke even, then you have a funnel that's generating leads for free (which is a huge win), and now we can start testing things to see if we can make it profitable.

If the funnel is making money already, I like to tell people that one of my mantras is I want to "give myself a raise every day." Think about it—in most professions, if someone wants a raise, they have to put in years of work and get continuing education with the hope of giving themselves a small raise. For you, each day you have the opportunity to give yourself a raise. If you have a page that is converting at 3 percent and making you $1,000 a week, with one small tweak you can give yourself a raise. If you can get it to increase to 4 percent conversion, over the next 12 months, that one percent will turn into an extra $17,362 per year in revenue—and that's from just one successful test!

Each day I come into the office and look at my active funnels and at what the "controls" are. The control is the current page that is winning. Then I brainstorm ideas for ways that we can beat the existing control. It's kind of like a video game, except that you get to keep the money you make from the game.

At one of my recent Inner Circle meetings, Mike Schmidt and AJ Rivera came to the meeting with a webinar funnel they had created that was a huge flop. It was costing them $24.85 to get someone to register for the webinar, and they only had 22.4 percent of the registrants actually show up. They were frustrated, thinking they would need to create a new type of funnel to sell their product. They showed the group their webinar registration page.

Figure 28.4:

Two of my Inner Circle members couldn't figure out why their webinar
registration page had such high ad costs and low show-up rates.

While this page looked like a good webinar registration page,
the market had told them that it was not. Lots of people were seeing
it, but very few registered. I looked at it for a few seconds and gave
them an idea to test. I told them that I thought the headline gave
away what they were going to learn on the webinar. It said that
the webinar would show "a secret method for helping companies
get more real five-star reviews." I could tell from the headline that
the webinar was about getting reviews and I thought that if I knew
the answer to the questions, I don't think that I would register for
it, and even if I did, I may not show up. I suggested that they try
a test where they didn't tell people what they would learn on the
webinar, but instead tell people what the webinar was not about
and create more curiosity.

They went home and changed the headline for the registration page and nothing else. The new headline created more curiosity, which caused more people to register and show up.

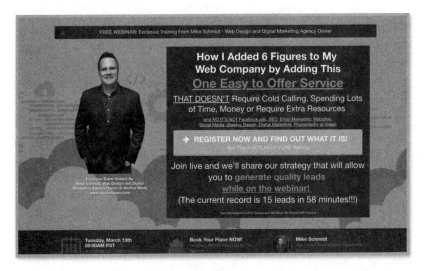

Figure 28.5:

By adding one small tweak such as adding more curiosity into their headline, they were able to lower their ad costs and increase their show-up rate.

This one small tweak dropped the cost for each webinar registration from $24.85 to $5.84 and increased the show-up rate from 22.4 percent to 31.7 percent! Can you imagine the size of the raise they gave themselves from this one small funnel audible?

Now that you have the first set of numbers from your initial test, this is where the marketing and funnel game becomes fun! We get to start calling audibles, making changes, and watching our funnel improve.

AVERAGE CART VALUE AUDIBLES

The first step to calling an audible on your funnel is to figure out what parts are broken. By looking at the numbers from your funnel audible images, you can quickly see which pages are converting well and which ones are not. Then we look at the underconverting pages and start setting up new pages to beat the originals.

The question I get a lot from people is: "What should the conversion percentages be at each page in the funnel?" This is a hard question to answer because this varies from market to market and traffic source to traffic source, so it's really important to start getting your own baseline numbers and then start trying to beat them. However, I know that it's nice to have an "idea" of where to start with so you can see if you're on the right track or not. We created some benchmarks that you can look at, and if you're under these basic percentages, then it's probably safe to say that you need to call an audible on that step. Even if you are above the benchmark, you can and should keep testing because small changes can yield big money over time.

- **Front-End Lead Funnels**

  - Lead Funnel Opt-Ins > 20%

- **Unboxing Funnels**

  - Two-Step Order Form Opt-Ins > 10–15%
  - Book or Cart Funnel Sales Conversion > 1–5%
  - Order Form Bump Conversion > 20%
  - OTO/Downsell Conversions > 3–15%

- **Presentation Funnels**

  - Video Sales Letter Sales Conversions > 1–3%
  - Webinar Registration Rate > 20%
  - Webinar Show Up Rate (LIVE) > 10–20%
  - Webinar Show Up Rate (AUTO) > 50–80%
  - Webinar Buy Rate (Hot traffic LIVE) > 10%
  - Webinar Buy Rate (Cold traffic LIVE) > 1–5%
  - Webinar Buy Rate (AUTO) > 3–8%
  - Product Launch Funnel Registration Rate > 20%

- **Back-End Phone Funnels**

    • Cost Per Application < $100

COST PER ACQUISITION: AUDIBLES

The other place that we start looking for where to call audibles is on the actual ads. Sometimes the funnel performs really well, but the cost per customer is way too high. If the CPA is too high, it can be because of the landing page, but it's more often because of your ads.

With each funnel, you will be creating many different ads with different hooks to capture your dream customers. Some ads will work great, and others won't work as well. As you will learn in *Traffic Secrets*, that's why we test and run lots of different ads. But each ad you post will have a cost per acquisition.

One of the biggest secrets to online marketing is that you need a lot of ad creative. My friend Dean Graziosi launched his best-selling book about the time I launched *Expert Secrets*, and a few months into the promotion, I called him to see how his book sales were doing. I was shocked to find out that he was selling four times as many books as I was, and we were selling a lot of books.

Now, to understand Dean's answer, you have to know a little about his background. Dean has been doing infomercials for over 20 years. During that time, he was on TV every night selling books on how to invest in real estate. He told me that when he would create an infomercial, it would last for about 18 months, and then the show would start to fatigue because so many people had seen it. In turn, the cost to acquire a customer would get higher and higher until it was no longer profitable. So they would stop running that show, go back to the studio, film a new infomercial, and launch it on TV. Again, that one would work for another 18 months or so.

Then he told me that he found his ads fatigued much more quickly online. He said that while on TV they would last 18 months, online they would only last a few weeks at best. So he started to carry his phone around with him everywhere he would go, and he would film ads on his phone, with his book, in front of the interesting places he would be at each day. He would then give these to his team, who would run them as ads.

He said many of the ads he made on his phone didn't work well because, for whatever reason, they didn't resonate with the market. The CPA was higher than the ACV, so his team would run them for a day or so and then turn them off. However, then other ads would come in at a really low CPA and he could run them for a few weeks until they started to fatigue (the CPA started to get as high as the ACV). At that time, they would replace the ad with a new one.

The reason Dean was selling four times as many books as me was because he was creating four times as many ads. I share this with you because you will be constantly creating and launching new ads, and each ad will have its own CPA. You will need to watch these ads, cut your losers fast, and scale your winners for as long as you can. Many of the ideas I share next on things you can do to make changes on your funnel pages will also be applicable to your ads.

WHAT SHOULD I CHANGE?

The concept of Hook, Story, Offer that I shared with you in Secret #2 seems so simple and obvious now, but for over a decade I didn't have that framework. I had studied hooks, stories, and offers, but I didn't realize that together, they were the secret to every funnel. In fact, I didn't write about that concept in the first edition of *DotCom Secrets* or *Expert Secrets* because I hadn't figured out that framework yet.

The first time the framework came to me, I shared it live during a small coaching group with about 100 students. After it was over, one of the people listening messaged me and said, "Russell, I've listened to every podcast you've put out. I've been to two Funnel Hacking LIVE events. I've done every course and read every book, yet that training on Hook, Story, Offer was the best training you've ever done."

I got so excited thinking about it that I couldn't sleep that night. The next morning I got up at 5:45 A.M. to meet Dave Woodward and James P. Friel in my gym for our morning lift. When I walked in, I think I had those crazy eyes I get when I'm excited because Dave asked me instantly what was going on.

"I think I figured out the secret to everything. Well, at least to selling anything. But it's so simple, I think I must be oversimplifying it." Then I taught them the concept of Hook, Story, Offer. "The hook grabs their attention for the story, and the story increases the perceived value of your offer." After that, I started to show them how Hook, Story, Offer happened at every phase of the funnel. "The ad has a hook, a story, and an offer. The landing page has a hook, a story, and an offer. The emails, the sales pages, the upsells, *everything* has a hook, a story, and an offer."

I could tell I was onto something, because we didn't lift a single weight that morning. I started to go deeper: "If your ad doesn't work, it's always because of the hook, the story, or the offer. If your landing page doesn't work, it's always because of the hook, the story, or the offer," and it went on and on.

That day I arrived at the office with our funnel team, and I had them pull up all our active funnels. I had them pull the stats on each page, and we looked at the pages that were below our conversion benchmarks. Then I explained to them the concept of Hook, Story, Offer. Through that lens, we started to look at each of the pages.

"What's the hook on this page?" I would ask. "What could we do to make it better?" And then we would brainstorm and figure out a dozen tests we could run.

"What's the story we're telling on this page, and does it build the perceived value of our offer?" We would then brainstorm ideas for how we could improve those stories.

"What do you guys think about the offer? What could we do to make it sexier?" I would ask and then we came up with dozens of ideas for how to improve our offer.

We did this page by page inside of our funnels and set up split tests to see if we could beat the controls, and in every test, the new pages won.

It's very simple to create a split test inside of ClickFunnels. Every page you create will have a button next to it that says **Start Split Test.**

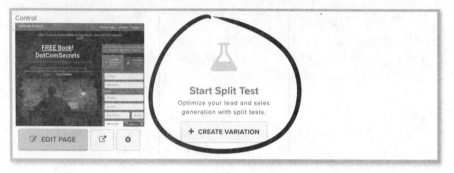

Figure 28.6:

You can instantly test two pages at once to see which one will perform better by clicking a button to create a split test.

When you click on that button, you can either create a new page from scratch or you can clone the existing page, which makes it very easy to run a simple test where you are replacing a headline or a sales video.

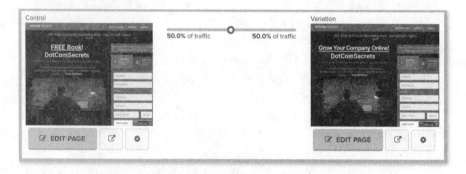

Figure 28.7:

When you're doing split tests, it's easiest to change one thing at a time (such as the headline) and test it to see which one will convert better.

You can use the slider to change the percentage of how much traffic is running one version versus the other. I will run a test for a few days or weeks, and then compare the control versus the new page. The winner becomes the new control, and we start over trying to give ourselves another raise the next day.

That is the big secret. If your funnel isn't working, it's always the hook, the story, or the offer. If you hired me to be your consultant and paid me $100,000 for the day, I would look at your funnel steps, and my response would always be, "It's your hook, your story, or your offer," and then we would brainstorm ways to make them better.

CONCLUSION

You made it to the end!

During this journey that we've been on together through this book, we've covered a lot of things, but now that you have the full context for these secrets, it really is pretty simple.

Everything you've learned in this book is literally the same thing I would do with you if I had a chance to fly to you and sit in your office. You now have the skills to do this, and I want to quickly re-walk you through the entire "DotCom Secrets" process.

- Step #1: Figure out exactly who your dream customer is.

- Step #2: Where are these dream customers already congregating?

- Step #3: What hooks can you throw out to capture their attention and what are the stories that you can tell to increase the perceived value of what you have to offer?

- Step #4: After you have their attention, focus on building a relationship with them (through the Attractive Character) so you can ascend them up your value ladder and serve them at your highest level possible.

- Step #5: Pick which tier of the value ladder you want to focus on first, and then select which funnel type you will create.

- Step #6: After you have the funnel structure built, plug in the videos, headlines, and other funnel scripts into the pages where your Attractive Character will be communicating with your dream customers.

- Step #7: Launch the funnel with the amount of money you would spend to acquire a single customer and see where in the funnels your hooks, stories, and offers aren't converting.

- Step #8: Split test the controls with the new pages and repeat the process until your ACV is greater than your CPA.

- Step #9: Keep creating new ads to keep your CPA low while continuing to improve your ACV. Repeat this process until this funnel qualifies for the Two Comma Club.

- Step #10: After your first funnel hits the Two Comma Club, start working on the next funnel in your value ladder. Email your existing customers about the new funnel and attach it as a funnel stack onto your first funnel.

- Step #11: Repeat steps #6, #7, and #8 for this new funnel until it hits the Two Comma Club.

- Step #12: Pick the next funnel in your value ladder to create . . .

This is the game, and it's the most fun game that I've ever played. You now have all the skills you need to start building funnels in your own or other people's businesses.

You've just learned what took me over a decade to discover and master. Tony Robbins often talks about how reading a book is like taking a decade of someone's life and compressing it down to a day. My entrepreneurial journey hasn't been all sunshine and roses. There have been many ups and downs, and I fought hard to learn all these secrets. It's been an honor to be able to share them with you.

I still remember the excitement as I learned each of these secrets and used them for the first time for the businesses I was starting. Whenever someone posts on Facebook or Instagram that they bought this book, I get slightly jealous about how much fun it would be to rediscover all these ideas. I hope that you had as much fun learning them as I did when I started this journey.

This book is a playbook. Don't just read it once and go on with business as usual. Keep it handy and refer to it often. This book is just part one of a three-part series.

DotCom Secrets is the framework. It was written to help you master the science of funnel building.

Expert Secrets is the fire. It was written to help you master the art of sales and persuasion tactics you will need to change the lives of the customers that you've been called to serve. (Get a free copy at ExpertSecrets.com.)

Traffic Secrets is the fuel. It will show you how to fill your funnels with your dream customers. (Get a free copy at TrafficSecrets.com.)

Having these three playbooks and using them hand in hand will give you the strategies that you need to geometrically grow your company. The last thing you need (outside of your personality and the offers you can create) is the tool that makes funnel building possible, and that is ClickFunnels. It was built for me, and it was built for you. If you don't have an account yet, you can get your free trial at ClickFunnels.com.

If you want to get up-to-the-minute ideas on marketing and sales, twice a week I publish a podcast called *Marketing Secrets*, where I share everything that we're learning in real time. You can subscribe for free at MarketingSecrets.com.

And with that . . .

I will end this book.

Thank you so much for reading, and I wish you all the success you can dream of.

Thanks,
Russell Brunson

P.S. Don't forget, you're just one funnel away . . .

ENDNOTES

Foreword

1. Kennedy, Dan S. *No B.S. Marketing to the Affluent: No Holds Barred, Take No Prisoners, Guide to Getting Really Rich, 3rd Edition*. Gildan Media Corporation, 2019.

Preface

2. Kennedy, Dan. "The Most Important Question You Should Ask When Advertising." *Dan Kennedy's Magnetic Marketing.* February 26, 2013. https://nobsinnercircle.com/blog/advertising/the-most-important-question-you-should-ask-when-advertising/.

Introduction

3. Lapre, Don. "Don Lapre." *Wikipedia, The Free Encyclopedia.* Accessed November 22, 2019. https://en.wikipedia.org/wiki/Don_Lapre.

SECTION ONE

Secret #2

4. Much, Marilyn, "Claude Hopkins Turned Advertising Into A Science, Brands Into Household Names." *Investor's Business Daily*. December 20, 2018. https://www.investors.com/news/management/leaders-and-success/claude-hopkins-scientific-advertising-bio.

5. Manning, Drew. "60-Day Keto Jumpstart." *Complete Wellness.* Accessed November 22, 2019. https://completewellness.com/products/60-day-keto-jumpstart.

Secret #4

6. Kutcher, Jenna. "Why You Need a Brand, Not a Business." *Jenna Kutcher* (blog). June 28, 2017. https://jennakutcherblog.com/why-you-need-a-brand-not-a-business.

7. Lee, Stan. "A universe of flawed heroes: Stan Lee was ahead of his time." *Associated Press*. November 13, 2018. https://www.apnews.com/d355ac3dbc154c7abee0e01a998b371d.

Secret #5

8. Stansberry, Porter. Presentation at GKIC SuperConference, Chicago, IL, 2011.

9. Robbins, Tony. *Unlimited Power*. Simon & Schuster, 2000.

Secret #6

10. Brafman, Ori and Rom. *Sway: The Irresistible Pull of Irrational Behavior.* Knopf Doubleday Publishing Group, 2008.

11. Lewis, Jared. "What Is Breakthrough Advertising?" *Houston Chronicle.* Accessed November 22, 2019. https://smallbusiness.chron.com/breakthrough-advertising-36576.html.

Secret #7

12. Miller, Donald. *Building a StoryBrand: Clarify Your Message So Customers Will Listen.* HarperCollins Leadership, 2017.

13. *Seinfeld*, "The Pitch," NBC, September 16, 1992.

SECTION TWO

Secret #8

14. Pagan, Eben. "The Kiss Test and Knowing When to Kiss Her." *Double Your Dating.* Accessed November 22, 2019. https://doubleyourdating.com/the-kiss-test.

Secret #9

15. Levesque, Ryan. *Ask.* Dunham Books, 2017.

Secret #16

16. Walker, Jeff. "Product Launch Formula." *Product Launch Formula.* Accessed November 22, 2019. https://productlaunchformula.com.

Secret #17

17. Sullivan, Dan. *The Dan Sullivan Question.* The Strategic Coach Inc., 2010.

SECTION THREE

Secret #20

18. James, Vince. "The 12-Month Millionaire." *The 12 Month Internet Millionaire.* Accessed November 22, 2019. https://www.12monthinternetmillionaire.com.

SECTION FOUR

Secret #28

19. Halbert, Gary C. "BIG Idea." *The Gary Halbert Letter.* Accessed November 22, 2019. https://www.thegaryhalbertletter.com/newsletters/zhzz-07_big_idea.htm.

ACKNOWLEDGMENTS

There are so many people I want to thank for being willing to share their ideas with me. Ideas that ultimately became the strategies behind everything inside of this book. I also want to thank my team—all the people who helped me to implement these ideas, find out which ones work, and share them with the world.

While there are hundreds of marketers I have learned from, there are many people who gave me very specific ideas that built the framework for my company and also for this book. I've tried to give credit to the original sources when possible, but some of these people may be left out. So I want to mention a few of the brilliant marketers who have inspired me in no particular order:

Mark Joyner, Dan Kennedy, Bill Glazer, Daegan Smith, Tony Robbins, Don Lapre, John Alanis, Andre Chaperon, Ben Settle, Steve Gray, Ryan Deiss, Perry Belcher, Armand Morin, Jason Fladlien, Ted Thomas, Mike Filsaime, David Frey, Chet Holmes, Jeff Walker, John Reese, Robbie Summers, and everyone else who has taken the risk to be an online entrepreneur and provide value online!

Lastly, I want to thank my team. These people have given me the ability to try all these crazy ideas, and they share in the successes and the losses. There have been hundreds of employees who have come through our doors, and it would be impossible to mention all of them. But I want to give a special thanks to my partners who have supported me and put in so much more than time:

Brent Coppieters and John Parkes for running my companies. Todd Dickerson and Dylan Jones for creating ClickFunnels and giving us the ability to make this process simple for everyone. Dorel Nechifor for taking the risk on me when I first got started and making it possible to build my company. Julie Eason for braving this book with me; your countless hours have made this book possible. And Joy Anderson for helping with all the updates for this second edition. It wasn't a small update; it was a full rewrite, and I couldn't have gotten it past the finish line without you. Thank you!

ABOUT THE AUTHOR

Russell Brunson started his first online company while he was wrestling in college. Within a year of graduation, he had sold over a million dollars of his own products and services from his basement. Over the past 15 years, he has built a following of over a million entrepreneurs, sold hundreds of thousands of copies of his books, popularized the concept of sales funnels, and co-founded the software company ClickFunnels, which has helped tens of thousands of entrepreneurs quickly get their message out to the marketplace. He lives in Idaho with his family, and you can visit him online at RussellBrunson.com.

MARKETING SECRETS

Have You Liked The Secrets That You've Learned About In This Book?

If So, Then **Subscribe** To My FREE Podcast Called "Marketing Secrets" Where I Share My Best Marketing Secrets Twice A Week.

You Can Subscribe For FREE and get exclusive content, interviews and the most cutting edge secrets and ideas at:

MarketingSecrets.com